THE HOOLIGANS OF KANDAHAR

THE HOOLIGANS OF KANDAHAR

*NOT ALL WAR STORIES
ARE HEROIC*

JOSEPH KASSABIAN

ISBN: 978-1-63161-049-3

Published by TCK Publishing
www.TCKpublishing.com

Get discounts and special deals on our best-selling books at
www.TCKpublishing.com/bookdeals

Sign up for Joseph's newsletter
and find out more information at
www.joekassabian.com

This book is dedicated to the 2,326 US Military men and women who have been killed fighting for some long-lost ideal in the mountains of Afghanistan. It is dedicated to the 20,083 service members who have been wounded in action. It's also dedicated to the untold thousands of veterans who have taken their own lives since the beginning of Operation Enduring Freedom.

CONTENTS

CHAPTER 1 A GOODBYE OF SORTS   1

CHAPTER 2 WELCOME TO KANDAHAR   6

CHAPTER 3 THE DEALER DEATH MARCH   14

CHAPTER 4 CORN FIELDS, BOMBS, AND ROBBING THE ICE
           CREAM GUY   22

CHAPTER 5 THE WORST SOLDIER IN THE UNITED STATES
           ARMY   33

CHAPTER 6 OPERATION GRIZZLY GANG-BANG   38

CHAPTER 7 GONG'S FIRST PATIENT   44

CHAPTER 8 OP COUCH   48

CHAPTER 9 BOREDOM ON THE RESERVE   51

CHAPTER 10 GRIZZLY BASE AND HOW I GOT DEMOTED   55

CHAPTER 11 CHAP STICK 25 AND THE GREAT GOAT-
            NAPPING   60

CHAPTER 12 THE NIGHT THE AFGHAN ARMY ALMOST
            KILLED US   67

CHAPTER 13 NAN PLAYS CATCH   75

CHAPTER 14 MAGGOTS   82

CHAPTER 15 GUNNY AND THE GREAT AIR CONDITIONER
            HEIST   86

CHAPTER 16 SPARTAN BASE AND THE DESCENT INTO
                MADNESS   91

CHAPTER 17 THE BATTLE FOR GRIZZLY BASE   102

CHAPTER 18 THE HOOLIGANS SAVE A LIFE   106

CHAPTER 19 KANDAHAR AIRFIELD, KUWAIT, AND
                FLORIDA   111

CHAPTER 20 THE SUICIDAL PERSON'S GUIDE TO BOMB
                DISPOSAL   126

CHAPTER 21 CALI AND THE MEMPHIS BLUES   135

CHAPTER 22 FUEL BOMBS AND THE MYSTERY GRENADE 142

CHAPTER 23 GRANDPA LEAVES, WINTER COMES   147

CHAPTER 24 BLOOD AND RAIN   155

CHAPTER 25 THE HOOLIGANS NEARLY GET KICKED OUT
                OF A HOSPITAL   167

CHAPTER 26 THE HOOLIGANS WITHOUT SLIM   170

CHAPTER 27 KEEPING YOUR COOL   176

CHAPTER 28 SLIM THE DICTATOR   187

CHAPTER 29 TAKING A BREATHER   199

CHAPTER 30 SAYING GOODBYE TO CAMP SPARTAN 207

CHAPTER 31 HUGO CHAVEZ THE PSYCHIATRIST 212

CHAPTER 32 OPERATION GRIZZLY GANG-BANG 2:
                ELECTRIC BOOGALOO   219

CHAPTER 33 LEAVING WALTON   227

CHAPTER 34 CLOSING THE BAR AT MANAS   231

CHAPTER 35 THE LONG WAY HOME   237

ABOUT THE AUTHOR   245

A NOTE FROM THE AUTHOR

All stories in this book are based on events that happened between May 2011 and May 2012 in Kandahar, Afghanistan.

Times, places, details, and names have been altered to protect my fellow soldiers from any adverse actions due to their conduct during our deployment together. I am not trying to glorify our war or make any of us sound like heroes. Not all war stories are flag-waving triumphs of the American soldier, but those stories and the soldiers that lived them are no less a part of our history.

CHAPTER 1

A GOODBYE OF SORTS

I WAS LYING ON MY back under the hot Texas sun with a cheap cigarette in my mouth waiting for a massive convoy of school buses. That was how the army chose to shuttle us to the airport. All around me, young soldiers were yapping, excited about getting to go fight in a war, but a lot of it was uncertainty and fear.

I call them young, but I was only twenty-two. When you've been in the army since you were seventeen and have spent your formative years bouncing around the world, you tend to age fast. Soldiers joked that we aged in dog years. My aching joints didn't make it feel like much of a joke, though.

We were waiting in an expansive field with our bags piled up in front of us. Soldiers' families milled about, hanging off their kid, husband, or whoever was about to go to Afghanistan. My family wasn't there. I didn't want them to be. It all just seemed so weird and awkward.

We all stood around baking in the hot sun. Never mind that the only reason we were there so early was that no one in our chain of command knew when the buses were supposed to show up.

God forbid a group of leaders who were expected to take this unit into combat could figure out how to wrangle a few fucking school buses together on time. So the soldiers and their families just sat there waiting. What are you supposed to talk about in that hours-long span while you wait to be shipped away?

"I really hope you don't die, son."

"Aw, thanks, Pa."

The married men held on to their women for dear life. Army wives were notorious cheaters. The men knew as soon as they let go, as soon as they got onto those buses, their women would run into someone else's arms. Even if it weren't true, it would be the only thing the deployed soldiers would be thinking about over the next year.

It was around this time the tall, gangly figure of my squad leader, Slim, sat down next to me. His family wasn't there either. A few weeks earlier he'd sent his wife and kid back to Florida so he could spend his last couple of weeks in the States getting shitfaced with me and a couple of the others in our squad.

"Did you call your mom yet, fool?" he asked.

You would think that was something a decent person would have done months ago. It turned out I was not a decent person. That wasn't a shock to me anymore, though. Still, Slim always found a way to make me feel guilty about it.

There I was a few hours away from deploying and I hadn't even told my mom.

I tossed my cigarette into the grass and pulled out my phone. As soon as I started dialing, I realized she was at work. I left a voicemail. I'm sure that learning through voicemail that your youngest son is going off to war yet again isn't the best thing to hear when you get home from a long day at work.

Slim and I wandered over to where our soldiers were hanging out. None of their families were there either. Our squad always had an outcast aura. It was something Slim and I embraced.

Slim was our squad leader: a man who nearly finished his college degree in radiological sciences and whose every other word was "fuck."

One day he woke up and decided he was through with school—or as he put it, "Fuck that book learning shit, I wanted to kill terrorists"— and enlisted. I served with him during my last deployment to Afghanistan where I learned he was bat-shit insane but also the best combat leader a soldier could want. He was the one who tagged us the Hooligans in the first place.

After taking over our squad from some totally incompetent jackass, he quickly saw the only thing we were good at was shooting at shit and getting arrested. "Y'all mother fuckers are some hooligans." The name just stuck after that.

My team, Charlie Team, was composed of me and two teenagers, Dirty and Urkel. Both were fresh out of basic training and both were married. And in true military fashion, both were already headed to their first divorces.

Dirty was a goofy kid from Florida who wore skinny jeans and was covered in tattoos. Urkel was a tiny black kid from Georgia who wore glasses that were nearly as big as his face. He called the death metal that Dirty and I played "crazy white people music."

They were the first soldiers I had ever been put in charge of for anything serious. They looked up to me for guidance and leadership, and I sincerely felt sorry for them.

Alpha Team was led by Grandpa, the oldest guy in the squad and the closest thing we had to a voice of reason. His soldiers were Cali and Machete. Cali was young and generally way too serious about everything. He was also the only guy in the squad—or possibly the entire goddamn U.S. Army—who really believed in our mission in Afghanistan anymore. He was the kind of guy who would wave an American flag and blast country music from his lifted pickup truck on his way to Wal-Mart.

Machete was a massive bag of shit. His uniforms always looked as if he'd stolen them off a homeless guy. For some reason, his hands were always covered with mysterious stains, and his fingernails were brown. No one liked Machete. We actually decided whose team he would be on by a game of rock, paper, scissors. Grandpa lost.

Bravo team was led by Kitty, the only female in the platoon and a lesbian with a receding hairline from years of pulling her hair back into a tight bun. She was a joke of a leader.

Her soldier Perro—an older guy who left a job that made him hundreds of thousands of dollars a year to enlist—did nearly everything for her. I considered Perro one of the best soldiers in the whole platoon. He was supposed to be my gunner, but because she outranked me, Kitty was able to steal him.

Her gunner, Guapo, so named because he was so overly groomed and because he could pull massive amounts of ass even though he was married, was only added to our squad about a month before deployment.

Kitty had an extra soldier named Nan who'd spent a few years as a firefighter in some middle-of-nowhere town in Iowa and seemed way too smart to be in the army. One second he would be talking about how the repercussions of the invasion of Iraq affected national security and the next giggling at a dick joke.

Slim's team consisted of Oldies, a guy who had managed to be in the army as long as Grandpa but had never been promoted past the rank of Specialist, and a guy named Memphis. Memphis was the most redneck man I had ever met in my life. And he had the hygienic self-discipline of a third-world slum dweller. He was friendly enough and a hard worker so we all just kind of ignored the fact that he smelled like a dead body.

Being on Slim's team also meant you had to deal with having his unrelenting rage directed at you for no reason whatsoever. Memphis and Oldies excelled at keeping their mouths shut and absorbing an immense amount of abuse. They were the abused spouses of the squad.

So there we were: all sitting in the Texas sun smoking and dodging work. Our glorious leaders kept coming up with pointless tasks for us to do to burn the time. Things like wandering around the parking lot picking up trash with our hands or sweeping the sidewalk. We managed not to do a single one of them. The other squads in our platoon kept giving us dirty looks for not acting like "part of the team."

They were huge about that: acting like we were in the whole thing together. Generally, outside of our squad, we hated everyone, and unless they were actively in the process of being murdered by the Taliban, we weren't going to lift a finger to help them.

Finally, the buses showed up. There were tearful goodbyes all around, and people clutched their loved ones. That part always seemed to me as if it made the goodbye that much worse. Watching your loved ones slowly file onto buses and pull away over the horizon, wondering if it would be the last time you saw them alive.

Why would anyone ever subject themselves to that? It suddenly dawned on me that not understanding these basic human feelings might have something to do with why I was single and why I had failed to call my mom.

At last, we got to the airport, a ramshackle pile of shit. Like most things in the city of Killeen, it was run-down and dirty. The airport was originally built to give military aircraft a place to go, and like most things the military makes, it was pretty bare bones.

Someone had the bright idea to make it both a military and civilian airport and out sprang a terminal. So, tiny planes that may or may not be certified to fly zoom around next to multi-million-dollar military jets and helicopters.

Like any other passengers, we had to go through security. I should mention that we were all carrying the weapons we would soon be using in Afghanistan. I had an M-4 carbine, an M203 grenade launcher, night vision goggles, and an M9 pistol on me. Several people in my squad were carrying belt-fed machine guns. There we stood, all this weaponry hanging from our bodies, waiting to be searched by TSA.

A fat TSA guy confiscated my fingernail clippers. He grabbed my crinkled-up water bottle, too. "Due to heightened security posture, you can't take this on the plane, sir," he drawled through puffy lips. I think the act of speaking made him out of breath.

"Funny, due to heightened security posture, I'm pretty sure I'm being sent to Afghanistan," I said. He didn't look entertained. I grabbed my unzipped backpack and stuffed my molested belongings back inside and shuffled down the line.

We all got through security and squeezed onto a chartered flight, courtesy of Ryanair. It's one of the worst reviewed airlines in the world. The military tends to do everything on a budget for its service members but loves to lavish attention on its civilians. To drive this point home, six civilians slid past us and disappeared behind a curtain labeled "First Class." They had the whole area to themselves. Meanwhile, we were so packed into coach that if I were seated that close to someone on a civilian flight, I would have been arrested for sexual harassment.

It seemed we got the Ryanair B-Team of flight attendants because we started to take off before they bothered with the in-flight safety briefing. An older woman with ratty blonde hair and a smoker's growl eventually started on it. She struggled mightily with the words on the pamphlet, her thick eastern European accent making each word nearly indecipherable.

"Show us your tits!" a voice yelled from the back of the plane.

Everyone cheered. I'm not sure why, because she looked to be on the wrong side of fifty and as if she'd been just a tad too close to the Chernobyl disaster.

I looked at the back of the plane and saw it was Walrus who's screamed at her. Walrus was a chubby little guy who prided himself on being the loudest prick in the platoon. I'd deployed with him before, and during the first six hours of that flight, he ran around the cabin yelling, "Where's Ashton? Are we getting punked?" over and over. He was like one of those kids who will throw tantrums all day long unless you ignore him. If he wasn't getting the attention, he wasn't enjoying himself, and even though I hated feeding his never-ending torrent of bullshit, he was pretty damn funny.

After booing the poor woman who was just trying to do her job got boring, we all settled in for the long flight. Beneath us, Texas vanished from view and was replaced with a cloudy blue sky. Probably the last relaxing thing I would see in a long time.

"Where's Ashton? Are we getting punked?" I heard someone scream at the back of the plane.

CHAPTER 2

WELCOME TO KANDAHAR

AT SOME UNGODLY HOUR OF the morning we landed at Kandahar Airfield. The sprawling Air Force base was the headquarters of our wonderfully failed allied mission in southern Afghanistan. Even at two in the morning, the temperature was already in the hundreds and the air was choked with dust, human waste, and jet exhaust.

Kandahar smelled like shit. It smelled like some celestial septic pipe in the sky had emptied every single toilet in the world onto its streets. In some places, you could even taste it. It was dried up and atomized into the dust that blew through the air and into our mouths, noses, and eyes.

It was our new home.

Airmen packed us into rickety old Russian buses and drove us slowly across the base. They were giving us the grand tour.

Even though the air field was technically in a war zone, the people there were so far from any real danger they may as well have been in the States. Most of the people who were deployed there rarely went outside the gates until it was time for them to go home–and even then it was by plane. They weren't even allowed to load the weapons they carried with them all over the place.

The war was some abstract thing they mostly heard about on the news–even though it was going on all around them. Kind of like rich suburban white folks who complain about the conditions in the inner city, even though they never go there.

The buses stopped outside of our building. One of the few actual brick buildings that we saw on the base, it almost looked brand new. Time barely crawled by there. There was literally nothing to do except breathe and eat. There were no amenities, no TV, no internet, and no recreational activities. It was just a massive brick building full of badly made bunk beds. The whole base wasn't like that, just where they stashed us. Like in some kind of shitty, Afghan version of section eight. I figured it couldn't get any worse than sheer unrelenting boredom. I was wrong.

It only took a few days for the collective irritated gastrointestinal tracts of a company of soldiers to overwhelm the plumbing in the building. Jetlag, combined with having to eat army food full-time, sent everyone running to the bathrooms. The poor, substandard plumbing didn't stand a chance. Because the next nearest toilets were over a mile away, people just kept using the clogged mess that was in our building.

Soon the bathrooms looked like something out of your worst nightmare. Shit and piss overwhelmed the broken toilets and spilled out absolutely everywhere. The whole building we were living in quickly turned into a HAZMAT zone and smelled like a third-world refugee camp. We resorted to pissing into bottles and chucking them out the windows. To make the situation even worse, our overtaxed air conditioning unit broke, and shit-infused vapors started snaking up through the shower drains. Our brand new building had quickly turned into a shit-stuffed hot box.

Our commander, Dweebly, saw that morale was plummeting faster than our sanitation levels. He made some long, drawn-out speech about how he understood we were unhappy with our horrible living conditions and he felt for us. He must have really been "feeling for us" from the nice, air-conditioned officers' building where he was staying— the one down the road with working toilets and showers.

After several days at the airfield, my platoon was being sent out to some place called the Provincial Reserve, a tiny outpost far away from any major civilization. Slim and I were excited. It was exactly where we wanted to be. During our last deployment we were also on our own, and even though the living conditions out in the boonies always sucked, no one was breathing down our necks. We were free to operate as we saw fit without commanders telling us how to live and work. It was as much freedom as anyone could ask for while deployed.

We rushed back into our building and began packing our stuff into our duffle bags. Our soldiers immediately started asking questions about what it was going to be like out there—living in a part of the country where we only controlled the area we happened to be standing on at that very second.

I didn't want to share any old war stories because I was afraid of scaring the young blood. Slim didn't have the same qualms and quickly launched into a story about him being stuck on a mountainside in an ambush for an hour. Our young soldiers' faces looked like mine had when, at eight years old, I watched Stephen King's *IT* for the first time.

We managed to finish packing our bags in between war stories and piled them all up outside near the helicopter-landing zone. According to our commander, a Chinook helicopter was supposed to pick us up and fly us to the Provincial Reserve. A few hours passed but no helicopter showed up.

"I'm getting this feeling our flight is late," Grandpa sighed.

"What gave you that idea?" I asked.

"Maybe he got lost?" Nan shrugged.

"Yeah, I guess he could have gotten turned around at that other massive American airbase in the area." I laughed at my own joke.

Finally, after what seemed like forever—and long after the sun went down—the deafening chopping sound of a Chinook came over the mountains. Chinooks look as if someone tried to build a helicopter modeled after a bumblebee and then decided to make it as agile as one to boot.

The army had been using Chinooks since the Vietnam War, and they had been doing an excellent job of lumbering slowly over war zones and getting shot down by whatever tribe or warlord we were fighting at the particular time.

While we had been in Afghanistan, half of SEAL Team Six was killed flying over Afghanistan's endless mountainous landscape while flying in one of these brain-damaged bumblebees.

The fat, awkward form of the Chinook plopped down in front of us on the tarmac.

The blades whirled overhead, their power blasting my ears and making my eyes vibrate in my head. We slowly picked up our bags and shuffled in a line up the loading ramp and into the thing's belly. The soldiers embarking the flight piled their bags in the middle of the seating area at the command of the Chinook's Load Master.

With a title like that—Load Master—I figured there was some kind of strategic plan to the loading of the bags. I was wrong. They were piled haphazardly in the middle and a net was thrown over them. We humans were stuffed along the wall in the small area that wasn't full of cargo. I think we were treated more like luggage than our bags were.

Slim tried yelling something to me, and even though he was smashed in next to me, I couldn't hear anything he said over the helicopter's engines. He pointed to where Kitty was sitting. The mountain of bags in front of her collapsed under their own weight and buried her. We both laughed, though neither of us made any audible noise.

The helicopter lurched, bounced a bit, and slowly lifted into the air. I think it was more beating the air into submission than actually taking flight. The sky relented and we climbed higher. The Load Master stood on the still-open loading ramp, tethered to the helicopter with a thin piece of cord and a machine gun swung around in front of him, pointing down to the retreating view of Kandahar.

We rose a few hundred feet above the dry, cracked earth. Mountains jutted up to our east and west. We were heading through the sole valley in the distance. Afghanistan's gaping maw was taking us in. The ground below us was uniformly brown and featureless. Stubborn villagers scratched out a living farming whatever would grow out of what looked like the surface of the moon. The Load Master spat a mouthful of tobacco into the wind; it was probably the most moisture the village had received in months.

We slowed down and started descending into the darkness, and before long we thudded to a stop. I couldn't see it through the thickness of night, but we had landed right in the middle of an American outpost. Confused, I stood up, grabbed two random bags from the pile, and slowly made my way out of the back of the helicopter. Just a few seconds after we had all filed out, the helicopter was taking off again. I looked around. This place looked nothing like the Provincial Reserve did on the map we had studied.

"This isn't the right fucking place!" Slim yelled over the fading sound of the helicopter.

"Where the fuck are we?" I asked him, rummaging through my backpack for my map.

"Maybe we weren't supposed to get off yet?" Grandpa shrugged.

"There wasn't anyone else on the damn flight," I countered.

"Calm down," Slim tried to reassure us. We were on a strange outpost in the middle of Kandahar, and we had no damn clue what was going on. None of us were calm.

"Let's go find their operations center and see where the hell we got dropped off. Kitty, stay with the soldiers, try not to let them figure out we have no idea where we are."

Slim, Grandpa, and I started wandering around the larger-than-expected outpost. The place was a ghost town. Just uniform rows of tan tents everywhere we turned. I lit a cigarette and blew a cloud of smoke into the chilly night air. Even after six years, the army still found ways to surprise me. I couldn't believe they could misplace a squad of soldiers in a war zone.

Slim lost what little patience he was capable of and began opening random tent doors and yelling for a commander of some kind.

Slim discovered their operations center in an unmarked tent. There was a fat sergeant first class sitting behind a computer. He was half asleep and obviously confused by our presence. "Who the hell are you guys?" he asked.

Slim told him our unit. The sergeant looked even more confused now.

"Is this the Provincial Reserve?" I asked him.

"What? Hell no, man, you're about thirty miles away from the PR."

"Well, our flight dropped us off here. Is there any way you can get ahold of the unit at the PR?" Slim was reaching the point where he could only communicate in swear words and by throwing things.

Grandpa stepped in to handle the rest. "We are obviously in the wrong place, can you help us out?"

"Yeah man, hold on. I'll see if I can get ahold of anyone. Go ahead and find an empty tent with your soldiers and get some shuteye. I'll let you know what they say."

We were a suspicious lot; not one of us went to find a tent to crash in. We walked back out to where the helicopter had dropped us off and laid down on the ground. Even in summer, the nights in Afghanistan are brutally cold and windy. I curled up in the fetal position in a vain attempt to stay warm and slipped off into an uneasy sleep.

Apparently someone, somewhere, really missed us because it didn't take long for a convoy to show up. A slightly overweight, bearded, and filthy sergeant first class whom I called Rambo greeted us by yelling to the sleeping pile of soldiers that was Second Squad, "How the fuck did y'all end up out here?"

"Good question," I said half asleep. "Are you our ride?"

"Better than just your ride, you're our replacements." He smiled.

That is how the deployment cycle works. Each unit gets replaced by another, regardless of what each unit's job actually is. It's not entirely unheard of for an infantry unit to be replaced by truck drivers, truck drivers by military police, or even National Guard weekend warriors who only know about a war zone from the latest iteration of *Call of Duty*. It's not a perfect system— or one that actually works at all for that matter. That tended to be the reality in Afghanistan when it came to most things.

Slim went around kicking our soldiers awake and telling them to grab their bags. I was attempting to balance an incredibly large rucksack on my back, a duffle bag in each arm, a rifle with a grenade launcher strapped to my chest, and a pistol on my leg.

I felt bad for Dirty. He was less than half my size but carrying even more because he had our team's M249 Squad Automatic Weapon. Urkel took a headlong fall onto the rocks and all his bags fell on top of him. He was far from the only one who went down as we awkwardly waddled over to the trucks that were waiting for us.

The trucks were truly a sight to behold. They are called Mine Resistant Ambush Protected All-Terrain Vehicles, or MATVs. They looked like semi-trucks that had been loaded down with armor plating and machine guns. They were far bigger than anything you could legally drive on any U.S. road. On the sides of the doors, in big, block letters, it read "Dealer," their unit's radio call sign and nickname.

Their trucks had clearly been through some shit. Windows were spider-cracked with bullet holes and bullet strikes, and fragment impacts had gouged every door and surface. Additional chain link fence-like armor was strapped on every flat surface of the truck. I was ordered to jump in the second truck of the convoy and I tossed my bags into the back of the armored monster. I loaded my rifle with a magazine I had to borrow from one of the Dealer guys.

Our company never gave us any ammo before sending us off into the countryside.

The convoy rumbled off into the night. Our lights weren't on; we were rolling in what is called "black out" driving. All headlights were off, and the driver and truck commander navigated using only night-vision goggles, or NVGs. Unlike in the movies and video games, NVGs are fucking terrible to use. You can't see anything clearly; everything just becomes unrecognizable shades of green.

We do this so that, theoretically, the enemy can't see the convoy coming. Seeing how we were driving down a clearly marked road in five incredibly loud, up-armored, diesel-powered semi-trucks, it was safe to say there was no mystery about who was driving down the street.

It didn't take us long to pull up to the gates of the Provincial Reserve, the outside of which was guarded by tired-looking members of the Afghan National Police. They were obviously the meat shields of the base. They had little to no gear, and in some cases, they didn't even have shoes.

They stood alone out on the only road leading to the Reserve, far away from the American guard positions. This was to guard against both the Taliban and the Afghan police themselves. The police had a tendency to turn their weapons on American forces about as often as the Taliban did.

We made it through the rickety metal gates and parked the trucks in a small, improvised parking lot full of other vehicles in various stages of disrepair.

I climbed out and was greeted by giant, ankle breaking rocks. U.S. forces have a habit of covering the ground wherever they happen to slap together an outpost with giant rocks. The arid terrain of Afghanistan tends to kick up terrible dust storms in the high winds. So people thought it would be a good idea to use gravel to keep the dust down on the outposts. The rocks never really kept the dust down and instead made the simple act of walking from point A to point B an exercise in ankle durability.

The Reserve was a sight to see. Not much more than four tents smashed into four incredibly old brick walls that had been haphazardly reinforced with sandbags and concertina wire. We shared half the compound with the Afghan police, which was something none of us were very comfortable with.

The Dealer soldiers all climbed out of the trucks and wandered back over to their tents. Sergeant South, the truck commander I'd ridden there with, helped me with my bags.

"We aren't patrolling tonight, so you guys can get some sleep. Tomorrow we'll probably go out for a while to show you the area," he said in his thick southern drawl.

"Thanks," I said, not really paying attention. I was still taking in all the sights. Looming over the compound was a massive ancient castle. Carved out from the same rock centuries before, it blended right in with the surrounding mountains. The Dealer guys told me it was built by Alexander the Great, who'd founded the city of Kandahar in the Hellenistic Era. It was amazingly well preserved, despite being pockmarked by bullets.

South showed me to our tent where they stored random odds and ends. They'd smashed a few cots in there and called it a sleeping area. Our soldiers were bunking with the Dealer guys for the night.

I didn't realize how tired I was until I sat down on the cot I'd picked out. It creaked under me as I tried to relax. I lit a cigarette, blew out a cloud of smoke, and saw Slim sitting across from me on his tiny cot with his rifle across his lap. My eyelids hung heavy.

"This shit is going to be real, boys," he said, a smile creeping across his face. He loved being out there in the middle of nowhere and probably surrounded by the enemy—no matter how much he tried to convince people otherwise.

"Seems that way," Grandpa said, sitting down on a cot that was frayed and torn and barely able to hold his weight. I reached over to my gear. I only had one magazine of ammo. The same one that was given to me for the ride over.

"I think we are going to need more ammo," I said, laughing. They nervously laughed with me. What we had just gotten into was starting to sink in.

The ground shook with a thunderous explosion from somewhere off in the distance. The shaking made the dust rise from the floorboards and swirl around in the air.

"A lot more ammo."

CHAPTER 3

THE DEALER DEATH MARCH

I ROLLED OUT OF MY cot some time in the early morning covered in sweat and with my tongue stuck to the side of my mouth. I was so dehydrated I had to immediately roll over and take a pull from my hydration pack. A hydration pack is a kind of backpack filled with water with a hose-like straw attached. It always made the water taste like old plastic and rubber.

We were packed in with various boxes and bags of supplies. I hadn't noticed the night before, but the tent they had stuck us in was their supply tent and had no kind of air conditioning or fans. Afghanistan's temperature had quickly hit over one hundred degrees before six in the morning. Even though it had been freezing the night before, it felt like I had woken up in an oven.

I put my boots on my bare feet and walked outside. I found all the other non-commissioned officers from my squad sitting on a bench smoking. About twenty soldiers in full combat gear and soaked through with sweat sat across from them in the dirt. They all looked tired and angry as hell.

"Perfect timing," Slim rasped. He was clearly still dehydrated from the long hot night in the tent.

"Why's that?" I asked. The smoke from my cigarette burned my parched throat. "Who are these guys?"

"These guys are from Dealer's Bravo Company, and they are going to show us our battle space." It turned out Alpha Company was living in the Reserve, and Bravo Company lived about twenty miles away in a place called Dealer Base.

For some reason, they had a squad from Bravo Company walk all the way over from Dealer Base to take us around their area. As in, not the area we were going to be in charge of or have anything remotely to do with. The soldiers who walked all the way the hell over to the

Reserve seemed to understand how dumb all of it was. You could tell by the pure hatred they wore on their faces.

"That doesn't make any sense, Slim," I said. "Why would we need to tour their battle space?"

One of the Bravo leaders, Sergeant Will, walked over to Slim and me. "You don't. It *doesn't* make any sense, and before you say anything, we know our commander is a fucking idiot." Will shook his head. "Pick a few of your guys to go with us, and we'll head out."

Slim had already made his mind up about who was going with us. "Kassabian, Grandpa, Cali, Thad, Tooth, and I'll be going." Slim read the names from a list. "Go ahead and gear up, be back out here in fifteen minutes."

Thad and Tooth were both team leaders from First Squad. Thad was a highly animated joker and also the best karaoke singer I've ever heard. Tooth used to be a tank mechanic and was a huge redneck. He had earned his nickname by getting a few teeth blown out of his head by an exploding fire extinguisher. Something I wasn't even aware could happen.

I was gearing up and loading myself down with ammo—most of which I had to steal from Dealer. Our company had deemed the small detail of arming us an afterthought. Dealer had built a sketchy-looking wooden shack to throw all their surplus ammo in. They never thought to put a lock on it, so Slim and I pilfered it when no one was looking.

They had so many penises spray-painted across the shed you could barely make out the particle board it was built from. For some reason, wherever soldiers go, they cover everything in dicks. If you pointed out how weird that was, they would probably accuse you of being gay. Kind of like all of the homoerotic shit frat boys do but insist it's totally straight because it's about "brotherhood."

Loaded down with stolen ammo and explosives, I walked back out to meet the Dealer soldiers. I noticed a few of the Dealer guys were loaded down with something that looked like a backpack made of metal with about six antennas coming out of it.

"What the hell is that thing?" I asked a bored-looking soldier leaning against a wall.

"It's a Thor system. It jams cell phone and radio signals so they can't set off bombs," he explained. Most of the improvised explosive devices, or IEDs, are remotely detonated using cell phones or radios so the little bastards can hide while they blow us up. We had jammers like that on all our trucks, but this portable thing was new to me.

"Sweet, does it work?" I asked.

The guy didn't give me a verbal response. He just pointed to an Afghan police officer, who was chatting on his cell phone. Right next to one of the soldiers carrying the Thor.

"Oh."

"Commander says we have to carry two on every patrol even though they're completely useless. The stupid mine detector too." He pointed to a long, gangly piece of equipment that was folded up on his back. "It doesn't detect shit."

"Wonderful," I said, lighting another cigarette.

As if to underscore his point, he unslung the mine detector, unfolded it, and turned it on. He held it to the ground and it beeped a few times.

"It just detects metal then?" I asked. Clearly, there were no mines in our compound.

He pointed the mine detector straight up above our heads and it beeped again.

"So it just detects *everything*?" I was pretty confused.

"We have no idea what this piece of shit detects. We've been trying to figure it out all year." He laughed and folded the detector back up.

Before I could ask any more questions about the faulty equipment my life depended on, my radio crackled to life.

"This is Dealer one-Alpha." The voice was Sergeant Will's. "Prepare to move out." The soldiers all fell into a file with a few feet of distance between them. We left gaps in between each soldier so if the Taliban started shooting at us with a machine gun, they wouldn't be able to take us all out in one burst. Or if a bomb went off, it wouldn't kill us all at once.

I was up at the front of the formation next to the guy who had shown me the mine detector.

"If I stop, you stop, all right?" he said with a cigarette dangling from his lips, the mine detector still slung across his back. "It means I saw some shit. If I start running, try to keep up." He nodded at the combat patch I wore on my shoulder. "It isn't your first rodeo, but Kandahar is a different monster... cool, Corporal?" Because of his thick New York accent, I decided to name him Brooklyn. He was tall and lanky; his skinny figure made it look as if all of his combat gear was just a little too big for him.

"Got it," I said. We passed by the Afghan police guard shack on the way out. Several of the police joined our patrol. All their uniforms were mismatched, and a few of them were wearing sandals. "Are they going with us?" I asked Brooklyn.

"Oh yeah. Those douches have to come with us on every patrol we go on. Not that they're worth a shit or anything."

"Then why do you bring them?"

"We have to. Part of that whole hearts-and-minds thing the government keeps talking about." He shrugged. "Making it look like the Afghans are taking charge of the war or something."

I laughed and pointed at one of the Afghans who wasn't even armed. "He isn't even in charge of his weapon."

"Oh yeah, their commanders sold half their weapons to the Taliban months ago," Brooklyn explained. That was pretty much par for the course for the Afghan security forces. "It's probably better they're unarmed. Any shit pops off, they just book it into the mountains anyway."

Our patrol stretched into the fields surrounding the Reserve. In most fields there was some kind of grape growing I'd never seen before. Tired old women with faces like well-worn leather worked the fields and children orbited around their feet playing with sticks and screaming at each other. They paid no attention to the twenty-odd heavily armed American soldiers marching past them.

"You gotta watch out for those little fuckers," Brooklyn sneered, pointing at the kids.

"Those kids in particular?" I asked.

"Any of 'em. All of 'em. They'll get right up close to you and throw a grenade at your ass."

"How lovely." I had never heard of anything like that. In Iraq, it was pretty common, but not in Afghanistan. I tried not to let anything shock me anymore, though.

"Oh yeah. Sergeant Will has a piece of metal in his ass from one of those kids." He gestured back at Sergeant Will, who was meandering around at the back of the file. The only thing I could think was, *Who would give a hand grenade to a child?*

Brooklyn wasn't kidding, Kandahar really was a different monster.

The trail we were walking on turned and passed through a small, ramshackle village. Large ditches were dug on both sides of the little path. They were filled with garbage and human waste. Afghanistan doesn't have a sewer system of any kind and people just throw it all out into the street. Sometimes people dug ditches to throw the shit in, other times it was just out on the street. The smell was not of this world.

Amid that acrid, nose-scorching stench, children were running around playing barefooted. I tried not to let it surprise me. I'd seen abject poverty before, but nothing like this. It made Northern Afghanistan look like Beverly Hills.

I had to stop watching when I saw a little girl not more than a few years old do a face-plant into one of the ditches while all the other children giggled. She popped up to her feet and spat out a mouthful of mysterious black liquid and kept playing with her friends.

"Fucking heathens," Brooklyn spat at the kids. "Who the fuck just plays in garbage and shit?"

"Maybe no one taught them better. Do you see any parents around?"

"Are you telling me someone had to teach you not to play around in your own shit?" he retorted. He had a point. Sure, every kid will stick their hand down their pants and fling crap around when they're a toddler. The majority of these children were probably closer to ten years old.

"That's some *Lord of the Flies* shit, man." I shook my head.

"Lord of the *what*?" he asked.

The kids in this village were obviously more interested in us than whatever game they were playing. They came running over. I didn't really mind the kids, even with the recent threat of murder via preschooler-launched hand grenade. The Dealer guys clearly had other feelings toward them. They hurled swear words in English and Pashto at them. The kids gave us the finger in return and I thought it was hilarious.

"Fuck you!" a tiny eight-year-old voice squeaked at us.

Brooklyn reached down, picked up a rock, and side armed it at a kid. Thankfully he missed. The kid's return shot did not, though. A stone thumped off of my body armor and fell at my feet.

I chucked an energy drink I had in my cargo pocket as hard as I could in return. The tiny can smacked into the chest of the child who had thrown the rock at me. He fell down in a pile of trash, sending bits of wrappers and paper flying into the air. The can exploded with grape flavored liquid.

"Nice aim, Corporal!" one of the Dealer soldiers called up to me.

The kid got up and scurried away. His little feet sent pieces of trash flying up behind him as he ran.

We moved on from the village and came to a small road surrounded by pomegranate orchards. It was walled off by badly built mud walls with broken glass and metal spikes sticking out of the top. Sergeant Will decided this was a good place for a traffic control point.

A traffic control point was when we set up a roadblock and searched any passing cars for weapons or the random Taliban fighter who might wander on by. We dispersed down the road with Cali, Brooklyn, and me picking up the front of the control point. We lazily walked down the sun-scorched road and tried in vain to set up the front of the control point in the shade.

I was quickly briefed on Dealer's rules on operating these control points. They mostly boiled down to: If a car comes down the road too fast, we shoot it. The threat of getting blown up by a suicide bomber was too high to risk it. At least that's what they said. I decided it wasn't worth not taking their word for it.

"Have you been hit by a suicide bomber?" Cali asked as we stared off down the empty stretch of road we were watching.

"Nope," Brooklyn answered, shoving a handful of chewing tobacco in his mouth.

"You ever think the people coming down the road just don't know you're there until you start shooting?" I asked.

"Nope," he said again. Brown spit dribbled down his chin.

The heat was starting to get unbearable as the sun crawled its way overhead. The water in my pack had gone from a somewhat refreshingly cool to nearly burning my mouth with each sip. I didn't want to drink it anymore, but it was the only thing I had. I looked down at my boots and saw they were soaked. I had managed to sweat through my boots. I didn't even know that was possible.

A dust cloud appeared over the horizon. The rumble of a poorly maintained engine rattled. A beat-up old Toyota Corolla came into view, and it was hauling ass. It sent dark black smoke into the air behind it. Brooklyn quickly rose to his feet, rifle up and pointing down the road.

I suddenly felt energized, my heart leaping to life in my chest. I raised my rifle to my shoulder and flicked off the safety switch. It clicked to the semi-auto position. I felt the trigger tension in my finger as I brought it to bear.

"Wadrega!" Brooklyn screamed. It meant "stop" in Pashto, or at least that's what people had told me. It was pretty clear no one in the car heard him. It wasn't surprising since the little Corolla sounded like a damn school bus. The car was still flying down the road at us. Brooklyn's rifle banged to life as he fired one round at the ground in front of him.

It was a warning shot, letting the assholes in the car know that we meant business. The car kept coming. I held back on pulling my trigger. Instead, I sighted my rifle onto the driver's face, which I could clearly see through the dusty, cracked windshield. The tension in my trigger finger tightened as I pulled the minuscule slack out of my trigger.

"Fuck! Cali, get ready!" I yelled. Brooklyn fired again, this time the bullet landed right in front of the oncoming car. The car screeched to a stop. We quickly moved forward on the car, rifles still raised, fingers on the triggers. There was a family of five crammed into the small car. They looked terrified and were exchanging glances with each other. Brooklyn tore open the driver's side door and ripped the driver out of the car. He pinned him to the ground and started searching him.

"Why didn't you fucking stop, you goddamn retard?" Brooklyn screamed at the confused, scared old man. His kids in the backseat started crying.

I looked into the car because it wasn't unheard of for the Taliban to use human shields to run weapons or bombs past our checkpoints. There was nothing in the car. It was pretty clear the guy just didn't hear us over his shitty old car and his radio blaring Indian pop music.

"Shit almost got real," Cali said excitedly.

"No," I said, shaking my head. "No, it didn't."

Sergeant Will and Slim walked up behind us and watched with me as Brooklyn tore the car apart and pulled the entire family out as he searched, screaming various insults as he went.

"The fuck is he doing?" Slim asked, confused. "I'm pretty sure Father Time and his thirteen-year-old bride aren't rolling for the Taliban."

"Yeah, Brooklyn does that sometimes." Will shrugged. "It's pretty clear no one's going to be smuggling anything this way since he started shooting at mother fuckers. Let's pack it up and move on."

"Yes, Sergeant," I responded. "Hey, Brooklyn! Pack it up!" I yelled at the angry man. I'm pretty sure he'd managed to rip about half the car out and throw it on the street by then. We slung our backpacks back over our shoulders, and our parade of tired soldiers crawled on into the mountains leaving the village behind us.

Hours passed, and the sun thankfully started to set, but our patrol didn't end. Will explained an old Buddhist temple was on the side of a mountain that overlooked the biggest village in the district. We were going to hold up there for the night and finish the walk to Dealer Base early in the morning. The temple was up a sheer cliff face and was accessed by ancient stairs carved out of the mountainside. After such a long day, the last thing any of us wanted to do was to climb a thousand-year-old rocky staircase.

I finally summited the small mountain and sat down on the ledge of the temple.

Once upon a time, this temple was probably very elegant. I could see some outline of the intricate carvings and pictures that lined the walls. Heavily decorated pillars rose into the sky to hold up a second floor that was no longer there. Each tile of the floor had a different hand-painted image. The whole place was truly a work of art. And at some point in the late 1990s, the Taliban blew most of it up only because it wasn't dedicated to the god of their choosing.

Several soldiers crawled up onto what remained of the temple's second floor to set up a guard position. The rest of us sat down inside the main room. We sat our bags down and finally got the chance to take off our sweat-soaked body armor. It felt like a million pounds had been lifted off of my back.

"All right guys, guard rotations are set up. If you aren't on watch, get some sleep," Will said as he stood in the middle of our small huddle. "No one goes wandering off to take a piss alone. We'll be heading toward Dealer Base in a few hours."

I put my head down on my pack and instantly fell asleep.

CHAPTER 4

CORN FIELDS, BOMBS, AND ROBBING THE ICE CREAM GUY

SLIM KICKED ME AWAKE AT some dark hour of the morning. It turned out that the soldiers who were on top of the temple had fallen asleep. Will hit them with rocks and screamed at them from the first floor to wake them up. We were fortunate the Taliban hadn't stumbled across us.

I fished around in my backpack and pulled out my night vision goggles, clamped them onto my helmet, and turned them on.

Despite what Hollywood might have you believe, night vision goggles are nearly fucking useless. They turn everything a sickly shade of green and ruin your depth perception. You can't effectively navigate a trail, let alone shoot well. They are only slightly better than blindly stumbling around in the dark.

We slowly started to make our way back down the uneven steps and toward Dealer Base. If climbing those stairs during the day had been hard, descending them while looking through my night vision goggles was damn near impossible. I tripped several times, and the only thing that stopped me from falling off the side of a mountain was sheer dumb luck.

And I wasn't the only one. As I stumbled through the darkness, I could barely make out the soldiers in front of me. I picked someone out and started following them down a trail.

More than once I spun around in a panic because I had lost the person I was following. When that happened, I had to break into a run to catch up. If I got lost, I was as good as dead. I had no idea where I was, and I wasn't exactly in friendly territory, but somehow—before long—we made it to Dealer Base.

Dealer Base was lit up like a Christmas tree. It was surrounded by high concrete walls and concertina wire. Guard towers lined its perimeter. It was a stark contrast from the Reserve.

At this point, my feet felt like bricks. It turned out sleeping on the ground for maybe three hours doesn't make you all that well rested. Again, the group of us dropped to the floor and gathered around in a huddle.

"Good job, new guys. That was a long-ass patrol, and no one passed out. Try to get some sleep because we have to walk back in the morning," Will said. He didn't even look tired.

I was immediately deflated; I didn't think we would have to walk all the way back.

"New guys are sleeping in the medical tent. Not to be morbid or anything, but we don't have room anywhere else," Will continued. He was right; Dealer Base had tents and plywood shacks built right on top of each other. There was barely enough room to park their trucks.

The medical tent had no beds, only stretchers. The air conditioning was cranked up and it was freezing. I was soaked in sweat and had no dry clothes with me other than a change of socks.

Thad, Tooth, and I dragged the stretchers outside onto the rocks to sleep in the night air. I stripped down to my underwear, hung my uniform up on one of the ropes holding the tent together, and went to sleep.

I rolled out of my makeshift bed when the sun came up. I slipped my now dry but stiff and salt-stained pants on and made my way to the chow tent. I was ravenously hungry and piled about eight servings of food onto my paper plate and went to town.

Slim stumbled into the tent after me, slamming back some horrible army coffee. "I don't think I'll survive another twenty-mile death march, man," he rasped. He was so dehydrated his lips were cracked.

"Me either. These people are insane. I'm pretty sure my feet are bleeding," I said between mouthfuls of waffles and ham. "Did you sleep much?"

"Nah," he shook his head. "I was freezing my ass off in that tent, and one of their sick dudes in there kept puking all night. How about you?"

"I didn't sleep, I slipped into a coma. But it was a refreshing coma." I laughed and drank some of his coffee.

Slim and I made our way to the operations tent to meet with Will.

Dealer Base looked like a movie set meant to recreate a third-world disaster area. I was beginning to realize that the smell of feces in the air was part of everyday life in Kandahar. Shacks made out of every material you can think of were propped up between the concrete retaining walls, and soldiers slept in them side-by-side, almost touching each other.

Will met us in the tent. A huge map was pinned to a board, and our route was all set. Will pointed out a village right in our path called Madaraja that his guys had attacked in a massive offensive a few months before. It was some fruitless attempt to chase out the Taliban.

It failed miserably, and every casualty they had taken during the deployment had happened within the small village. This included his platoon leader having both his legs blown off and Will himself having an up-close and personal meeting with an exploding hand grenade.

"So...we're going to walk right into that bitch and set up traffic control points all over the place. Stir some shit up. You guys cool with that?" Will asked us with a smile on his face.

"You picked the right boys," Slim laughed. Slim had a reputation for always looking for a fight. I just had a reputation for always being in one. That might have been because I kept deploying with Slim.

"All right, get your guys together. Let's roll." Will walked out of the tent.

Before long we were walking out of the cramped confines of Dealer Base and back into the mountains. As we crested the mountain, we saw vast fields of corn as far as the eye could see.

Sergeant Will called all the non-commissioned officers over to where he was kneeling, gathering everyone into a huddle. "This is where they like to fuck us up, guys." He gestured out to the cornfields. "The shit is so high we can't see in it. Plant bombs all over, that's how they blew the legs off of our platoon leader."

I looked out at the field. The thick corn stalks were so close together it was a hypnotic sea of green and yellow. There could be any number of people in there staring back at us.

"All right. So how do we get across it?" Grandpa asked.

"We spread out into a line and move across slowly. You see anything, yell so we all stop," Will motioned with his hands how he wanted us all to line up. "Let's move, boys!" he yelled back at everyone.

We fell into a line, side-by-side, stretching out across the edge of the field and slowly began making our way into the field. I could barely see more than a few feet in front of me and could just make out Cali off to my left.

They always tell you in training that any upturned dirt, loose soil, or holes in the ground can be signs of hidden bombs.

As I walked slowly, staring down at my feet, I realized every single inch of that damn field looked like every indicator I had ever been taught. I came to the conclusion that unless it had an ACME-style sign sticking out of the ground telling me where it was, I was most likely going to find a bomb about the same time it was going to find me.

"Stop!" Slim's voice came over the radio. "Back up! Back up!" he screamed.

I knew Slim was the next guy to my right. I turned around and ran. Stalks of corn slapped me in the face as I sprinted through them.

I came out of the field and back onto the mountain trail. The rest of the patrol busted out of the fields and back out with me. Slim took off his helmet and sat down, his eyes the size of saucers.

"What the fuck did you see?" Will asked between gulps of air.

"A goddamn bomb was on the wall! Stopped right next to it!" Slim tripped over his words. "I panicked, ripped the fucking wires out, and ran."

"You *what?*" I screamed at him.

"I don't know, man! I didn't know what else to do!" Slim yelled back.

"Calm down, guys; team leaders, make sure your soldiers are all here," Will said calmly.

The team leaders—not including me because none of my soldiers came along—walked around to ensure all of their men made it back. They all gave him the thumbs up.

"Good. I'll call it up to Dealer Base. Spread out and get some security for the area. We probably aren't going anywhere for a while," Will said as he sat down on a rock.

When you find a bomb, you have to call it up to your superiors who will then call in an Explosive Ordinance Disposal team, or EOD. They come riding out to save us by blowing up the bombs we find using multi-million-dollar robots. The only problem is they take hours to get out to where you are waiting for them because of the massive demand for their services.

We settled into the rocks of the mountainous trail and watched over the huge field in front of us.

I lit a cigarette and leaned against a rock next to Slim. "I can't believe you ripped the damn wires out." I shook my head.

"Hey, it worked, didn't it? I'm still standing here."

"Only because the rookie manning the bomb was sleeping at the wheel. You got lucky."

"You say luck, I say skill." Slim laughed.

I was starting to think the locals knew about the little gift waiting for us in the field as absolutely no one came out to work the fields in the middle of harvest season. It wasn't surprising. The Taliban would always give the locals a heads-up so they wouldn't step on traps meant for us. Not because they cared about the civilians, but because it was a waste of resources to blow up some farmer.

When entire villages of people disappeared in the middle of the day, it was generally a good sign we were about to be attacked. It wasn't typical for the locals to completely abandon their livelihood to wilt in the oppressive midday sun.

After a few hours, several bearded EOD technicians appeared over the horizon. EOD techs were easy to distinguish: they carried tons of gear strapped to their chests, never wore helmets, and always had beards.

They walked up to Will and shook his hand.

"Which one of you guys found the bomb?" the tech with the biggest, bushiest beard asked. I assumed—based on his mighty beard—that he was in charge.

"I did," Slim said.

"Show me."

Slim sighed, nodded at me to go with him, and we walked back out into the cornfield with the EOD guy following us.

We spread out and walked slowly. The EOD guy didn't seem to have a care in the world. His rifle was slung on his back and he was strolling behind Slim as if it was a walk in the park.

I should have been paying attention to where I was walking. Suddenly, right in front of me, I came across a metal box half sticking out of the ground. Strung from the box and toward the perimeter wall was a wire. I stopped dead in my tracks, my heart in my throat. I could feel my heartbeat slamming in my temples.

"IED!" I screamed. Slim and the EOD guy rushed past me at a dead sprint and I was right on their heels. We gathered back together at the edge of the cornfield.

"What did you see?" The EOD guy asked between breaths.

"Metal box—wire going back toward the wall, toward the first bomb," I gasped.

When several bombs are wired together, it's called a "daisy chain." If someone trips one, several others go off, increasing casualties. Apparently, the two we found were strung out in a line going from the wall toward the middle of the field, meaning they had figured out Dealer's tactics for clearing large open fields.

"Take your people back to the trail," the EOD guy told Slim. "I'll get my guys into the field and handle this." He waved over to the other six EOD technicians who were sitting with our soldiers on the rocks.

They all stood, picked up their bags, and started walking toward the cornfield.

The rest of us sat on the outskirts of the cornfield. It was too thick for us to see the EOD guys at work. Before long the bearded gang of bombers emerged from the cornfield and walked over to where we were watching.

"We're gonna blow them, so we should probably back up," the lead EOD guy said. He had a small box with a ton of wires attached to it in his hand: a detonator.

We all knelt down behind a small crumbling retaining wall.

Thad sat down next to Slim and me, giggling and holding a camera. This is the first time he was ever going to see something like this and he didn't want to miss it.

"Fire in the hole!" the EOD guy yelled.

A fountain of dirt shot up into the air. A blast wave knocked us off our knees. The ground shook. We all cheered and laughed as we got up and brushed ourselves off. The EOD guys slung their backpacks back on, waved their goodbyes, and headed back up the trail they'd come in on. They were gone as fast as they'd appeared.

We finally made our way through the corn field, which was made much easier by the fact nearly all the corn had been blown over by the explosion set off by EOD. Sure, we totally destroyed an entire village's food and income source, but our day was made marginally easier by it.

The field looked like a moonscape; you could clearly see two massive craters punched into the earth.

"Popcorn, mother fuckers," Cali laughed as he stomped through piles of charred stalks of corn.

The village of Madaraja lay on the other side of the devastated cornfield. I could tell it had seen some major combat.

Every building was damaged in some way. Bullet holes, blast marks, and a burned-up Afghan National Army pickup truck still on the side of the road.

"Wow, you guys weren't kidding," Grandpa said as he surveyed the damage.

"Yeah, it was a rough couple of days," Will sighed.

"We fucked those bastards up!" Brooklyn laughed, wildly pointing his weapon at one of the buildings.

The denizens of the village had come out of hiding, pouring out into the streets as we walked down them. They were no doubt a bit curious who was wandering through their neck of the woods blowing up their food supply and local economy.

"You think they came out to tell us how much they like democracy?" I joked.

Slim laughed and waved at the people who were gawking. "Vote Republican!" he yelled cheerfully. I shook my head at him, and he laughed some more. "What? They're all inbred, backward farm people. Seems like the right demographic."

I laughed.

Our interpreter, an older guy they called Reggie, walked over to Will and they exchanged some words.

"Stop, guys," Will instructed. "Some shop owner wants to talk to us about something. Spread out, set up security," he ordered over the radio. "Slim and Kassabian, you're going in with me." He wanted to keep us close so we could see what we would be dealing with shortly.

Will, Slim, Reggie, and I walked into a small dirty shop to meet an ancient-looking old man who was sitting on the floor. He was seated on a small brown rug surrounded by bags of various kinds of beans or rice. Everything he sold was covered in bright Chinese lettering. Reggie crouched down next to him and shook the man's hand. I noticed that even though no one could see us inside that little shop, Reggie never took the scarf off his face. He didn't trust the old man.

Most interpreters working for U.S. soldiers in Afghanistan kept their faces covered when out on patrol with us. They were normally from the same areas we were patrolling, and it would be bad news if someone recognized them. Not only would they be killed, but so would their family and friends. If they were lucky they would just be shot, but the Taliban was capable of terrible cruelty.

"He's asking who blew up the corn field," Reggie said, fighting back a laugh.

"Tell him we did it because it's obvious his village is still harboring Taliban," Will said, his voice tinged with anger.

Reggie translated the words into Pashto, and the old man gestured wildly with his hands. "He says there is Taliban in the village," Reggie said.

"No shit," Slim laughed.

"Who are they, then?" Will demanded. "Show us their houses."

Reggie said a few words to the old man who quickly shook his head "no" and said something to Reggie. "He says they will kill his whole family if he helps us," Reggie replied. It was clear from his tone that he felt sorry for the old man.

"Not if we kill the Taliban first," Slim sneered. "Tell him that."

Reggie dutifully related the message. "He says you could never kill them all. Eventually, you will leave and go back to America, but they will not. They will slaughter me." Reggie's voice trembled as he translated. He clearly understood where the man was coming from.

The old man was right. We wouldn't be there to protect him forever. We would leave his war-torn country and return to the comfort of our homes in America. And the Taliban would roam through his town with knives looking for collaborators.

Sick of this back and forth, I stood up and walked out of the shop into the street. Compared to the cramped, dirty confines of the man's shop, the open air sewers in the streets of Madaraja felt like a breath of fresh air. As I stood in the sweltering mid-afternoon sun, I glanced down the street to see Brooklyn robbing the local ice cream guy.

Brooklyn was shoulder deep into a tiny freezer on wheels trying to grab some ice cream bars while an angry old man attempted to push him away. The old man didn't have the strength to fight off the American soldier pilfering his goods and resorted to screaming and waving his arms around.

Brooklyn laughed it off and walked back to me, several ice cream bars in hand. "Hey, Corporal, you want some ice cream?" he asked, jamming a bar into his mouth.

I was utterly speechless. I had seen soldiers do plenty of illegal, immoral, and unethical things during my career, but I had never seen a strongarm robbery before.

"God dammit, Brooklyn! Give that man a few dollars!" Will yelled out from the shop's entrance. The way he said it made me think Brooklyn did this sort of thing often.

Brooklyn stomped over to the merchant, pulled out his wallet, and handed him a few tattered Afghani bills. It ended up being less than one dollar. I walked over to the irate old man and gave him a five-dollar bill—all the money I had in my pocket at the time.

"Damn, Corporal, I already paid him," Brooklyn called out to me.

"Shut your fucking mouth!" I snarled at him.

Thankfully, after our little run-in with the shop owner and the robbery, we left the town.

The heat was like something I had never felt before in my life. I was so dehydrated it was a chore just to blink, but I wasn't as bad off as Grandpa. Grandpa was tired and stumbling, showing all the symptoms of heat exhaustion. Dealer's medic was walking alongside Grandpa trying to get him to drink water, but I was pretty sure he was past the point of helping.

"All right guys, we might be having a heat casualty so we're gonna bring the patrol down to the river. Once we get down there, spread out and pull security," Will's voice crackled over the radio.

Slim and I walked next to Grandpa to help guide him down to a river that crossed through a nearby village. Pomegranate trees grew all around the river covering it in a refreshing level of shade. The field we were in was the greenest piece of land I had seen in Afghanistan, like an oasis. The ripe pomegranate trees hung heavy with purple fruit.

We plopped down in a lush green field as our soldiers secured the area around us. Grandpa fell on his back gasping for air and stripping off his body armor in an attempt to cool off. His skin was bright red and his lips were painfully cracked.

Dealer's medic crouched down next to Grandpa and started an IV line in his arm.

"Man, he looks like shit." Will stifled a laugh. "I think we might have to evacuate him."

"Grandpa?" Slim said. "Hell no. He'll recover. He's a tough old bastard," he said, waving Will off.

"All right, I'll give him ten minutes. We have to get out of here." Will sat down next to us. "Down that road—" Will pointed to the dirt path that curved next to the walled-off compound that enclosed the pomegranate field "—that's where our platoon leader got fucked up."

I could see a massive crater in the road where a young lieutenant triggered a tripwire and was torn apart and maimed forever in a massive explosion.

It was clear that a lot of the Dealer soldiers were getting overheated. We were all soaked through with sweat. Our hydration packs were already running low. When we stopped to give Grandpa a chance to rest everyone else had stripped off their gear as well.

I followed suit. I dropped my backpack and body armor in a pile on the grass. Feeling the breeze on my body was probably the best thing I'd felt in days.

Some of the Dealer boys sat next to me near the water's edge.

"I bet that water feels amazing," mused a soldier named Dexter. I saw the distorted water coursing over the lens of his coke-bottle glasses.

"And full of human waste," I said.

Afghans usually disposed of waste and garbage by throwing it outside or into a water source. There was usually an accumulation of trash alongside riverbeds or the smell of feces. This river appeared oddly clean.

"Looks fine to me," Cali murmured.

"Yeah," Dexter said.

Before anything else was said, several of the Dealer soldiers jumped into the river. A splash of water landed on Dexter, Cali, and me. The chilly water made me recoil. Dexter was the next one in, and then Will ran past me and splashed into the stream.

The spontaneous bathing drew several villagers out of their homes to watch. Before long, the villagers and their children were jumping in.

I got up and jumped into the river. The water was so cold it knocked the wind out of me. It felt like falling through ice in the middle of winter.

Before I could brush my overgrown hair out of my eyes, an Afghan kid splashed water at me and laughed. I laughed and splashed him back.

"Y'all are going to get AIDs from that river!" Slim called out from the bank.

The Afghan kid and I splashed at Slim and laughed. I hoisted the kid up on my shoulders and tossed him into the air, he landed with a splash and all the villagers watching laughed and clapped.

"Oh! Gross!" Dexter screamed. "I just saw a turd!"

The Afghans didn't seem to mind, but Dexter ran for shore.

"Ah!" Will screamed. "A damn wipe just floated by!" A small white rag with an unmistakable smear of brown drifted by.

We all booked it for the shore. We climbed out of the river while most of the soldiers on the banks laughed at us.

Brooklyn came out from behind a tree carrying a bag of baby wipes and buckling his belt.

"You mother fucker!" Will screamed.

Brooklyn turned on his heels and ran. Sergeant Will following close behind.

"You know, I think that Brooklyn guy isn't right in the head," Cali said.

"Really?" I laughed. "Just catching onto that, are you?"

As we moved away from the river, Afghan kids ran alongside our patrol. For the first time since I had arrived in Kandahar, I felt like I had made a connection with the locals.

That was until Cali kicked one of the kids in the chest, King Leonidas-in-*300*-style. After that, the kids went back to throwing rocks at us until we put some distance between ourselves and the village.

Several hours passed as we made our way through the heat and back to the Reserve. I could tell by my map that we were getting closer as the day wore on. Soon our death march would be over.

We crested a small hill and walked down a road that was partially melting because of the heat. Regular blacktop has no place in a country whose temperatures run close to those on the surface of the sun. Sticky black tar stuck to my boots and trailed behind me in strings as we plodded on.

The outskirts of the small farming village that surrounded the Reserve came into view. It felt comforting to see that massive castle in the distance, even if it could perfectly conceal about one hundred different snipers at any given time.

Will called for us to stop and set up positions around the village. He apparently had something to do that couldn't wait. I knelt down behind a small crumbling wall with Slim and waited for us to move on.

I peered over my shoulder to see Will, pants around his ankles, toilet paper in hand, and his ass pressed up against an old mud brick house. He was taking a shit on someone's house, in broad daylight, in the middle of a busy village.

Slim and I just glanced at each other and kept staring off into the field we were guarding. Somehow after only two days with Dealer, I was already completely desensitized. It didn't even get weird until an old man, who was obviously the owner of the house Will was shitting on, came outside and witnessed what was going on. Will gave him a friendly thumbs-up in between grunts and farts.

Finally, we turned back down the trail that led to the Reserve. Alexander's castle loomed over us as we passed through the gates of our newly adopted home. Will and the Dealer soldiers waved their goodbyes and walked back out of our gates.

Slim and I plopped down on a bench near the front gate, taking off our helmets and brushing the sweat from our eyes. I lit a cigarette and leaned back against the retaining wall, Slim shook his head and said:

"What the fuck have we gotten ourselves into?"

CHAPTER 5

THE WORST SOLDIER IN THE UNITED STATES ARMY

I SHOULD HAVE KNOWN FROM the second I sat down and looked at Charlie Team and said to myself, "Man, I have some good soldiers," that it wasn't going to last.

There's a saying in the army that whenever you get screwed over in a way that you can only attribute to stupid command decisions, it's called "being fucked by the big, green weenie." Obviously, it came from the days that we actually wore green uniforms, but it didn't make it any less real.

By then I had been at the Reserve about three weeks. I was lying on my cot with a horrible bout of dysentery and hooked up to two different IV drips when Slim walked into the tent and sat down next to me. "How you feeling, brother?" he said, looking at my horrible sunken cheeks and dark eyes.

"I feel like I'm shitting myself to death," I said weakly. Out of all the terrible illnesses I had contracted in third-world countries, dysentery was the worst. It's a food- or waterborne illness spread by fecal matter.

Before you judge me for eating and drinking water coated in human shit, just remember that before the wonderful conveniences of plumbing and germ theory, it was incredibly common and sometimes even fatal. I had probably caught it from eating our cook's fantastic creations—the ones he would leave out in the open air for hours at a time.

"Well fuck, man." Slim shook his head. "I hate to give you even worse news then."

"Fuck, what else could you do to me right now? Shoot me?" I gave a weak smile and showed him the two needles sticking into my arms.

"We're giving you a new soldier," Slim said.

"New?" I asked. "What about Dirty and Urkel?"

"You'll keep them. But we're giving you a third."

"Who?" I was incredibly wary about his tone of voice. I was the lowest ranking team leader in the squad. No one just gives up a good soldier, especially not to a corporal team leader.

"Creep," he said, not making eye contact. I slowly sat up on my cot, bracing myself with what was left of my strength.

"Fuck no," I said, grabbing his arm.

Everyone in my unit knew who Creep was. Creep was in third platoon when the deployment started. He had volunteered to deploy with us from another unit at Fort Hood because we were short on soldiers.

In the short time he had been with third platoon, he had no less than four sexual harassment complaints filed against him. Add that to the Equal Opportunity offenses and at least one restraining order.

Equal Opportunity was a program that the Department of Defense created to address the staggering number of sexual assaults that happen in the military. Every company had an Equal Opportunity representative that you could go to and voice complaints completely anonymously, and your representative was supposed to make sure the wrongdoer was punished.

Of course, that never happened, as Creep had four complaints filed against him for only God-knows-what. Instead of being kicked out of the army, he had been shuffled around to different units. Kind of like the Catholic Church does with its offenders.

I could almost be okay with having Creep on my team if that were his only shortcoming, but that just scratched the surface. On our pre-deployment field training exercise, Creep had lost the firing pin to his rifle, started crying, and tried to say everything he did was justified because his mother was a colonel in Medical Command.

I think the worst part was that even though he was being transferred to my team, no one would tell me what exactly he did to get completely kicked out of his platoon.

"I'm sorry, man," Slim said.

"No. I'm not taking him," I said stubbornly. I was aware Slim was only telling me this way because he was my friend, not because I had any say in the matter. Nothing I could say was going to change that.

"We'll bounce him around on different teams for the most part, but he's going to be on your team for administration reasons."

"You mean for when he fucks up," I corrected him.

"Yeah." Slim laughed a little.

"You fucking owe me," I groaned. "He's going to poison my kids," I said regarding Dirty and Urkel. They were young and impressionable, but great soldiers.

He laughed and gave me a few more bottles of water. The worst part of dysentery was trying to stay hydrated as you spent the majority of time ejecting liquids from one orifice or another. Hence the IVs.

Slim walked out of my sweltering tent leaving me to stew on the fact he'd just dropped one of the worst soldiers in our company onto my lap.

I wasn't fully recovered or even walking under my own strength when the first problems with Creep started popping up. Our operations frequency was pretty crazy, and our lives generally boiled down to if you weren't on patrol you were on tower guard duty. We made sure each tower had at least two people in it during the night to make staying awake a little easier, but Creep never even made it that far.

On his first shift, Perro found him lying on the floor of one of the towers, all his gear stripped off, and sleeping soundly in the dirt.

The worst part was that Creep hadn't fallen asleep by accident—something most of us did eventually. He had taken off all his gear, gotten comfortable, and intentionally gone to sleep. Not only did that show he was a shithead, it showed he really didn't care about any of us. If you fall asleep while on guard, you put every soldier in danger. We let him know that.

But in the end, we chalked it up to him being young and stupid and let it go.

Besides being totally unable to stay awake while on guard, Creep had another problem: he didn't know how to wash up. At the Reserve, we had two working showers. Sure, the water wasn't hot, and it was harder than rock, but they worked. You could generally shower whenever you wanted, and at least once every few days.

We also had one working washing machine. You had to fill it with water from one of the showers with a bucket, and we had no dryer, but you could still wash your clothes. Creep did neither of those things.

As you can imagine, several days of patrolling in the blistering-hot Afghan sun builds a mighty funk on one's body. With twenty people living in a tent, that funk could quickly reach levels that would make you wretch.

Gong, Perro, and Guapo all came into my tent one morning when I was still hooked to my IVs and covered in a cold sweat.

"Your boy is fucking up," Perro said.

"Huh?" I said groggily.

"Creep. He hasn't washed his ass or clothes since he's been here," Perro went on.

I rolled over. "It's been over a week. No way."

"He smells like a dead body covered in burnt hair," Gong added. His tone was surprisingly serious for him.

"Mother fucker." I pulled myself onto my feet, holding IV bags above my head as I went. I shuffled across the Reserve to their tent. My gaunt, dehydrated, sickly figure was a shell of my former self.

I ducked into their tent and my nose was assaulted by a smell that was as if someone had drunk nothing but vinegar for a month and taken a massive shit on a campfire.

"Creep!" I tried to scream, but I didn't have the energy. It was more of a crackling rasp. He bolted to his feet and stood at parade rest.

"Yes, Corporal?" he drawled. He was from somewhere in bum-fuck-nowhere Missouri. I never cared to find out where exactly, but I assumed wherever he was from had no problem dating within the family tree.

"Have you washed your ass since you've gotten to the Reserve?"

"Well, I was going to Corporal, but..." he started. I saw his teeth for the first time. They looked as if he had brushed them with a handful of rocks his whole life.

"I didn't ask for a fucking story, goddammit," I croaked weakly.

"No, Corporal," he answered, trying his hardest not to make eye contact.

"How old are you?" I asked him.

"Twenty-nine, Corporal."

"You're older than me, Creep. You understand that? I shouldn't have to be asking you if you fucking showered."

"But I—" he began again.

"Shut the fuck up," I raised my voice into the closest thing resembling a scream that I could. "This isn't something that I should have to explain any further. You get your nasty ass wet, put some mother fucking soap on, and then you rinse it the fuck off." I was yelling so loudly that I was getting light-headed. I was still sicker than I thought.

I watched little droplets of spit smack against his face. The places where that spit landed were probably the cleanest part of his body at that moment. "Perro, Gong, Cali," I yelled. They all rolled over in their cots to look at me. "Escort this fucking retard to the shower and make sure he washes his fucking balls correctly!"

They all laughed and got up.

I shuffled back to my tent and collapsed into my cot. All of the screaming and the simple act of moving had worn me out.

Perro came back into the tent about ten minutes later and told me that their grotesque mission was complete. They had had to take the shower curtain off to ensure Creep washed up. The first time they just waited outside until he was done, and after five minutes Creep walked out bone dry and looking the same way he did when he went in. After that, they pushed him back into the shower trailer and watched him.

"You owe me a beer when we get home," Perro said. He looked disgusted.

"Put it on Slim's tab." I smiled at him.

CHAPTER 6

OPERATION GRIZZLY GANG-BANG

ABOUT FOUR WEEKS HAD PASSED since our little jaunt out into the wilderness with the Dealer soldiers. Their company that had been living with us had packed up and moved back to Dealer Base leaving us to run the Reserve and its surrounding area as we saw fit. We had already fallen into a rhythm of sending a patrol out early in the morning and late at night, splitting the two squads into shifts that rarely saw each other.

One massive thorn in our side was Captain Scream. Scream was the commander of Dealer and therefore technically in charge of us. He always came up with big, pointless missions and had us carry out raids on houses where he thought high-value targets lived.

Scream had never once been right about any of the raids. We were getting sick of being sent on wild goose chases in the middle of the night.

One day, while Nan was pulling the graveyard shift in the radio room with our platoon leader, Lieutenant Ginger, Scream's voice crackled to life over the radio. His voice sounded as if it had been put through a belt sander and he had a healthy, three-pack-a-day smoking habit.

"Spartan Six, this is Dealer Six," Scream's gravelly voice echoed.

Spartan Six was Ginger's radio call sign.

Nan was asleep on the floor of the radio room; Ginger was passed out in a broken swivel chair. They were both startled awake by the radio. No one ever tried to contact us in the middle of the night. Most units we ran into didn't even know the Reserve existed, let alone our radio frequency.

"This is Spartan Base," Nan croaked, still waking up. "Send your traffic."

"I'll be arriving at your location in fifteen minutes," Scream said.

At that, Ginger shot to his feet and rushed out the door to start waking up our squad and team leaders.

Ginger, Thad, Slim, Nan, and I were all standing in the tiny mud-brick radio room to meet Scream when he walked in. All of us were wishing we were still in our beds.

"All right guys, code name Cobra was last reported in your area," Scream announced. For some reason, he came up with code names for all the high-value targets, as if they were somehow listening in on our meeting. "We tracked his cell phone to a compound less than a mile from here."

"What's the plan, sir?" Ginger asked with disinterest. He knew any plan Scream concocted wouldn't be followed anyway.

"Your trucks will surround the compound to make sure no one runs off. Then you send in dismounted soldiers to raid it," Scream said. He was clearly pretty proud of his plan. By the tone of his voice, you would think he just planned the next D-Day invasion rather than a raid on a shitty building made out of mud.

"Second Squad, suit up," Ginger said, meaning the Hooligans. Of the two squads in our platoon, we both had our strengths and weaknesses. First Squad was good at contacting the locals, meeting elders, and carrying out rebuilding projects. Second Squad—the Hooligans—on the other hand, excelled at good old-fashioned violence, and that mission was right up our alley.

Codename Cobra was a guy named Mohamed Omar, the Taliban warlord in charge of building and planting roadside bombs in the entire providence of Kandahar. He was also the third most wanted man in all of Regional Command South. To say that was a pretty big deal was a huge understatement. And as it turned out, the third most wanted man in the south of Afghanistan had been living a few doors down from us ever since we'd moved into the Reserve.

Second Squad was lined up at the gates of the Reserve. We were all nervous as hell. The third most wanted man would have legions of bodyguards and, obviously, wouldn't go down without a fight. We were all loaded down with more ammo than normal, including hand grenades and a few rocket launchers. First Squad's convoy roared out through the gates toward the target compound. A few minutes later, we rushed through the gates after them on foot.

We ran down the road. Normally, running a few hundred meters wouldn't be a chore at all, but weighed down with about sixty pounds of gear strapped all over our bodies, it became a Herculean task.

We met a soldier along the way who looked as if he was holding a small satellite in his hand. He was apparently looking for Omar's cell phone signal. Meaning Scream really had no damn clue where he was sending us.

The satellite guy had ridden into the village in one of First Squad's trucks and stopped them when he got a hit on his satellite, but couldn't pinpoint it to a single compound.

So two squads of soldiers sent into a village known to be harboring the third most wanted man in Kandahar just sat there like idiots. By then there was no doubt lookouts and gunmen were moving into position as we tried to figure out where the fuck we were supposed to be going. Any hint of surprise we'd had was totally and completely gone.

"What the fuck do you want us to do? Just start kicking in doors?" Slim yelled at the satellite guy.

First Squad was trying desperately to keep an eye on all the compounds around us from the turrets of their vehicles, but it was impossible. The satellite guy started making his way up a hill toward a massive complex that was elaborately decorated with flags and multicolored lights.

A Toyota Corolla screamed up to the compound's front door blaring its horn. The satellite guy looked back at us.

"That's the compound!" he yelled. We all realized that the Corolla was there to whisk Omar away.

Slim turned to Second Squad and pointed at the building on the hill. "Let's go, boys!" he cried.

We rushed up the hill. Alpha Team went around to the right side of the compound. Bravo Team went to the left, leaving my team to go straight through the front door. For some reason that was a detail we hadn't gone over beforehand.

As we neared, Slim broke out the Corolla's driver side window, shoving the barrel of his rifle in the driver's face.

I sprinted toward the front door with Dirty at my heels carrying the massive M240B machine gun across his small frame. Urkel brought up the rear as Dirty's assistant machine gunner.

I broke through the flimsy wooden door and it shattered to pieces. I lifted my rifle and immediately went to the left following along the inner compound wall. Dirty and Urkel went to the right.

My team had the entire compound covered in a few seconds.

Instead of going toe-to-toe with a legion of terrorist bodyguards, we found ourselves crashing what looked like some kind of garden tea party.

About twelve people, including women and children, were sitting around on blankets. Between them was a massive spread of bread and tea. They were laughing and joking as we burst through the door. Now it looked like they were just trying to figure out what the fuck we were doing there.

Our interpreter, Hamid, was quickly in the door behind us and screaming at them in Pashto. I had no idea what he was saying, but the people in the courtyard stayed frozen in place. I slowly advanced on the men of the group and began searching them.

"Slim, the compound's secure. Get in here," I said over my radio. A few seconds later Slim, Oldies, and Memphis came rushing into the compound.

"Start doing biometrics on all these assholes," Slim commanded.

I fished around in the backpack Urkel was carrying and pulled out our biometric machine.

Biometrics are identifying marks every person has. We take fingerprints, iris scans, and facial measurements. The U.S. military has been keeping a database on the most wanted Taliban fighters for years using pictures or partial fingerprints left on bomb fragments. Using our little machine, I could take someone's fingerprints or a picture and know within a few seconds who they were and if they were a wanted person.

The first man I stood up and put against the wall gave me his hands without any questions. He had a little smirk on his face and made direct eye contact. I started scanning his first finger when the screen on my machine popped up a red warning.

It read: *Muhammad Omar: Tier-Two Wanted*. Now, this might get some people excited right away, but our machine was pretty damn unreliable. Normally you had to scan all ten fingers and one iris before you could get a reading that was at all believable. There was a very good chance this guy in front of me was innocent.

"Are you Mohammed Omar?" I asked, laughing. I did not expect a known Taliban commander would admit to an American soldier's face who he was.

"Yes, I am," he answered in slightly accented, but very good English.

I stared at him wide-eyed.

Omar smiled at me.

"The Taliban commander?" I asked.

"Yes, that is me," he answered again. He was still smiling. His black-toothed grin disgusted me. I still held his hand to my machine. Those gnarled hands had built countless bombs that had killed many American soldiers over the years.

"You know I'm taking you away, right?" I matched his eye contact as I said it. I could feel the hatred in his gaze, and I hoped he could feel the same in mine.

"No, you're not," he said slowly, still smiling. I had no idea what he meant. Clearly, he wasn't going to escape from us. He was unarmed and surrounded by over thirty soldiers. What the hell was he going to do?

The answer came in the form of an Afghan National Police patrol walking in through the compound door. At its head was Colonel Ashraf, the incredibly corrupt district commander of district six of Kandahar. He was well known to have Taliban ties. Many people accused him of setting up U.S. soldiers and sometimes his own police to get ambushed by Taliban in exchange for money.

Ashraf started yelling at Hamid as his police started spreading out through the compound.

"He says he will take this Taliban into his custody," Hamid stuttered.

That was what Omar meant. He knew if we ever hit his house, the police would come to his rescue under the guise of taking him into their custody.

"Tell him to fuck off," Slim said. "He's ours." Slim hated Ashraf. Every time we had a meeting with him, it always ended in the two of them screaming at each other.

"He says Scream told him they would be allowed to take them to their police station," Hamid said with a smile. Hamid knew Ashraf was lying through his teeth. At this point, I was starting to wonder where the hell Scream was. He never missed a chance to steal someone else's glory.

"Goddammit! You mother fuckers need to turn around and get me!" my radio shouted into the air. It was Scream, and it turned out First Squad had left him back at the Reserve. To be fair, he never said where he fitted into this whole operation, but leaving your area commander behind on a mission was probably a bad idea.

"Scream, this is Slim. Ashraf is saying he has the authorization to take Omar into custody. Is this legit?" Slim asked over his radio. I could only imagine Scream was tearing our little operations room apart in anger for being left behind on a mission that had captured the third most wanted man in Kandahar.

"Negative!" Scream roared in response. "Detain *Codename Cobra* immediately!" The emphasis he put on "Codename Cobra" was hilarious. He was apparently pissed we were using Omar's name over the radio.

We quickly surrounded Omar, who at this point was sitting back down in the compound's garden having tea with Ashraf. We forced

Omar to his feet and placed plastic zip cuffs around his wrists. I made sure to make them painfully tight.

Ashraf quickly got to his feet and started screaming at Hamid.

"He says you can't take him," Hamid translated. Hamid scowled at Ashraf, totally sick of the back and forth.

"Tell Ashraf I told him to go fuck himself," Slim growled. Slim said stuff like that all the time. Hamid was experienced enough to know not to actually tell the Afghans what he said.

Hamid had been an interpreter since he was eighteen, or at least that's what he told people. Most Afghans don't actually know how old they are. Over the years, he had been blown up, shot at, and wounded by the Taliban. He hated them more than we did.

"Hamid, tell him I told him to *go fuck himself*," Slim reiterated. He wasn't kidding this time. Slim was giving up on the relationship we were supposed to have with the local Afghan police and torching the bridge behind him.

Hamid translated to Ashraf and laughed, his shotgun held over his shoulder like some kind of Afghan action hero. Slim grabbed Omar by the collar and started dragging him out of the compound. Surprisingly, Ashraf didn't try to stop us.

Slim and I lifted Omar up and tossed him into the backseat of one of First Squad's trucks. We buckled him in and wrapped his face in a t-shirt. I slammed the door behind us.

"Second Squad, let's go home!" Slim called over the radio. We filed out of the compound and started marching back down the road toward the Reserve. First Squad's trucks gunned it toward Dealer Base, holding our prize and leaving a trail of dust in their wake. We walked back holding our heads a little higher that day.

I felt as if I'd really done something to support the war effort. We captured a goddamn Taliban warlord!

Of course, that ended up being a total lie. The Taliban aren't a set of dominoes. You can't just knock one of them down and expect the rest to go down with them. It turned out they simply replaced the guy we arrested less than a day later, never missing a step in their operations in our area. But for that brief moment, we stuck it to our enemy, and it felt good.

We walked back to the gates of the Reserve like conquering war heroes. Even if it was only just for that day.

CHAPTER 7

GONG'S FIRST PATIENT

ONE OF THE MOST COMMON things we had to do was check on the Afghan National Police. We would go out to their police stations and double check to ensure they were actually doing their jobs. We learned too long ago that if you left them to their own devices, they would sell all their equipment, sit back, and collect a paycheck that was generously donated to the Afghan government by various NATO nations. And that's when they weren't openly helping the Taliban.

We only had one police station in our patrol area, but it was the district headquarters commanded by Colonel Ashraf. It was evident that the other Americans Ashraf had worked with overlooked all his illegal doings for the sake of the mission. Slim was not one of those people. He wouldn't look the other way when Ashraf sold a whole shipment of gasoline or when we gave him thirty pairs of boots to make sure his policemen all had shoes, and every pair mysteriously went missing.

Slim might have been insane, but he wasn't a bad soldier. Ashraf even had a cop under his employ whose sole job was to torture and abuse people. The dude was massive, even by American standards. Standing over six feet tall, his beard and long hair joined together into one huge tangled mess that made him look like some kind of missing link. His feet were so big he didn't even bother wearing anything on them anymore. We named him Mongo.

Mongo carried a club around and beat anyone who displeased Ashraf. This included civilians, other cops, and prisoners. Gong and I checked in on a group of inmates who were locked up in the police station's storage closet after Mongo made his rounds one day.

The three men were lying on the ground moaning in pain. So much blood was spattered everywhere I couldn't tell if it was fresh or old. One of the men wasn't moving or making any sound.

I entered the room and rolled the man over. His face was a mess, and it looked as if one of his eyeballs had ruptured. White fluid mixed with blood streamed from his eye socket like a water faucet. There wasn't anything we could do for the men, so we left them where they were.

Slim reported Ashraf for every single violation of the law. Nothing was ever done about it. Eventually, our ability to work with Ashraf eroded away to nothing. Afterward, we still patrolled the district headquarters, but it was purely for show.

Instead of going on patrols with Ashraf's men or training them, we went to an entirely separate part of the headquarters and shut ourselves into a room full of discarded beds. Half of us would get to sleep while the other half stood guard outside.

We had been patrolling the area long enough without getting shot or blown up that soldiers started getting complacent. Complacency is a soldier's worst enemy while at war. Instead of always keeping your head up for the enemy while patrolling, you start to think that they aren't there. Your mind drifts to the home you miss so much. You start thinking about how fucking hot it is, and you kind of just drag your feet from Point A to Point B. This is generally when people start getting killed.

I was just as guilty of complacency as any of my soldiers, even though I knew better.

One day, during a typical mission to the district headquarters, I was sleeping on one of the many torn-up and discarded beds in our little corner room with the rest of Second Squad when a long burst of machine gunfire jolted me awake.

I fell out of bed and grabbed my rifle, and we all shoved our way out through the door and into the compound's expansive courtyard. Machine guns and rifles were popping off all around us.

We took cover in the courtyard. Our policy was that in case of attack we let the police handle the perimeter wall and we just tried to defend our side of the compound.

Police scampered across the walls from one guard position to another randomly firing wild bursts into the surrounding village.

The firing died down after a short while and Slim, Grandpa, and I slowly made our way to Ashraf's office on the other side of the building, leaving Kitty in charge of the rest of the soldiers. We walked into his office to see him and a few of his officers sitting on the ground drinking tea having seemingly no knowledge of the headquarters-wide gunfight unfolding a few feet away.

Hamid rushed in on our tails loading his shotgun.

"Hamid, ask this asshole what the hell that was all about," Slim said, annoyed.

Hamid did, but Ashraf acted as if he couldn't be bothered to answer any questions. Hamid translated: "He says some terrorists started shooting from the village, so we suppressed them."

"So they fired indiscriminately at a village full of people in the middle of the day?" Slim yelled. At this, the little tea party finally stopped. Ashraf looked annoyed that Slim dared raise his voice when informed of a war crime.

"He says all of his men are accomplished snipers," Hamid said, stifling a laugh.

Slim gave up and walked out of the office. Grandpa and I followed. As we walked by the gate of the police department—whose guards were already back to taking naps and not doing their jobs—a car roared up to the gate laying on its horn. The windshield had several bullet holes in it.

Hamid ran up to the driver's side window to see what was going on. "Hey, Slim!" Hamid yelled back at us. "We need Doc!"

"Medic!" Slim yelled as loud as he could. He directed the car to pull into the compound even though every single policeman was trying to get them to turn around.

Gong came sprinting through the compound. His massive aid bag bounced around on his small frame. He had left his rifle behind in the sleeping room in his urgency to get over to us. "Who's hit?" he half-yelled, half-gasped after his run over.

The family that was sitting in the car climbed out. They were covered in blood. By the amount of gore, it looked as if someone had exploded in the car rather than been shot. They opened up the battered old hatchback and inside lay the limp form of a man wearing a once-white gown, now stained red. His beard and hair were matted with blood. The area that was once his face was now mostly blown away.

Gong recoiled in horror at the gruesome scene. He quickly unzipped his aid bag and fished around for something before Slim started laughing at him.

"That dude is dead," Slim laughed.

Gong reached around his patient's head and his hand found an open skull with gray matter pooling onto the car's upholstery.

"Way to save that mother fucker, Gong," Slim managed to get out in between cackles.

"Well, fuck." Gong sighed. The guy was a new soldier, and this was his first deployment. That was definitely his first time sticking his hand into another man's skull.

"Go wash that shit off, man," I said trying to be reassuring. Seeing someone's violent end for the first time can be pretty jarring, and Gong's eyes were wide. "Hey, Dirty!" I yelled to the soldier guarding the main gate. "Go with him and keep an eye on him."

Dirty wordlessly followed my order and trailed after Gong. I shut the car's hatchback.

"Who did this?" Grandpa asked quietly.

Hamid quickly translated to the grieving family.

A young man I assumed was the dead man's son answered Hamid.

"They say they were just driving down the road and got shot at," Hamid said, motioning to the road that the car had come on.

"Slim, these assholes were shooting down that way," Grandpa said, meaning the police. A restrained anger coated his words.

"I know," Slim shook his head. "I'll report it, but I don't know what else we can do."

"I'd like to give these guys my rifle and a shot at Ashraf," I said.

Slim reported Ashraf and his men to our commander when we got back to the Reserve. Our commander quickly reported the incident to Scream, who totally blew it off.

His explanation was that because Taliban activity was so low in the areas that Ashraf was in charge of, whatever he was doing was working and shouldn't be interfered with. He said this with full knowledge that Ashraf was probably a member of the Taliban.

Unfortunately, no matter how many times we brought forth examples and proof of Ashraf's complete corruption, nothing was ever done. The idea of "the lesser of two evils" was apparently a part of our operations and procedures now. Though thankfully someone out there did have the power to dethrone the little tyrant of district six.

One day, while Ashraf was driving home from the district headquarters, a group of people ambushed him and left him to die on the side of the road. We never figured out who it was, not that we cared to catch them. It was probably some faction he pissed off, maybe even his own men.

It was a fitting end to such a corrupt warlord. Unfortunately, he hadn't officially been one of our enemies. He had been trained, employed, and paid by the U.S. government. To make matters worse, we had been ordered to let him continue his reign of terror over his tiny fiefdom of District Six. And we hadn't been the first ones.

CHAPTER 8

OP COUCH

GENERALLY, WHEN OUR SQUAD WENT on patrol for hours at a time, we would set up Observation Points, or OPs. OPs were areas that were slightly defensible and allowed us to watch a large area while remaining concealed. That's what the manual says about OPs, anyway.

What we really used them for was to duck away in the night for a few hours and take turns napping. A few soldiers stood watch while the others removed their overbearing gear and laid down in the dirt to catch a few minutes of much-needed sleep.

The official mission was to watch over a Taliban "rat line," or trail used for smuggling weapons into the area. We had watched the ratline and raided various houses in the last few months and found nothing. We were all pretty sure that the ratline didn't actually exist anywhere outside of Scream's head.

Because Scream was adamant that something was going to happen in that village, he kept ordering us to sit in the darkness and stare at nothing.

We established a primary OP on an elevated ridge that overlooked the trail that Scream was certain was a pathway for whatever nefarious deeds the Taliban did at night. During our first ten-hour watch of the area, Walrus—one of the laziest people I've ever met—found a couch in one of the cornfields. He dragged the furniture up the ridge and into the OP, giving the position its name.

It was at that OP that some of us older soldiers had to teach the other guys the art of soldiering in the pitch darkness. Smoking without being seen became a skill. You could easily see a cigarette's lit cherry over a mile away. If you weren't careful, you could give away your position while feeding your terrible vice.

You could stick your cigarette and lighter into your ration bag to light it. Then you'd cup your hand around your mouth and cigarette when you needed a hit to conceal yourself from whomever wanted to blow your face off in the middle of the night. A few of us switched from smoking to chewing tobacco for night patrols. The first few times I tried it I puked on myself.

Only one guy in our squad didn't smoke or dip—Slim—but he made up for it in the states with a drinking habit that would make Hemmingway suggest rehab.

We had to teach our soldiers real skills to survive at night as well. You would be surprised how much noise a soldier can make shambling through the darkness with all the gear we carry. We had to duct tape down anything that would rattle or clang off another piece of equipment and spray paint any little piece of metal that would catch the moonlight.

I knew a few guys who went above and beyond by not cleaning themselves for weeks in order to smell like the natives. As if the Taliban were out in the mountains trying to sniff us out of our hiding spots or something.

Of course, all of these night survival skills went out of the window after a few weeks of mindlessly patrolling the same ratline. Once, Slim thought we found something, but it was just a group of farmers working their land at night.

Scream thought it was suspicious that these guys were out working late. But we all knew it was understandable because the temperature would climb into the mid-one hundreds during the day. We let them go after searching their belongings with what was probably a little too much excitement.

After our run-in with the midnight farmers, things slowed to nothing out on the OP. We occasionally fired a flare out over the village from our grenade launchers. The flare was about the size of my palm. We would launch it into the air, and it would explode in a bright plume of whatever color we happened to have on us at the time. Just one would light up the whole valley. Boredom quickly set in.

One night while Walrus and I were taking our turn napping on that tattered couch, we were shocked awake by a thunderous bang. We were both covered in dust and rocks. The squad around us started firing into the night. The pressure from the exploding rounds popped my ears. My eyes shook in their sockets. I rolled over and grabbed my rifle, but before I could find a target, it was all over.

"You mother fuckers almost got killed!" Slim screamed changing out the magazine in his rifle.

"What the hell just happened?" I yelled, totally deafened by the quick exchange of gunfire.

"Sniper, man," Slim pointed out into the village. "Hit right next to Walrus's fucking head." That explained why we were covered in rocks and dust. The bullet slammed into the boulder he was resting his head on next to the couch.

"Well shit," Walrus sighed. He reached into his pocket and put a fat pinch of dip in his mouth. He spat out some brown liquid.

"I think they know where we are, Slim," Grandpa said calmly.

"Right, we should get moving. Pack it up boys," Slim said peering off into the darkness through his night vision goggles. "Don't think we'll be coming back here again."

"You guys hit that bitch?" Walrus asked, brushing dirt and dust from his face, talking about the sniper.

"I fired off two magazines, bro. I think so," Cali responded. "Didn't see shit, though." It turns out that everyone just wildly fired into the night. The only one with a good shot was the guy who tried to kill Walrus.

Walrus and I slowly put our gear on and our squad made its way down the mountain path away from OP Couch. The man who had tried to murder Walrus was probably still out there watching us. The worst part about us moving out of the OP was that the Taliban were destined to swoop in and steal our sweet couch. The war was truly lost.

CHAPTER 9

BOREDOM ON THE RESERVE

IN BETWEEN OUR PATROLS OUT into the middle of nowhere, there was almost nothing to do. Just absolute, maddening boredom. There weren't a lot of different ways to kill time on the Reserve. We had a small gym packed into one corner that Thad and I had been attempting to improve on. I filled a duffle bag with sand to create a ghetto punching bag. I didn't notice until after we had filled it up that it said "Davidson" in black marker down the side. Davidson was one of the Dealer soldiers who had been killed a few months back.

The gym was outside in the elements because we had no other tents to spare. Everything was covered in a fine layer of dust, and every metal surface would scorch your skin if you attempted to exercise without wearing gloves. All of the equipment rested on a floor of gray powder, which was once concrete. Afghan concrete is nine parts dirt, one part concrete mix. It tended to atomize the second you dropped something heavy on it.

To make matters worse, the Afghan police would pack into the small corner we worked out in, not to exercise, but to stare at us. They would totally surround us, leer, and chain smoke. It was probably one of the weirdest feelings I've ever felt in my life. I was being objectified.

I wasn't sure how to react to it, but Thad did. He chucked small weights at them as hard as he could and sent them scattering. They would always come back, though. When one of them tried squeezing my bicep, I punched him as hard as I could in the chest. I think his shoulders may have touched. They kept their distance after that.

Another cherished activity was collecting porn. Even though we didn't have the internet on our laptops, that didn't stop us. Everyone had an external hard drive full to the brim with every kind of porn imaginable. The funny part was that it was totally illegal.

For whatever reason, when we first invaded Afghanistan back in 2001, someone in high command made possession of pornographic material illegal for U.S. military. But I never heard of the ban being enforced by anyone.

We would hook our laptops up and have screening parties in our tents. Dozens of soldiers would watch some guy with a penis roughly the size of my rifle plow some nameless porn star and then critique the whole thing as if we were Siskel and Ebert.

There was nothing erotic gained by anyone from any of this. By that point, porn transcended sex for us. We would make fun of the story, the performers' reactions, and whatever else we could glean from the material.

Cali even sent an email to one of the porn stars to ask if it was really "her first time" in one of the clips that we watched. He insisted he got an email back from her, but we all pointed out that those email accounts are probably controlled by some PR group.

We stopped making fun of him when she sent him a Facebook message confirming that it was really her. Cali tried to impress her by naming his truck after her. I'm not really sure if it worked. All our other attempts to contact porn stars through the internet were unsuccessful.

Outside of binge-watching porn, there was our community entertainment tent, which also served as our chow hall and internet café. Lining the walls inside the tent were a few poorly made benches and tables with donated desktop computers on them.

We were connected to some over-censored version of the internet that ran through a massive satellite propped up behind the tent. If the wind blew just a little too hard, it would shift and cut off our connection, and because we were in a mountain valley, this happened about every five to ten seconds.

We also managed to get a PlayStation working. Its wires were frayed and held together with electrical tape, and the copious amounts of dust in the air caused it to make a horrible groaning noise. We had two games: *NHL 2010* and *Mortal Kombat*.

Gong and I played endless hours of NHL to the point we would only play with the worst teams to see how much they sucked. We eventually talked several other people into playing with us.

Almost everyone bought webcams so they could use our incredibly slow internet to see their loved ones. It almost always turned into several minutes of people yelling, "Can you hear me?" before they would just get pissed and walk away.

People tried to say there was some unwritten rule about not screwing with each other while they were trying to talk to their loved ones on camera. No one listened.

One time Grandpa was talking to several of his kids, and Slim licked the old man's face before tackling him off his bench, sending his headset flying. Grandpa got Slim back by waving his heavily pierced penis behind Slim's head in a rotating motion known as "the helicopter" while Slim was talking to his wife.

One night while pulling Sergeant of the Guard duty, I stumbled half asleep into the tent to get coffee only to find a soldier at the computer furiously masturbating with his webcam pointed at him. I saw his overweight wife on the other side doing the same thing. I slowly backed out of the tent as if I had just seen a murder take place. I never told the kid what I saw, but I did share it with just about everyone else.

I think the best of all the pranks was when Bugsy and Thad climbed on top of the shower building with two bottles full of baby powder. They were waiting for one of First Squad's NCOs to walk out. When he did, clad only in a towel, they unleashed hell with tons of baby powder. The guy looked like a ghost. He coughed out a cloud of baby powder and backed slowly inside the shower building.

The boredom even crept into how we punished people for fucking up. Kitty found Creep asleep while on guard in the middle of the day and told Slim. Slim called the whole squad into the tent and announced that because Creep was always so tired and couldn't be trusted to use a weapon, we would be acting as his personal bodyguards.

The squad would suit up in full gear and follow him around the Reserve everywhere he went. It went exactly as well as Slim thought it would. Every soldier immediately started screaming and throwing things around the tent. I think the only reason they didn't beat him to death was because we would have been short a soldier on patrol.

I found out through Gong that all the soldiers had gone into detail about how they were going to kill Creep. He was due to go home for two weeks very shortly, and they threatened that he shouldn't come back from leave if he wanted to live.

I felt uneasy that we were effectively hazing the living shit out of a young and clearly troubled soldier. But I also understood why the soldiers had all turned against him. They saw him as the weak link and one that could very easily get someone killed. Even though you would never know it, the squad deeply loved and cared for one another. We were a family and Creep was threatening that.

We also took to the poorly conceived sport of combatives. Combatives is what the army calls its unarmed self-defense system and consists of a few chokeholds, arm bars, and takedowns. In the hands of a skilled fighter these can be pretty useful, but in the hands of a few bored soldiers, they were just tools we used to hurt each other.

We had no real floor on which to do combatives, so we did it on the same large rocks that covered the entire Reserve. We rolled around and smashed each other's heads on the sharp gravel for fun.

Dirty managed to pound my face into the wall of our smoking area in a failed attempt to lock me in an arm bar. Another time, Nan got knocked out cold when he was slammed to the ground.

Grabbing someone's neck in a hold became a sport. When someone wanted no part in our stupid games, we would ambush them. We would spear them into the rocks and try to choke them out while they fought for their life. Memphis discovered that if you did this to Afghan policemen, they would just scream and try to crawl away from you.

Another excellent pastime was playing with our puppy. Even though it was strictly against the rules to adopt local animals, it takes a real asshole to turn down a puppy. Ginger and Bumpo, our platoon sergeant, turned a blind eye to it because they saw how much the little dog raised morale. It was honestly the best command decision Bumpo had ever made.

Thad had half-adopted, half-stolen the pup. He found the little mongrel while on patrol through one of the surrounding farms and stuck it in his pocket. Thad dubbed the puppy Ares, the Dog of War.

Ares lived in the tent with the team leaders, and we treated him like he was our child. Even though Thad saved him from his bleak existence on that farm, Ares did not show any appreciation. He was never broken of shitting under Thad's bed or pissing on his boots.

We didn't have dog food, so we fed him the same things we ate. The dog grew surprisingly fast. He also learned to attack anyone who didn't wear a U.S. Army uniform and he followed us on patrols.

Unfortunately, Ginger and Bumpo's hands-off leadership style didn't win them any points with our company command. Our platoon quickly became known as being undisciplined, unprofessional, and disrespectful. I won't argue; all those things were true, but we ran more patrols for a longer period of time than anyone else in our company. We were also the first to engage the enemy, even if Walrus and I had slept through it.

As the old adage goes, "The nail that sticks out gets hammered down."

We later found out that the hammer was coming for us.

CHAPTER 10

GRIZZLY BASE AND HOW I GOT DEMOTED

THINGS HAD GOTTEN A LITTLE out of hand out on the Reserve. Within three months, the soldiers living in that little slice of hell had gone completely native. I had not shaved or cut my hair during the entire time. Because of my Armenian genetics, it made me look like a crazed mountain person.

Soldiers started to disregard orders from our platoon sergeant, Bumpo. The soldiers and leadership of our platoon lost all respect for him after he openly admitted he didn't want to go on patrol with us because he was scared after Walrus had almost gotten shot in the head.

It was unfortunate because Bumpo was generally a good guy. Out there, though, we didn't need good guys. The squad leaders and team leaders held our platoon together, but not by much. It was hard to keep discipline and order instilled when it seemed as if every level of command had totally forgotten about us or, even worse, didn't care.

Mail and supplies stopped coming for weeks at a time for no good reason. Our company commander never once came out to visit us, leaving us at the mercy of that bastard Scream.

Morale died around the same time the truck that emptied our portable toilets stopped showing up, leaving every single one of our toilets overflowing. We contracted the job out to a local trucking company, but they never came. Rumor was that someone had killed the truck driver.

Soon we were digging and squatting in the bushes with the locals.

We hit a new low when one of our team leaders, a young corporal from First Squad named Red, went on leave and never returned. To make matters worse, we were already running too many missions with not enough people. We had no extra hands, so a team leader from our squad would have to fill in for Red in addition to running his regular missions.

I think having a team leader go AWOL was the straw that broke the camel's back for our company commander. Even though he never actually came out and saw how we were operating, he decided Second Platoon needed to be moved.

I was informed of this one day while in the smoking area. First Platoon would be taking our place at the Reserve so it was time to pack our bags. We would be moving to Grizzly Base with the company command and a platoon of Task Force Chimera. Chimera was the unit that finally took over for Dealer.

We were being pulled back under the watchful eyes of high command, and we weren't very happy about it. Even though we hated our lives out on the godforsaken Reserve, it was better than being picked over with a fine-toothed comb by our company commander.

Our commander, a guy named Dweebly, was a tall, skinny, awkward dude and the exact opposite of who you would picture as a combat leader. He was a guy who cared more about how professional you looked than how well you could shoot a rifle.

Awkwardness aside, he wasn't the guy you wanted looking too far into how you ran your squad. He was prim and proper and wouldn't stand for anything we were doing as a platoon if he knew about it. Ginger informed us all of what would be expected of us at Camp Grizzly, which was pretty much the polar opposite of what we had been doing at the Reserve.

Unfortunately, moving on also meant saying goodbye to little Ares. He had gotten so big so fast, and Dweebly would never allow us to have a dog at Grizzly. We mournfully turned the little guy over to First Platoon when they showed up to move in. We made them promise they would take good care of him. I think Thad took it harder than I did.

We packed our bags and moved about thirty miles to Grizzly Base. Grizzly was much more built up than the Reserve. It was a large compound made up of only Hesco baskets. Hesco baskets were large burlap bags that could be filled with dirt, like a sandbag on steroids. The ones at Grizzly Base stood about fifteen feet tall and were filled with concrete.

Orderly tents were lined up inside. Formidable guard towers surrounded the compound. Unlike at the Reserve where the towers were held together by a few nails and mud and couldn't withstand a slingshot, these looked as if they could actually survive some gunfire.

The area where we parked our trucks was surprisingly lacking in broken-down vehicles. They even had some replacement parts, and Chimera had a mechanic. Life at Grizzly was already starting to look up. And while they didn't have internet in the sleeping tents, they did have a proper computer tent with reliable internet that wouldn't go out at the slightest hint of wind. The tent's air conditioners worked just as well as anything I had ever felt in the States.

We moved into the team leaders' tent and discovered we had mattresses on top of our shitty green army cots. I selected a handmade wooden bunkbed to share with First Squad's leader. His name was Olly, a bald staff sergeant in his mid-thirties who volunteered for the top bunk. I think it was because we both thought the bed was going to collapse and he just wanted to survive the outcome.

The worst part by far about Grizzly Base was the surveillance camera perched about fifty feet in the air. It was originally a boon for protecting the base. The camera could see anything for miles around. It could even see the heat signatures bombs gave off from underground. But once Dealer gave that camera over to our command cell—the guys who answer radios and handle logistics—it was horribly abused.

A staff sergeant by the name of Walt was given control of the camera as his only job. He quickly turned the camera inward on Grizzly Base to spy on soldiers going about their daily lives. If he spotted someone wearing their uniform incorrectly, he would run out and tell that soldier's platoon sergeant to get them in trouble.

Walt wasn't done there. When Second Squad started going on dismounted patrols out of Grizzly Base, he would keep the camera on us the whole time. The moment one of our soldiers rolled up his sleeves because of the searing heat, my radio crackled to life with Walt's voice.

"Spartan two-two, tell your soldiers to wear their uniforms correctly."

Slim glared at the radio as if he was attempting to send the stink eye through the waves. "Hey, Grizzly Base, how about you use that camera and look for the goddamn Taliban?" Slim snarled.

Walt didn't say anything back.

"I wonder what it's like to be unemployed in a war zone," Grandpa laughed. Walt had been deployed with us even though they had no task or purpose for him. He decided to give himself the job of being an asshole, and he excelled at it.

"You think he can still see us?" I asked.

"Oh, I'm sure," Slim said. "That camera can look out for about ten miles."

"Good." I stuck a cigarette in my mouth, climbed on top of a nearby wall, pulled my dick out, and pissed in the general direction of the camera. To put some icing on the cake, I stuck my hand in the air and gave them the one-fingered salute.

The squad all laughed, and a few other guys climbed on top of the wall and followed suit. The radio stayed silent that time. Though I'm sure Walt ran out and told Bumpo.

Surprisingly, that wasn't what got me demoted.

Dweebly devised a plan for my squad to move out to an Afghan police checkpoint in the middle of Kandahar City. The checkpoint was roughly half the size of the Reserve with no guard towers and built directly on the road. It had no standoff distance from any possible attackers. The checkpoint also had a history of being car bombed.

Dweebly's plan involved us showing up there late at night with shovels and empty Hesco baskets. We were going to divert traffic with the baskets and, we hoped, create a barrier between the station and the main road to give us a chance at survival there. The plan was terrible, and we all knew it. We tried to raise our objections, but they were ignored. Gong had other ideas, though. Other really dreadful ideas.

Using our internet connection, Gong took to Facebook and made a long post about how dumb the plan was. He didn't give up any operational security details, but he did insult every single person in a command position for having such a terrible battle plan. I thought the post was hilarious and clicked that stupid little "like" button at the bottom.

That was all it took to get me demoted.

Within a few hours, I was dragged into the command tent and told what a piece of shit I was for not punishing Gong. I was unprofessional and a terrible leader for agreeing with him. I laughed the whole thing off until Ginger told me I was to be demoted from corporal to specialist, and that I was losing my team leader position.

Bumpo was also being fired as our platoon sergeant. I was going to be placed in Grandpa's team, and Bugsy, a guy from First Squad, was going to take over my team. Gong was moved to a different platoon altogether, and we would operate without a platoon sergeant for the time being. It was like being hit in the head with a brick.

Still kind of stunned, I packed my bags and moved into the Second Squad soldiers' tent. I plopped all my crap down and sat on my cot trying to take in everything that had just happened. That was when I heard the constant chug of the air conditioner sputter and die out, smoke rising into the air. Everyone in the tent exchanged a panicked look and ran outside.

The air conditioner had literally melted from the inside out. The temperature within our tent shot through the roof, and soon it felt as if we were living in an oven. We rolled up all the windows and lay around on our cots in varying stages of nakedness, but it didn't make anything better.

We got a new medic to replace Gong. His name was Sal. He wasn't from our unit but was lent to us from a medical brigade stationed at Kandahar Air Field. Sal was a body builder from Texas who'd worked as a paramedic before he joined the army. He quickly fit in with the rest of us by stripping down to his underwear and passing out on his cot. When we woke up, we were disoriented from dehydration.

I started pulling guard shifts with the soldiers and falling in line with my new duties. Cali and Grandpa were incredibly welcoming. Grandpa was one of the best leaders I'd ever met, and it was an honor to be on his team. I just tried to accept my lot in life and prepare for the incredibly stupid mission that Dweebly had laid out for us.

CHAPTER 11

CHAP STICK 25 AND THE GREAT GOAT-NAPPING

WE PACKED OUR TRUCKS UP in preparation for our move out to the Afghan police checkpoint. To make an already horrible plan worse, we had totally run out of room in our trucks for our own bags. We quickly enlisted First Squad to help us haul the rest of our crap out there. We waited for nightfall and our long convoy snaked out of Grizzly Base toward the checkpoint.

In the middle of the night, the roads were totally abandoned and the markets void of life. Electricity in the area was spotty at best so when the jerry-rigged lights went out, everyone vanished.

While sitting in the back of Grandpa's truck, I noticed a particular barn-like smell. Cali was behind the wheel and laughing like a maniac.

"*Baaa*," came a muffled noise from somewhere in the back of the truck.

"What the fuck was that?" Grandpa yelled. Cali started laughing so hard the truck began to swerve all over the road.

"Baaaaaaaaa!"

"What the hell *is* that, Cali?" I yelled up at him. I was frantically looking around the back of the cramped truck.

A goat's head popped up from under a pile of camo netting.

"Holy shit!" I screamed. "Why is there a fucking barnyard animal back here?"

"Did you say an *animal*?" Grandpa yelled, trying in vain to turn around in his seat, but the bulk of his gear restrained him. By this point, Cali stopped trying to drive and pulled the truck over. The whole convoy had to stop behind us.

A military operation was halted because Cali had stolen a goddamn goat and stuck it in the back of our truck.

How he got the goat was even better. About a month before we had moved into Grizzly Base, Walt had bought three goats to fatten them up for Thanksgiving dinner. We hated those stupid goats. Walt was too damn lazy to take care of them himself so he ordered us to look after them instead. We had been plotting the death of those goats ever since.

Unbeknownst to anyone else in the convoy, Bugsy and Cali had snuck into the goats' pen the night before and stolen one. Cali wrapped it in camo netting and tossed it in the back of Grandpa's truck without a word.

With the convoy at a standstill, it wasn't long before Slim's voice crackled over the radio wondering what had happened. Grandpa knew that he couldn't explain to Slim the situation with our transmissions being monitored, so he mustered his calmest voice possible. "Hey, Slim, we're having a mechanical issue. Can you meet me at my truck?"

"Roger, be right there," Slim answered back. Slim calmly walked over to our truck and exchanged a few words with Grandpa.

I watched as Grandpa spoke and gesticulated with his hands.

Slim slowly turned, opened the back door of our truck, and came face to face with our goat friend. "Mother fuckers," Slim laughed, walking back to his truck.

Once Cali had composed himself, we drove on to the destination.

Our convoy pulled up next to the checkpoint and started heaving piles of gear onto the side of the road. Because the checkpoint was hardly defensible, we planned on tossing our bags quickly and having First Squad speed off before anyone was the wiser. That plan quickly went to hell when the rolls of concertina wire got tangled up on our radio antennas and Hesco baskets and had to be cut apart.

By the time we had everything untangled, we had been struggling for about an hour. It was pretty safe to assume that everyone in the area knew we had moved in. We hastily set up a ring of Hesco baskets as First Squad drove away. No one in the squad had ever filled up one of those bastards by hand before. Turned out it was slow, dirty, painful work.

We scraped away at the side of the road with splintered and broken tools, making meager progress. The hours went on performing this laborious task. Eventually, we stripped down to just our pants and kept working through the muggy night.

A few soldiers fanned out to cover us while we worked, but chances were that if any Taliban were watching, they were just as confused by our plan as we were. After several more hours, we stopped to check our progress only to find we had barely made a dent in the baskets.

"Holy shit," I panted. "Slim, we haven't even filled one fucking basket!"

"I've noticed. And we're running out of dirt," Slim motioned to the fact we had dug out the sides of the road, probably making it pretty unsafe for a car to drive over it. "We either start breaking up the road or call it a night."

"I would just like to let it be known that I voted for this OP to go fuck itself," Nan said, dropping his shovel to the ground.

"I say it goes and fucks itself now," Cali said.

"Yeah, screw this," Slim exhaled.

We trudged back inside the checkpoint to rest and get some water.

Our interpreter came out of the checkpoint's Afghan commander's tent, weed smoke billowing out behind him. "Hey, dude, the commander asked what you guys are doing with the goat." He giggled.

"Good question." Slim turned to Cali. "What was your plan when you stole the damn thing?"

"I don't know. It was Bugsy's idea; I just kind of went along with it." Cali shrugged, spitting out brown tobacco dip.

"We could eat it," Bugsy pointed out. For some reason, he was kneeling down next to the goat and spray painting the word 'Radio' across its body in black paint.

"What're you doing man?" I asked.

"I named it." Bugsy gestured to the word sprayed onto the goat's side.

"Well, are we eating Radio or not?" Slim asked.

"Yeah, but I have an idea first," Bugsy said.

Bugsy's idea was brilliant. Walt had no idea who stole his goat and was probably not even aware it was missing yet. So Perro, Bugsy, and Hamid took off their army uniforms and put on some local clothing. They wrapped their faces in scarves and had Slim videotape what happened next.

Hamid screamed random shit in Pashto and gestured wildly with his hands. Afterward, Perro marched up, pulled out a small pocket knife, and cut the goat's throat open. The whole time Bugsy yelled "Radio!" in his best mock-retard voice.

The slaughter had several purposes. Cutting an animal's throat and bleeding it out was the only way the Afghans would eat with us. We also made sure it was facing Mecca while we did it. Making a counterfeit Jihadist execution video of Walt's goat to send to him was just a theatrical bonus.

After we had killed the goat, the Afghan police cleaned it and prepared it. They chucked the whole thing into a hole in the ground with onions, potatoes, and spices and lit the thing on fire. About an hour later, we all gathered around and ate it.

Everyone sat in a circle picking at the goat with bare hands. I plopped big handfuls of meat and rice onto bread and shoved it in my face. It was actually a good bonding experience. That, and it was always good to show our Afghan hosts that we weren't total dicks so they didn't kill us in our sleep.

After we finished our dinner and had some tea with the police, Walrus turned to Hamid. "So, where do you guys take a shit around here anyway?"

"Oh, they just go out back, man," Hamid pointed out to where our trucks were parked.

"God dammit! If I have to go outside to take a shit, someone has to come guard me...Joe?"

"Ugh, fine." I grabbed my rifle, and we both walked out of the checkpoint. Behind it was where the Afghans tossed all their trash and went to the bathroom. Unlike most people forced to take a dump outside, they didn't dig holes or keep it all in one area. There were little piles of shit all over the place. They were completely uncovered with empty water bottles next to them. They wiped their asses by splashing them with water.

"Fucking animals," Walrus cursed. Walrus perched himself against a wall and squatted down behind a small cutout of Hesco he'd brought with him to act as a wall for privacy. I stood by and made sure no one murdered him while he took a dump.

I heard someone start running down the small alley that went from the checkpoint to the trash field. I quickly brought up my rifle only to see Perro sprinting by.

Perro ran over to Walrus's Hesco wall and kicked it over sending it and his toilet paper flying, exposing Walrus to any leering eyes—of which there were plenty. Several soldiers were standing on top of the checkpoint's walls snapping pictures and laughing.

"Fuck you guys, man! Someone bring me some toilet paper!"

I started laughing uncontrollably. Mostly because I knew no one was going to bring him any toilet paper and I was curious about what he was going to do next.

Walrus slowly shimmied over to where his toilet paper roll had landed, cursing us the whole way. The laughter from the peanut gallery followed him as he waddled. I wasn't guarding anyone at this point; I was too busy doubled over with laughter as I watched Walrus do a strange crab walk in an attempt to wipe his ass.

Once the night slowed down and people stopped harassing each other while they took a shit, we settled into our cots. They were lined up in the middle of the checkpoint under the clear Afghan sky. I saw more stars that night than I ever had in the States.

We set up guards throughout the evening and went to sleep. At some point during the night, I was awakened by Oldies screaming. While switching out guard duties, Oldies had caught Walrus, illuminated by his iPod, beating off in the guard tower.

We woke up again early the next morning to a gunshot and the sound of screaming Afghans. By the time we all rolled out of our cots and grabbed our rifles, the Afghan police were dragging a man into the checkpoint while simultaneously smacking and kicking him.

"Hamid, ask them what the hell is going on!" Slim yelled, still half asleep.

"They say he shot at them while they were directing traffic, but his gun jammed after the first shot, and he surrendered," Hamid sputtered among the chaos.

"That guy is *so* going to be executed," Perro laughed. He wasn't wrong. Generally, the police just took people out back and shot them when they captured them. In a few hours, we would probably find his body among our shit piles.

"Should we, like...stop them?" I asked. Honestly, I was more concerned about being an accessory to a war crime than saving the man's life.

"Hamid!" Slim called out. "Don't let them kill that fucker!"

Hamid ran over to talk to the commander. The policemen were still laying into the guy. The kid was taking a beating worse than anything I'd ever seen. Sure, he was probably some kind of Taliban operative, but the poor guy was given a shitty thirty-year-old Russian pistol to attack a checkpoint manned by twelve American soldiers and five Afghani policemen. He never had a chance.

"We have to stop them," Grandpa said forcefully. He looked disappointed in us.

Slim glanced around and saw the faces of the young soldiers. Most were either terrified or disgusted at the unholy beating being given to the prisoner. The prisoner was nothing more than a skinny teenager. "Hamid, call off the attack," Slim said. "We need to have a meeting with the commander. Grandpa, take a few soldiers and make sure they don't beat him anymore."

Guapo and Perro pushed the policemen away from the prisoner and stood in front of him. Slim, Hamid, and the Afghan police commander, Naweet, ducked inside the command tent for an impromptu meeting.

Other policemen kept a close eye on us, waiting for us to get bored on guard so they could swoop in and take their prisoner back. It was the type of situation that could easily lead to the Afghan police and U.S. soldiers shooting at each other. I had my hand resting on my holstered pistol and was squared off with an Afghan who was doing the same. It was like a production of the most fucked-up western movie ever made.

Thankfully, Slim and Naweet emerged from the tent all smiles and laughing. It turned out Naweet—who was about twenty years old and just put in charge of this checkpoint—was a pretty agreeable person. Once Slim explained that you couldn't just beat and kill your prisoners, Naweet apologized.

The fact that had to be explained spoke volumes about the Afghan police's inability to function as an actual police force. Naweet traded the prisoner to us in exchange for some fuel for his trucks. We radioed First Squad and had them come and pick up our new ward.

Part of the mission we had while living out at the checkpoint was patrolling the surrounding markets and villages. This was made a little more dangerous by the fact that we had to leave a team of soldiers back at the checkpoint to guard, so when we went on patrol, we had three fewer soldiers than normal. Not to mention that three soldiers weren't exactly a stout defense if a determined group attacked them.

We all thought about it and decided that this incredibly ill-advised mission wasn't worth it. We wouldn't go on patrol. We would just hunker in behind the walls of the checkpoint and hold our ground.

We built a few better fighting positions at the checkpoint's gate, ran up an American flag on a stick next to the Afghan flag, and Bugsy built an enormous wooden sign that he spray-painted "Chap Stick 25" onto. He positioned it so that anyone could clearly see it from the road. He wouldn't explain why he named it that, but it stuck.

We lived out in that shithole for a week, and surprisingly we were never attacked once. Not counting the one random teenager firing a shot at a traffic cop. But it was clear the mission didn't have its intended outcome. We were supposed to act as a breakwater for Taliban attacks in the area. The Taliban just attacked the police stations around us and left us alone.

Dweebly ordered us to dismantle our improvements to Chap Stick 25 and to move back to Grizzly Base. We didn't do that. We'd grown to like the young police commander Naweet and decided to leave him all our Hesco baskets, camo netting, fuel, and piles of water bottles. He was thankful for it and happily invited us back whenever we wanted to go fight the Taliban with him.

Naweet excitedly left the big sign that said Chap Stick 25 up, saying it was a sign of our friendship. For one fleeting moment, I felt as though we'd really helped the Afghan police take a step in the right direction.

We packed up our bags and left the little checkpoint. Unfortunately, we never got the chance to work with Naweet again. He was killed in a suicide bombing when he went home to visit his wife a few days later.

After our mission went so badly, there was never a repeat of it throughout our area, not that we were complaining.

The Chap Stick 25 sign stayed in its place as long as we were in Afghanistan.

CHAPTER 12

THE NIGHT THE AFGHAN ARMY ALMOST KILLED US

OPERATING OUT OF GRIZZLY BASE brought with it one major change to our operations: We were no longer working with the Afghan police. We were working with what everyone loved to tell us were the "elite" of the Afghan Security Forces. They were the Afghan National Civil Order Police or ANCOP.

Technically, they were a branch of the Afghan police, but operated completely independently and were more respected by U.S. soldiers. The only difference we could see between the two was that the ANCOP could go on patrol by themselves. They could also generally be trusted not to murder us in our sleep. That part was kind of debatable, though.

The ANCOP had the same very strange tendency to stare at us while we worked out in our still rustic, outdoor gym. These guys wanted tips on lifting weights and getting "big like an American." Not like the Afghan police, who apparently just wanted to eye-fuck us. They had their own guard towers and were trusted to manage one of the rings of security that surrounded Grizzly Base. They, at least in our eyes, were almost real soldiers.

They turned out to be just as crazy as Slim. He, of course, loved that. When we went on long, boring patrols, the ANCOP would take pot shots at birds or stray dogs and challenge us to marksmanship contests. They showed us the fields we could patrol through and steal grapes and pomegranates. Of course, they made a detour into their favorite fields: pot and opium. Whole football fields of the stuff grew in neat rows like corn.

Drugs are so widespread in Afghanistan that when we western folk showed up to put together a military and police force and told them they weren't allowed to do drugs, they laughed it off. The ANCOP would openly smoke cigarettes laced with opium while on patrol, and their tents at Grizzly Base pumped out clouds of pot smoke. We tried to stop them at first, but it got us nowhere. Clouds of acrid smoke followed them wherever they went.

We were just learning the ins and outs of working with our newest batch of Afghans when Dweebly pulled another mission out of his ass for us. The local Afghan army base had a kid walk up to them and tell them his dad was in the Taliban. The kid knew where he was hiding weapons and explosives. He was willing to take us there in exchange for some money.

This was not our business for several reasons. We didn't work with the Afghan army, ever. We had no working relationship with them. If it had been any other nation's military, that wouldn't have mattered; we could have still cooperated. But the Afghan National Army was a different beast entirely.

The Afghan army was notoriously shady and had shot at U.S. soldiers on more than one occasion. The area that this kid said his dad was hiding weapons in wasn't even our area of operations. It was another unit's entire mission to patrol that area. Dweebly insisted we do it anyway.

To make matters worse, the ANCOP hate the Afghan army more than they hate the Taliban. The Afghan army is almost entirely made up of ethnic groups from the north of the country, while the police and ANCOP are made up more of ethnic groups from the middle and south.

Afghanistan, like most tribal-based societies, has ethnic issues going back centuries. No matter how many times America tried to tell all the groups to kiss and make up, they simply would not get along. That they were working for the same government meant absolutely nothing to them.

We waited for nightfall and set out for the Afghan army base. It was a few minutes up the road closer to Kandahar City proper. We rolled through the gate and parked our trucks against the base's tall concrete-reinforced Hesco basket walls. Slim jumped out and headed toward the command cell with Hamid while the rest of us sat around near the trucks and waited.

I put a pinch of Cali's dip in my mouth and shuddered at the bitter wintergreen flavor. Grandpa cranked up his iPod through our truck's speaker system. Justin Bieber's "Baby" pumped throughout the truck. Grandpa insisted he had Bieber on his iPod because it reminded him of his daughters back home. None of us believed him.

Grandpa's playlist was an odd mixture of country music, teen pop, and thrash metal. Since we couldn't get any new music, the playlist never changed, and by then we had everything memorized. We sang it at the top of our lungs while on mounted patrols. We were through Bieber's song and somewhere in the middle of Avril Lavigne's "Girlfriend" when Slim, Hamid, and an Afghan army soldier came out of their command tent.

"This guy," Slim said, pointing to the skinny Afghan guy standing next to him, "is going to take the kid in his truck and we're gonna follow him to the house where the weapons are."

"We're going to follow the Afghans into an area we don't know?" Grandpa asked, confused. He had a right to be concerned; it was a terrible idea. "The kid could be leading us right into an ambush."

"That's what we're actually betting on right now—the whole thing being a setup." Slim shrugged.

"So the whole plan you guys worked up involves driving into a trap?" Cali asked

"Yep."

"That does sound like one of your plans." I laughed and spat out a gob of brown.

"Hey, fuck you, man. I'm like General Patton in this bitch," Slim said, offended.

"Patton killed, like, a ton of his soldiers," Grandpa pointed out.

"You would know, you old bastard," Slim countered.

We climbed back into our trucks and waited for the Afghans to set out. Their tan pickup trucks were packed with soldiers. At least seven in each one. Most of them were sticking out of the bed holding onto whatever they could. A massive fifty-caliber machine gun that was originally developed to shoot down planes was mounted to the bed of one. We thought we were following out one Afghan army truck, but four more rolled out of the gate. They were obviously expecting an ambush as well.

Our massive, armored trucks followed the four tiny Afghan army trucks into the city. Their vehicles were completely unarmored Ford Rangers spray-painted tan and given to the Afghan army for free. Most of them were already perforated with bullet holes and burns from explosions.

Their trucks turned down streets and alleyways that were getting progressively smaller and tighter.

Our bulky trucks started grinding up against the encroaching buildings. We tore down several low-hanging power lines and business signs. Our anti-rocket armor started breaking people's windows and ripping bricks out of the walls.

"Where in the fuck are we going?" Grandpa asked over the radio. Hearing him lose his cool was unnerving.

Cali gave me a look that told me he was feeling the same way.

"The house is up here. At least that's what the Afghan marked on my map. Stay frosty, boys," Slim's voice crackled over the radio in response.

Finally, as if sensing our growing anxiety, the Afghan army trucks stopped. Two of their trucks zoomed out down other, smaller alleyways while two stayed with us.

Perro, Slim, Guapo, Cali, Grandpa, Walrus, Nan, and I dismounted from our trucks to join with the Afghan soldiers while everyone else stayed in or around the trucks. The Afghans marched with us right to the house where the kid said the weapons were. Grandpa sent Walrus, Cali, and me out into the streets to help the Afghan soldiers secure the area.

Walrus sat down on the hood of the Afghan's truck and the thin metal crumpled under his fat ass. He just giggled and shifted his ass around to cause more damage. The Afghans, for some reason, didn't seem to care about him ruining the hood of their truck with his ass; they just laughed at him.

The soldiers outside with us seemed okay enough. They were covering the many alleyways and side streets and were generally acting like they knew what they were doing. Due to our prolonged working experience with the Afghan police, that kind of surprised us.

Inside the house, a few of the Afghan soldiers met with the supposed Taliban member's wife. She said there were weapons in the house and she was happy we were there to take them away. It turns out there was one major problem: the guy had buried the weapons under the foundation of the house. So it wasn't an ambush. The family was just sick and tired of their Taliban-loving patriarch and wanted to sell his ass out.

A few of us went back to our trucks to dig out some pickaxes and sledgehammers. We were going for those weapons even if we had to destroy those well-meaning people's house. Of course, like any good group of Americans, we handed the hammers and picks off to the foreigners so they could do the manual labor while we watched. Thankfully that house was built with the same concrete-dirt mixture as the old gym floor back at the Reserve and we quickly broke through it.

Unlike an American house, where you have a foundation set deep into the earth, that house had maybe a foot of concrete acting as its foundation. We were soon just digging a hole into the ground. The Afghans quickly tired and handed the tools back to us. Guapo took up a shovel and jumped into the growing hole.

The scene around the hole was one of growing friendship. We were sharing cigarettes and lighters with the Afghan soldiers. One Afghan soldier was showing Walrus some porn he had on his cell phone. It was easy to forget we were digging in a war zone looking for weapons that were originally meant to kill us.

Before long Guapo's digging found purchase. Four small plastic bags were unearthed and handed up to Slim. A few grenade fuses and an old rusty Russian landmine.

"Are you fucking kidding me? This is it?" Slim growled. It was hardly the cache we were led to believe it was. "Hey, Hamid! Ask that kid where the rest of his dad's shit is!" he screamed back at Hamid, who was sitting with the Afghan commander.

"He says his dad must have taken the rest of it," Hamid said. The smirk on his face said Hamid didn't buy it.

"Taken it and just laid some mother fucking concrete down real quick?" Slim yelled, kicking dirt around. "This bastard dragged us all out here in the middle of bumfuck nowhere in Taliban land for some grenade fuses?" Slim was livid. "Hamid, slap that bitch for me!"

Hamid dutifully slapped the kid upside the head.

Slim sat down on some dusty steps that led to the upper floor of the house and called Grizzly Base on his radio. Grizzly Base's response clearly pissed Slim off further because he spiked his radio into the ground. "Dweebly wants EOD to come out and grab this shit. Go ahead and start evacuating the other houses around here." Evacuating the area where we found explosives, or ordinance, was standard procedure, even in cases like this one.

Cali, Walrus, and I were still outside the housing compound so we walked up to the house next door and began knocking on its bright, baby blue gates. The tin gates rattled loudly when Cali knocked on them. The Afghan soldiers started screaming at us. They gestured wildly with their hands. I didn't understand a goddamn word of it.

"Hamid! What the hell are these assholes saying?" I asked loudly.

"They say there are women in there, and we cannot disturb them," Hamid answered.

Afghanistan, like most Muslim countries, is incredibly conservative. The thought of us Americans seeing a woman without her full body robe, or hijab, was more important than their possibly being exploded by the unstable ordinance we'd found next door.

"Tell them EOD is coming out and we need to move them in case something explodes," I told him.

"He says they are just going to take the explosives away," Hamid said. He was clearly getting uneasy with the situation.

Slim came bursting outside where Hamid and the Afghan commander were now standing with several incredibly pissed off Afghan soldiers.

"Oh, fuck no. I have orders to secure this site for EOD. They aren't taking them. Joe! Get those people out of that fucking house!" Slim screamed.

"Roger!" I screamed back. I slammed on the blue gates, and they rocked in protest. I heard the metallic clack of the slide of a rifle. Someone had just chambered a round. We always loaded our rifles before we left Grizzly Base. It had to have been an Afghan. I wasn't the only person who heard it, either.

"What the fuck!" Cali screamed. "I got a mother fucker pointing his shit at me over here!" I glanced over to see an Afghan armed with a SAW—or squad automatic weapon—pointed right at me. I stood staring down the barrel of a belt-fed machine gun. I turned beside Cali and leveled my rifle at one of the other Afghan soldiers. I put my sight over the middle of his chest and flicked off the safety of my M4.

"Hey, bitch, don't touch me!" came the heavy New York accent of Guapo from inside the house.

An Afghan soldier came from the top floor of the house and tried to wrap his arms around him and bring him to the ground. Guapo was a strong guy with a deep knowledge of mixed martial arts. So that shit didn't fly.

He quickly twisted the man's arm around and tossed him to the ground. Before we could figure out what the hell was going on, we were surrounded by an incredibly hostile force of soldiers our country had trained and armed.

Slim was screaming commands at Hamid trying to get the situation under control. He had grabbed the Afghan commander by the collar of his oversized uniform and put his rifle into his chest. Every soldier was now squared off with an Afghan counterpart who only seconds ago we'd been joking with.

"Grizzly Base, this is Slim, I need a QRF at my location *right now!*" Slim screamed over the radio. A QRF, or quick reaction force, is a squad of soldiers who are always on standby waiting for something to happen whenever another squad is out conducting a mission. They can be out of a base's gates in minutes.

Slim advised Grizzly Base what was happening on the ground, which was essentially a Mexican standoff in the middle of Kandahar City surrounded and outnumbered by Afghan soldiers. Maybe that was called an Afghan standoff.

"Negative, Slim. We want EOD to go on scene," Walt answered over the radio. "Try to talk down the Afghans," he advised.

"I think we are pretty *fucking* far past talking at this point!" Slim screamed back over the radio. "Get in the fucking house, boys!" Slim yelled. We slowly backed into the house we had originally come for. We were still heavily outnumbered and outgunned. At least we had a defensible position behind the house's thick walls.

Afghan soldiers fanned out all around us and surrounded the house. One of their pickup trucks pulled up and aimed its massive fifty-caliber machine gun, its bullets the size of goddamn railroad spikes, in our direction.

"Can we call up our trucks?" Grandpa asked.

"The roads are too goddamn small," Slim said. Slim loaded a grenade into his mounted grenade launcher. "Everyone with a grenade launcher, load up! When this shit kicks off, take out their trucks first!"

Grandpa, Walrus, and I dutifully loaded our launchers. I grabbed a grenade from my pouch and slammed it home into the breach of my launcher. I flicked my rifle's switch from "semi" to "burst."

"If you have a SAW—suppress their soldiers! If they try coming into this fucking house—open up!"

My rifle was leveled on the truck with the machine gun pointed at us. My trigger finger was on the second, forward trigger. It fired my grenade launcher. Several Afghan soldiers started moving toward the house. My heart slammed in my chest. I could feel my pulse in my temples, and it made my eyes shake in their sockets.

"Get ready, boys!" Slim yelled as the Afghan soldiers slowly reached for the house's gates. My finger flicked off the launcher's safety.

"Hey!" screamed a voice in the distance. "Back the *fuck* off! Put your *fucking* weapons on the ground right the *fuck* now!" The shouting voice was followed up by a quick translation into Pashto.

U.S. soldiers poured out of the alleyways and surrounded the Afghans. Their weapons were up and at the ready. At the head of the advancing force was Third Platoon's Sergeant First Class Eastwood, who was carrying a sawed-off shotgun and had it pointed directly at the Afghan commander.

"Tell this asshole I'll kill every single one of his piece of shit soldiers if they don't obey every single one of my *fucking* words like they're the gospel of Mohammed!" Eastwood growled in anger. Eastwood's interpreter translated.

Slowly the Afghans lowered their weapons and backed away from our building. I rocked back off my knee and sat down on the house's roof, breathing a sigh of relief. I took my helmet off and brushed my hair back. Sweat dripped down into my eyes and burned like fire. The stinging sweat felt good. It reminded me that I was somehow still alive.

"I can't believe that just fucking happened," Walrus laughed. The laugh was infectious, and we all started into strange, nervous bursts of laughter.

Eastwood made his way into the house and met us upstairs. "What the hell happened here, Slim?" he asked with genuine curiosity.

"They wanted to see whose dick was bigger over this bullshit weapons cache." Slim pointed to the grenade fuses and landmine.

"Why didn't you just give them the shit?" Eastwood asked.

"Trust me, we would have. Dweebly wouldn't let us. He said he was sending out EOD." Just then Slim's radio came to life with a burst of static.

"Slim, go ahead and give them the cache. We can't get ahold of EOD at this time," Walt ordered.

Slim's eyes narrowed and for the first time he was rendered speechless.

Eastwood started laughing so hard his cigarette fell out of his mouth.

I reached into Cali's pocket and grabbed his can of dip. I shoved some in my lip and spit on the bags full of fuses.

We left the cache where it was and slowly made our way back to our trucks. We thanked the soldiers of Third Platoon for quite possibly saving our lives and waved goodbye. The way back to the trucks was hardly relaxing. We were afraid the Afghans were going to try to ambush us on our way out. We methodically checked every alleyway and street. One team would rush forward and cover an alleyway, and once that team was set in place the next team would rush to the next alleyway in line.

Eventually we made it back to our trucks, climbed inside, and slowly worked our way out of the intertwining maze of alleyways and side roads back out to the main roads. We drove back to Grizzly Base in silence. Grandpa's iPod blared out some awful rap version of a country song, and we all tried to forget we were almost killed by people who were supposed to be our allies.

CHAPTER 13

NAN PLAYS CATCH

EVERY MORNING THE GENERAL OFFICER in charge of our area sent down a message to all the units under his command. That message was called the Significant Actions Report, or SIGACTS. Those messages would include all the enemy attacks that happened on allied soldiers in the last twenty-four hours.

That was important because the Taliban generally never changed their tactics unless we did—meaning attacks on our forces followed trends. It gave us something to look for rather than just looking at every bearded adult Afghan male with suspicion.

Our district in Kandahar had seemingly turned into Compton overnight. The Taliban had taken up the fine art of drive-by shootings. These drive-bys differed from the Crips or Bloods in one very significant way: They liked to use hand grenades.

Two men riding on a scooter—which was overwhelmingly common in our area—would drive through a U.S. or Afghan patrol, drop a few grenades, and keep on trucking down the road. It was also not unheard of for them to roll up and shoot an American soldier in the back of the head, execution style.

You might think that would be easy to see and jump off into a ditch, but you'd be wrong. In a busy market or village, cars, motorcycles, and scooters zip by every few seconds. People are yelling and screaming trying to hawk their wares in the street. It's a loud and distracting environment to operate in. If someone simply drops a grenade into traffic, which you happen to be working in, you won't see or hear it. You might feel it, though.

"Man, y'all are fucking pussies!" Nan argued with Thad. They were arguing about the enemy contact first squad almost had the night before. Most of the platoon was hanging out in the chow tent choking down some awful shit the cooks had put together for us. We tried to eat as fast as possible so we wouldn't have to taste it.

"There is a difference between being pussies and being insane. You guys jump over that line and shoot at it," Thad said, laughing. He was talking about Second Squad's habit of starting shit while we were on a mission. He wasn't wrong. We had a habit of overreacting to everything.

"You can call us crazy all you want, but we don't run from a fight!" Cali mocked.

In Second Squad, we loved to say First Squad always ran from a fight. Of course, that wasn't entirely accurate.

A few nights back, First Squad had been on a patrol at night, which was normally Second Squad's job, and decided to set up an OP in a burnt-out farmhouse.

At some point during the night, all hell broke loose. Guns started cracking to life. Machine guns and rockets ripped through the air all over. Tracer rounds were tearing through the night from all sides about one hundred yards in front of them. They had no idea what was going on and no one was actually shooting at them. No one seemed to know that they were there. It was as if they'd stumbled upon some random turf war in the middle of nowhere.

Neither Olly—First Squad's leader—nor Grizzly Base had any idea what was going on. Because he wasn't insane, Olly ordered his squad to slowly pull away from the firefight. Turning that two-way cluster fuck into a three-way wouldn't have made anything any better. They turned around and no one involved noticed.

The various militant groups that operated in our area—a strange mix of Islamic insurgents, smugglers, and gangs—routinely tried to kill each other. The Afghan security forces would shoot at anything that went bump in the night. It could have easily been two different Afghan police patrols shooting at each other. Olly was a smart leader for not getting his men involved in that firefight. That didn't mean we weren't going to fuck with them for it.

"So how was it? Holding the Taliban's pocket, I mean," Perro joked.

"Whatever, let's see how you assholes react when it happens to you." Thad waved off all the jokes. He was a smart guy, a promising young leader who just lacked a bit of experience. Before we could get another word in, Thad had to leave to suit up for their patrol that was coming up.

"Try not to run away from anymore enemies, dude!" Perro called after him.

"Fuck you!" Thad called back.

Dweebly decided one random day that because a village elder and Olly couldn't iron out plans to build a school, he would send Slim in to talk to him.

I would like to think it was the occupation version of "good cop, bad cop," and after a few hours of dealing with Slim, the elder would immediately agree with Olly. So Olly and his guys had to roll out at night instead of us. After hearing about their mystery firefight, I was glad we were stuck on day patrols.

Meanwhile, we headed out to the construction area that was slated to be a school with a few Army Corps of Engineers civilians. On the site a school already stood. It was built about ten years before and was already completely stripped of everything worth a shit. Even down to the toilets.

People had just started throwing their trash over the walls of the abandoned compound afterward. Due to the incredibly shoddy construction work, or just plain fraud, the walls of the school had actually melted in the rain. The Afghan contracting company that had built it hadn't used any cement whatsoever. They just piled mud and hay together into something resembling a building. It held until the first rainstorm.

About the only thing not stolen was the nice big sign on the outside of the school that said: Provided to the People of Afghanistan by the People of the United States of America. It had a painting of an Afghan flag next to an American one. It looked as if we had donated a landfill to them.

We sat down with the elder only to find out he objected to the school because he wouldn't be in charge of it. By the looks of this guy, the only thing he could teach people was how to cultivate incredible body odor. We laughed at the old man and told him that would never happen. He explained that Olly told him he would be in charge of everything in the village, including the school.

Of course, that wasn't true at all. Village or tribal elders were notorious for lying and saying they were promised things by other U.S. soldiers, even when they were totally ridiculous.

The next day, First Squad went back and managed to get the elder to agree with the school project. They probably told him that if he didn't, the other soldiers would come by again.

We sat around Grizzly Base trying to kill time until nightfall and it was our turn to go outside the wire. Around the time night started to fall, Slim burst into the soldiers' tent. "Hey, get the fuck up. First Squad found an IED and we are going out to help them secure the area," he yelled.

We all lazily rolled out of our cots, put our gear on, and trudged to the trucks to get them ready.

Before every mission, the trucks had to be prepared for combat. That meant radios were checked, weapons were mounted and loaded, and we did a quick check over the vehicle to ensure everything still worked. Military vehicles had an uncanny ability to break while parked. Every time we climbed inside and cranked it up there was a good chance the piece of crap wouldn't start. When you first deploy, this process can take anywhere from twenty to thirty minutes. By that time, though, we were up and ready to go within five.

We rushed out of the gate to First Squad's location. How they found the IED just went to show just how much of a different group of people they really were.

While out on a normal patrol through a village, the point man on their patrol had found a small dugout with puppies inside. He called to the rest of his squad and they came forward to see the puppies.

It was around this time they saw half of an artillery shell sticking out of the ground and wires leading into a house. They quickly backed up and tried to secure the area. The puppies were left depressingly unsecure in the blast zone. The guys were laughing at First Squad for rushing to see the puppies. I was laughing because I probably would have done the same thing.

We showed up on the scene and blocked off traffic with our trucks. A few people dismounted to join in on the securing effort. Grandpa and Cali got out of the truck, leaving me alone to man the gunner's position. I settled in for a long stay. Grandpa's iPod was blaring some awful bubblegum pop music at me. I think that time it was Kesha.

I unstrapped my body armor and took my helmet off to get comfortable. I stared down the incredibly busy market street, scanning rooftops and alleyways.

My truck shook, and I heard the dull *thump* of an explosion behind me. My radio hissed to life. At first, I couldn't understand what was being said because the sheer amount of panic in the person's voice made it completely incomprehensible.

"I'm hit!" screamed the voice. It was Nan. He was the gunner in the truck behind me.

I ripped my headset off and put my helmet back on, grabbed my rifle, and jumped out of my truck. When I landed on the ground, I noticed there was no traffic at all anymore.

Every living thing in the village had vanished as if it had never been there. I rushed to Nan's truck. It was totally obscured by smoke and I could barely see.

Sal, our medic, was already climbing into the truck. He turned to me and pushed me back. "Get back to your fucking truck!" he yelled at me. He was right. I had totally abandoned my position to run over to my friend. I quickly ran back to my truck before Slim or Grandpa noticed.

I climbed back behind my gun. I wasn't focused on it. My mind was racing, Nan said he was hit. Was he dying? The geeky, chubby guy who I always debated politics with. He could be dying, and I wasn't doing anything to help him.

Slim immediately pulled everyone back to the trucks. Everyone jumped in, and we screamed off down the road. We drove as fast as we could to Camp Nathan Smith, the nearest base with a medical center. The Afghan security guards barely got the base's gates open in time for us to blast through. Cali had no intention of stopping the truck to wait for them.

When we stopped, I jumped out of my truck and ran back to Nan's. Sal was helping him out of the truck. Nan's eyes were wild, and he was breathing heavily. He wasn't bleeding.

"I'm pretty sure he has a concussion," Sal said. "Besides that he's okay."

I breathed a sigh of relief and walked with them to the aid station.

Once Sal sat him down on a bed and stripped off his gear, Nan started to calm down. He was coming down off his adrenaline high. He began replaying the events for us.

"I thought they had just thrown a rock at me." He shook his head. "They do that shit all the time." He put a massive handful of dip in his mouth. "Two fuckers on a scooter drove by and chucked it at me. It hit me square on the side of the head, bounced off, and landed on the outside of the gunner's shield. When it exploded, I was thrown back into the truck." The gunner's shield is a shield of metal and ballistic glass that surrounds the truck's turret. It could stop most bullets and, as Nan discovered, hand grenade blasts.

Slim put Perro and me in charge of changing out the passenger side tire of Nan's truck because the explosion had shredded it. The entire side of the vehicle was peppered with shrapnel and burn marks. Chunks of metal had lodged themselves into the truck's armor plating and taken deep gouges out of the gunner's shield. All the windows on the passenger side were spider-cracked.

A mechanic let us use his forklift to pick up our truck so we could change out the tire. It was incredibly unsafe, and I was pretty sure the truck was going to fall over at any second, but Perro worked fast, and soon the tire was switched out.

Perro reached into his backpack and pulled out a package of pink tiger-striped Band-Aids and started placing them over the gashes the shrapnel had taken out of the truck. "That should work, right?" he laughed.

"Good enough for government work," I said. I grabbed a few of the little pink Band-Aids and stuck them over the gashes on the front passenger door.

Perro lit a cigarette, hitting it so hard the burning end sparked.

"So what happened out on the patrol after Nan got blown up?" I asked him. Perro had been out with Slim and the group of people attempting to secure the IED.

"Dude, everyone froze except Grandpa and Slim. They took off running to see what happened," he explained. "Why didn't y'all shoot the fucker that threw the grenade?"

"I didn't see it. He said it was two people on a scooter." I shrugged.

"So in other words, pretty much anyone," Perro said. About half the vehicles on the road were scooters packed full of people, even during the winter. "Should have started shooting anyway. Just waste the fucking city, bro." The thought had crossed my mind more than once.

We walked back to where the rest of our squad was hanging around outside the aid station. Nan wasn't there.

"Where's Nan?" I asked no one in particular.

"They're keeping him overnight," Cali said. "To make sure he doesn't die or some shit."

"It's because he has a concussion. They have to keep him for observation," Sal said, his professionalism showing.

"Is he going to be okay?" I asked. Nan was one of my best friends. We couldn't have come from more different backgrounds in life, but in the army that didn't really matter. Hating your life while serving in uniform tends to bring people together.

"Should be," Sal said. "Concussions aren't usually serious." Sal had recently quit smoking, though you wouldn't be able to tell from the cigarette dangling from his lips. That was his first time ever having to treat someone he knew and who was a friend.

Slim appeared from within the aid station looking upset. "They aren't letting us bring him home with us tonight, and they won't let us stay with him." It turned out Slim wasn't keen on leaving one of his men behind. He decided we would all be staying, too.

We were told that there were no cots for us. That didn't matter. We would sleep on the floor. We don't leave anyone behind, not ever.

It took a direct order from Dweebly for Slim to admit defeat. "We'll come get him in the morning as soon as they let us," Slim said, relenting.

We climbed into our trucks and headed back to Grizzly Base. Sal took Nan's spot behind the gun of Kitty's truck.

At first light, we were in our trucks and driving back to get Nan. We each exchanged a hug with him when we saw him again. The doctors said he was perfectly fine, though he still had a headache that refused to go away and an endless ringing in his ears.

Once we found out he was fine, we started giving him shit.

"What's wrong man, never played catch before?" Cali and Perro laughed at him.

He laughed with us, clearly just happy to be alive.

CHAPTER 14

MAGGOTS

KANDAHAR IS ONE OF THE most impoverished areas of Afghanistan. There are many reasons for this, but mostly it is because it's the birthplace of the Taliban and was their de facto capital during the brief point in history when they ruled as the official government of the country. A small sliver in the northeast of Afghanistan was under the control of a group called The Northern Alliance that allowed some of the modern world within its borders. NGOs were allowed to work, hospitals were built, roads were constructed, and girls were even allowed to go to school.

The south wasn't so lucky. Under the iron grip of the Taliban, the south of the country was dragged back into the Stone Age. Sports, school, and even music were outlawed. Economic development crashed to a halt, and any kind of health care system was entirely unheard of. This meant while we were on our patrols conversing and mingling with the population, we saw all sorts of horrific medical issues that people just lived with as if it were a part of everyday life.

There was an old man who worked a farm near our outpost who always waved to us when he walked by. He had an index finger that was so badly broken and twisted it hung limply from his hand. When he waved to us, it would flap uselessly in the wind.

Another young girl near us had her face almost entirely fused to her neck due to scars from a horrible acid burn.

About a quarter of the kids who milled around us while we were on patrol had visible birth defects and mental disabilities. It seemed as if the majority of the children were cross-eyed and limping.

Some of us were compassionate. We at least tried to treat all the kids the same. I learned quickly not to show any special treatment toward the obviously messed up ones, but I was one of the few people who would still give out the candy my mom sent me in the mail. That was mostly because she asked me to, and only a real asshole doesn't listen to his mom.

At first, I would try to hand out the good pieces to the little girls. I really can't think of a worse life someone could have than being a girl in Afghanistan. Maybe I could brighten it for a few seconds with a Jolly Rancher.

I learned that was a big mistake. The little boys and even some fully-grown men would beat the ever-loving shit out of the little girls and take their candy. The same thing would happen if we purposefully gave out anything to anyone else. After a while, we just stopped giving anything out. I'd rather that they have no candy than an ass whooping.

Long after our compassion had died from seeing one too many toddlers get their face smashed in over some Dollar Store suckers, Sal rekindled it. Sal would stop and bandage up people's cuts and bruises whenever he had time.

He always got Hamid to ask people if they had any medical issues. He couldn't do a whole lot to help most of them. Yet many of the people left him looking a lot happier than when they arrived. His kindness was infectious, and soon I was helping him check over the local populace on our patrols.

Working with Sal was one of the few times I felt as if I was doing something to help those poor people. Most of the people we helped were raised thinking Americans were pure evil. We were the cause of everything bad that had ever befallen their country.

We were trying to dispel that notion one Band-Aid at a time. The idea that we were going to win over Afghanistan one village at a time by dispensing Tylenol and smiles was total bullshit. But the idea that I could make some kind of difference in these poor, miserable people's lives was enough for me.

One day, Sal and I were posted up near an Afghan police checkpoint talking to the locals through Hamid. The rest of the squad was spread out throughout the area stopping and searching people in a vain attempt to try to find smugglers. Sal and I had looked over a few people. It seemed that they just wanted to say hi to the Americans who weren't going to rifle through their pockets.

A young boy, no older than ten, walked up to us carrying something small wrapped in a blanket. He pulled the blanket back to reveal a newborn girl. She was sound asleep and wearing a knitted hat even though it was easily over one hundred degrees outside. The little boy said something to Hamid.

"What did he say?" I asked.

"His sister has a headache," Hamid said.

"A headache? She's sound asleep," Sal said puzzled.

The boy said something else and reached up and took the knit cap off the little girl. A bright red rash covered most of the girl's scalp.

"Oh," Sal laughed. *"That* kind of a headache." He leaned in close to look at the rash and immediately leapt away from the little girl, retching. "Ah! What the hell is that *smell*?" he choked.

I leaned in and looked. The girl's head smelled like rotting meat that had been left out in the sun. The smell burned my nose, and I saw tiny little black holes in the middle of the rash. Something wiggled inside the holes. I reeled back. *"What the fuck?"* I screamed a little too loudly.

"What?" Sal asked.

"Something is in her fucking head!"

Sal shot me a look like he didn't understand and leaned in for another glance, that time breathing through his mouth. He slowly turned his head and gave me one of the most horrified looks I think I've ever seen. "She...she has maggots in her head," he stuttered.

"No fucking way," I gasped.

"The rash must have gotten infected, and they never got it looked at. I can imagine how an infection would run rampant in an area like this," Sal said rubbing his chin. He took off his medical bag and dropped it on the ground. He unzipped it and started picking through it.

"What can we do for her?" I asked.

"Not a whole lot. Something this far gone probably needs to be seen in an ER, like...well, probably before the maggots got there," Sal said, still fishing through his bag. "We can at least clean it up and send them to the hospital."

"Clean it out? Oh, baby is not going to like that."

"Not even a little bit," Sal said ripping open an alcohol preparation wipe. He started cleaning away dried blood, puss, and maggots. It all came off in a red-black smear and the little girl screamed bloody murder. Sal wrapped clean gauze around the girl's head and gently placed the knitted cap on top of it to keep it in place.

"Tell him his sister needs to see a doctor as soon as he can get her to one," Sal instructed Hamid.

Hamid quickly translated, patting the little boy's shoulder. The boy smiled and ran off, baby in arms. He got to the corner, took the girl's cap off, ripped off the gauze, and threw it to the ground. He placed the dirty cap back on the open, infected wound and strolled away down the road.

"Why do I even bother?" Sal shook his head.

"Because you're a good guy. Don't stop being a good guy," I said.

"Why? It's so much work."

"Because if you do you'll end up like one of us." I gave him a weak smile and lit a cigarette.

CHAPTER 15

GUNNY AND THE GREAT AIR CONDITIONER HEIST

IT HAD BEEN ABOUT A month since Bumpo was fired as our platoon sergeant for the breakdown of the platoon's discipline, and we had kind of been in limbo. Before the dust had even settled on that, First Squad's leader, Olly, was also fired and sent to the command cell to push paper. I'm still not really sure why they fired Olly.

He was an incredibly skilled leader with decades of experience, and he should have rightfully been made our platoon sergeant. The only reasoning I can think of was the disaster known as Red. He was one of Olly's team leaders.

Red always seemed out of place in Afghanistan. During our first patrol, someone stepped on an empty water bottle, and the crunching sound made him dive into a ditch. He had perpetual look of overwhelming fear in his eyes and his soldiers absolutely hated him.

One day, Red lost his night vision goggles and the shit hit the fan. Losing something like night vision goggles is a huge deal because it can mean the Taliban could get their hands on them. The idea of the Taliban being able to see us as we crept around at night was unnerving. His total incompetence led to Bugsy becoming the real leader of his team while Red only kept the title.

Red always seemed to be in trouble but was never demoted. Instead, Olly was given a severe dressing-down for not making sure one of his leaders had all his gear at all times. It seemed unfair because Olly didn't pick Red to be a leader. The Company had left Olly to deal with all of his fuck-ups, and there were plenty.

Thankfully, they found his night vision goggles right before Red was due to go on leave. The same leave he would never come back from. He vanished off the face of the earth and we didn't hear from him for months. This, of course, was blamed on Olly for some reason. By the time we did hear back about Red, and why he went AWOL, it was too late, and Olly was already riding a desk in the command cell.

Red's excuse for disappearing was that he wanted to see his son —something he didn't actually have. He was banging a girl who happened to get pregnant with someone else's kid. He thought it had to be his, even though the girl said it wasn't. I'm pretty sure Red was grasping for an excuse not to go back to Afghanistan. He was just too goddamn scared to operate efficiently as a soldier, let alone as a team leader. It was impossible to respect someone as a soldier or NCO when he dived for cover at the sight of his own shadow.

To make things even more convoluted, Dweebly was the next person to be fired. One day, without warning, he just vanished from Grizzly Base. He was a weak, ineffectual leader who burned many talented young soldiers to make himself look better. I don't think anyone was sad to see him go.

Our new commander was a man named Rocky. He appeared at Grizzly Base as quickly as Dweebly left. He was short, stocky, and sturdy looking. He was a full head shorter than I was, but the way he carried himself made me feel small in comparison. He wasn't at Grizzly Base long before he appointed Gunny as our platoon sergeant.

Gunny had earned his nickname because we all joked that he was so much of a strict hardass he should have joined the Marines. Of course, we would never call him that to his face. He had been working in the company's command cell since we had been in Afghanistan and it had been driving him insane the whole time. Gunny was a tried and tested combat leader who was stuck riding a desk only because he had a great track record of planning operations. Not that Dweebly ever let him do his job effectively.

We all hoped that Gunny would do well. It could be a breath of fresh air after Bumpo. Although Bumpo was a good guy, he had allowed the platoon to fall into a bit of chaos, to say the least. He was too laid back. Even so, Bumpo had been a stark contrast to our original platoon sergeant.

Everyone knew that Bumpo would shit the bed when he got promoted to platoon sergeant. He wasn't even Dweebly's first choice for the job. He had come into the position because a month away from our deployment, our first platoon sergeant, a guy named Scar, was fired.

Scar was a model soldier. He sounded like Clint Eastwood, sported a massive scar on his neck from a parachuting accident, and absolutely never bent the rules for anyone. He was the rare leader that really fostered a family feeling within his unit. He knew, while we were in Afghanistan, that each other was all we were going to have. We all loved him.

Scar's love of all things regulation and order would eventually bite him in the ass. While out in the field training, he screamed at a soldier for leaning against our company commander's truck. Scar could not tell from a distance, but that soldier was actually a company commander from another unit.

This fact was quickly pointed out to Scar by the commander he was yelling at. Scar didn't care what rank the guy was. He was breaking the rules, and that was all that mattered to him. The next week, Scar was quietly fired and we were stuck with Bumpo.

Our platoon did not take Scar's firing lying down. Scar had always taught us that regulations apply to everyone equally, regardless of rank. We, as a platoon, marched into our sergeant major's office and filed a complaint. Before long we were gathered into a room to talk with our sergeant major about why Scar was fired.

"Scar is a great combat leader," the sergeant major told us. We already knew that. No other leader in our company was more qualified to lead a group of men into combat than he was. The sergeant major went on. "I wish he were surrounded by glass that said *IN CASE OF WAR, BREAK GLASS*. Then I would free him," the old, fat bastard droned.

Where did he think we were going? Canada? We were going to war and by his choice he put a lamb in charge of lions. Then we were stuck with Bumpo and we all learned a valuable lesson about how full of shit higher army leadership was.

Now Gunny gathered us all outside our sweltering, still very much un-air conditioned tent to say his hellos. We stood in a lazy formation, most of us half undressed due to the ungodly heat inside our tent. Our NCOs had no such problem and were wearing their full uniforms. This, of course, was the first thing Gunny noticed.

"Why aren't most of you dressed?" he asked calmly. He had this weird nervous habit of not making eye contact when he was mad. Instead, he would cast his glance anywhere and everywhere else. The whole time with a small sneer on his face.

"Their tent has no air conditioner," Slim answered quickly.

"But yours does?" Gunny asked Slim. The tone of his voice said there was no right answer to this question.

"Yes, Sergeant," Slim said.

"Just letting your soldiers bake to death in there while you were comfortable. Wonderful." If you followed his eyes, it looked as if he was really pissed at the gravel for some reason. "Heat is no excuse not to wear your uniforms. Go change," he said, glaring at the sky. We hurried back to the tent to get dressed. It was so hot in the damn tent my belt buckle burned my hand when I touched it. Being burned by my clothes seemed to me like a good reason not to wear them.

Later that day, we were ordered by someone to go grab mail from Camp Nathan Smith, which would also be Gunny's first mission with us. As we got the trucks ready, Gunny was all over the place. He watched us intently while we worked. He stopped Cali as he was working on the radios to ensure he was doing it right.

"Ugh, micromanagers," Cali complained, spitting dip spit into an old water bottle. "Say what you want about Bumpo, but he left us the hell alone."

"That's because he was afraid of Slim." I laughed.

"He was afraid of everything," Cali corrected.

"And he had no idea how to do any of this stuff. Gunny obviously knows what he's doing."

"You say that like it's a good thing." Cali shook his head.

We climbed into our trucks and drove out. The ride over to Camp Nathan Smith was uneventful, except that we hit half the speed we normally did for fear of pissing off Gunny any further. We pulled into the camp's gate and parked our trucks. The mail would have to be signed over to Gunny before we could do anything, so we just sat around and waited.

Before I could light a cigarette, Gunny was already walking back to the trucks carrying a box. He looked pissed. "Why aren't you guys getting an air conditioner for your soldiers?" he yelled at the NCOs.

"We tried before here, Sergeant. They won't give us anything because we aren't in their unit," Slim answered.

Gunny dropped the box onto the ground and started looking around at the massive motor pool we were parked in. There were probably close to a hundred different military vehicles of varying types around us. "So take one," Gunny spat. "These assholes have everything they've ever wanted here, and they won't help us. So let's help ourselves. Find an air conditioner."

The air conditioners the army uses aren't a window or house unit you would normally see. They are massive, about the size of a compact car and attached to their own trailer. In other words, we wouldn't be hiding it. We would just be attaching it to one of our trucks and hauling ass out of the camp.

Quickly, but not quietly, Perro, Nan, Cali, Slim, and I spread out and started searching through the expansive motor pool.

"No AC over here!" Perro called out.

"Nothing over here," I screamed back.

"I got something!" Slim yelled. There was a huge AC trailer that was sitting unguarded, attached to someone's truck. Slim and I quickly started unhooking the trailer. Everyone else spread out and made sure no one was coming.

We pushed the trailer over to where our trucks were parked. We struggled with the big unit, attempting to maneuver it in between the various vehicles around us. We failed and smashed the trailer off just about every vehicle we tried to get around.

"Hey! Those motherfuckers are stealing our AC unit!" we heard an incredibly angry voice scream.

"Oh, shit," I laughed. "Our master plan is ruined!"

"Shut up, asshole, push faster!" Slim yelled. We hoisted the trailer up onto the hitch of one of our trucks and frantically connected it.

"Let's roll, boys!" Gunny called out, jumping into his truck. Before we even had all our gear on we were hauling ass out of the camp's gate. A group of screaming soldiers left in our dust.

"Suck it, assholes!" Nan laughed at them from his gunner's hatch sticking up both middle fingers as we pulled out. We laughed and high-fived each other. Within hours of taking command of our platoon, Gunny had done more for us than Bumpo ever had.

Back at Grizzly Base, we excitedly hooked our shiny new AC unit up to our tent. It chugged, coughed, and roared to glorious life sending a dark plume of black smoke into the air. Within minutes, our tent was cooler than it had been in months.

That night, lying on our cots, we were freezing cold. I had to rummage around for my sleeping bag, which had been buried deep in my belongings ever since I'd moved into that horrible hell tent. I was unbearably cold the entire night. It felt absolutely amazing.

CHAPTER 16

SPARTAN BASE AND THE DESCENT INTO MADNESS

AFTER FINALLY GETTING AN AIR conditioner and making our tent semi-habitable for the first time in months, we learned we were going to move again. This time to a small outpost in the middle of Kandahar City. We would be replacing a unit that was going home. Again, our mission would be to work, live with, and train the Afghan police.

Thankfully, this time command decided it was a good idea to scout out the area before blindly moving us in—unlike the Chap Stick 25 debacle. So, with Gunny leading the way, we got in our trucks and headed out.

The downtown area of Kandahar City was incredibly built up. Not like a real modern city or anything, but it was a decent third-world metropolis.

We were flanked on all sides by recently constructed, foreign-bankrolled skyscrapers. All of them had obviously cut corners during their construction. Windows were missing and in one case an entire building was just a hollow shell. Electrical wires were hung up from anywhere and everywhere with no apparent plan.

Wires hung low over the street, and we tore them down as we drove by. Open-air sewage channels ran on both sides of the street right next to stalls that sold food. The accumulated stench stung your eyes and lingered in your very soul.

The base, which we decided to name Spartan Base after our platoon, was located smack dab in the middle of all this. It was lined with tall concrete barriers and Hesco baskets. Guard towers were at every corner, and a parked truck acted as the base's main gate. We parked our trucks inside the base's cramped motor pool, just barely fitting in.

We were met by an older guy, a sergeant first class named Johnson, and his medic Rick. They looked tired and worn out and were clearly happy to see us. All the team leaders went with Johnson into the command building. The UN had originally built the building for the Afghan police as a shower and bathhouse. A big blue plaque out front proudly proclaimed the showers were built by the international community for the betterment of Afghan law and order.

The rest of us went with Rick, who started showing us around the base.

Rick showed us to the rear side of the command building where they had set up a sleeping area. Inside were the shower stalls built by the UN. Each of them was so narrow I wouldn't be able to extend my arms all the way if I stood in the middle. Each of the ten stalls housed at least two soldiers, with a bunk bed shoved inside it and disconnected plumbing fixtures sticking out everywhere.

"Y'all live in fucking shower stalls?" Cali said, taken aback.

"Yeah, but at least we have electricity now." Rick shrugged.

Our tour then took us to the single, sad-looking shower trailer that was tucked into a corner of the base. The trailer was obviously broken. Several pipes and fittings littered the ground around it as if someone had once tried to fix it. Clearly they had failed.

"This would be the shower trailer if it worked...now we just use it for storage," Rick said. "It probably has something to do with the cholera outbreak we had a few months back."

"Did you say fucking cholera?" I sputtered in shock. I tried to remember if cholera was one of the hundreds of vaccines and shots I had received before I deployed.

"Yeah, it got pretty bad. Couple guys got sent home," Rick responded, like a goddamn cholera outbreak was no big thing.

Without another word, we moved on with our tour. We went through a small gate and started walking through the Afghan police portion of the base.

They hated each other so much they built a wall straight through the middle of the base like some kind of war zone version of an 80s sitcom with feuding roommates.

"This is their side," Rick said lifting an arm. "We try as much as possible not to come over here." While Rick was telling us this, he high-fived a child who tottered by, carrying a tea tray in his other hand.

"Why are kids wandering around?" I asked.

"They're *chai boys*," Rick said, pointing to several other small children who were serving tea to Afghan policemen. "They are the Afghans' slaves."

"I'm sorry, did you say *slaves*?" Nan asked.

"Yeah. They kidnap them off the street and turn them into sex slaves and tea boys," Rick said, giving another kid some candy.

"Sweet Jesus! Why haven't you stopped that?" I asked.

"We tried. Reported it to every level of Afghan and U.S. command. No one cares. We tried banning them from the base, but the police smuggle them back in. We just gave up."

"You gave up...on child sex slaves living next door?" I was baffled. I had seen some seriously messed-up stuff in Afghanistan, but never something like this.

Rick looked irritated that I was blaming the atrocity on him, which I was.

"Sorry, I know it's not on you," I said through gritted teeth.

Rick just nodded. He lit a cigarette and moved on with our tour.

We sat down inside the dining tent that was also their internet tent. Two huge picnic tables were in the middle, and the sides were lined with a few incredibly old desktop computers. Somehow they had managed to get their hands on a large flat screen TV and hung it on the wall. They even had a crappy U.S. military version of cable hooked up to it.

It showed every major sports game, though the service would cut out randomly. Instead of typical commercials for whatever stupid product Apple was selling in between shows, there were Pentagon-approved commercials. These commercials were skits starring soldiers talking about things like how not to be a rapist, please don't beat your wife, and don't spread top-secret info to the enemy.

The network was laughably bad. I wasn't sure what was worse, that the commercials had to exist or that someone had joined the military and picked the job whose duty it was to run a bullshit government cable network.

With our tour complete, we walked back to the motor pool and waited for our team leaders. The place didn't seem so bad. Sure, at one point they had a full-on third-world disease outbreak, no working showers at the same time they were, ironically enough, living *in* showers. It had to be better than living in Grizzly Base with the looming eye of Walt's stupid camera making our lives miserable all the time.

The team leaders finally came out of their meeting and we headed back to Grizzly Base.

I packed up all my worldly possessions. All of it added up to one whole duffle bag, a backpack, and a box overflowing with workout supplements. We were all just as excited about moving out to Spartan Base as we were about the Reserve. We would be out on our own, far away from everyone else.

We happily tossed our bags into our trucks and headed back out, this time permanently. By the time we got back to Spartan Base, the outgoing soldiers were already packed and ready to get the hell out of there.

We picked out where we were going to live. Second Squad got the infamous shower bay while First Squad moved into the right wing of the bathhouse. It was a large bay with a few more of the tiny shower stalls lining the walls. The outgoing soldiers had hand-built rickety wooden bunk beds that filled the middle of the bay and had hung some sheets up for some measure of privacy.

I moved into a shower stall with Cali and claimed the bottom bunk. I tossed my sleeping bag across the old stained mattress I would be sleeping on and noticed there was a whole shower piping system and showerhead sticking out of the wall right next to my bed.

"Fuck, let's switch, man," I complained to Cali. The damn pipes took up half my bed space.

"Hell no, dude, you called bottom bunk; now you deal with it," he said, laughing. As he moved around, the shoddy metal bed frame creaked and moaned. I noticed most of its welds were cracked or totally broken.

Before we were settled in, we had to take over the guard rotations in the various towers. This was also when the horrible realization set in about our undermanned platoon: We did not have enough people to effectively run Spartan Base.

There were six guard towers, each requiring two soldiers. This effectively meant an entire squad was on guard at once while the other one would be out running a mission with the Afghan police. And those were only the planned missions, of course.

We could be ordered to go out of the gate at any second on the whim of three entirely different command cells. Our own at Grizzly Base, the one at Camp Nathan Smith, or another unit's at nearby Camp Walton. It was a convoluted mess that we had no control over.

Cali and I moved into a tower that overlooked a nearby market. The market was surrounded by the slums. The slums didn't look any worse than any other part of the city, but they happened to be built in the shadow of towering skyscrapers.

The skyscrapers had no working plumbing or trash system. The skyscraper residents just tossed their trash and waste from the upper floors onto the hovels in the slums below. Cali and I watched this happen more times than we could count.

The walls of the guard towers were filled with scribbles and graffiti produced by hours of boredom. Almost every one was a variant of penis doodles or commentary on how much they hated Afghanistan. There was a scorecard full of tick marks titled "Tower Six Jerks," next to which there was a pile of porno magazines. It had sixty-five tick marks.

Rules were also laid out on the tower wall for a game called the "Tower of Power." It stated that you had to masturbate every hour on the hour during your tower guard shift. The scores that were scribbled underneath the rules defied biology. I had to wonder if they had two-man tower guard shifts like we did.

Hours crawled by in the tower with nothing to do except stare off into space. That was technically your duty while you were there anyway. Cali and I talked about all the plans we had for leave. We were both coming up on our leave dates.

While you're deployed, you get two weeks of leave. The army will pay for your plane ticket anywhere you want. I'd made plans with Bugsy to go with him to Tampa Bay, Florida. I had never really had a vacation before, so I decided that two weeks of sun and beaches sounded just right.

Cali was married and was excited about going back to California and seeing his wife. I was single at the time, though Bugsy was trying to fix me up with one of his wife's friends. The ongoing joke was that I would marry her during the two weeks I was going to be in Florida.

"The first time you guys bang you're going to fall in love," Cali said with a laugh.

"Not going to happen." I shook my head. "She is way out of my league." She was a model, and I was an awkward, lanky dude who was already balding and had deep wrinkles at the age of twenty-three.

"Man, that's why you gotta lock that shit down. What other model is gonna let your ugly ass bang her?" He spat out a mouthful of dip spit onto the tower floor. "Better hope your dick game is strong."

"Hey, fuck you, man. At least I don't have a lisp."

"At least I'm not going to marry some hooker," he said.

"I'll have you know that is the oldest profession in the world." We both laughed together, and I stole some dip from out of his can.

By the time First Squad got back from its first mission outside of Spartan Base, fifteen hours had passed. Two incredibly tired-looking soldiers came up and replaced us. We walked down to the gate ready to go on patrol.

By the time we set out on our first patrol into Kandahar City, it was pitch black out. The city was totally dead. Due to an incredibly limited amount of electricity, almost everyone was in bed by the time the sun went down. Or they were at least hiding indoors because of the constant fear of getting caught in the middle of a firefight between us and the Taliban.

It felt strange walking through a city of nearly one million people and not seeing a soul. Like some kind of Discovery Channel documentary about how a city will look after the end of times. The roads were scarred with bomb craters, and the buildings were pockmarked with bullet holes.

"This place making you homesick?" Slim whispered to me as we made our way.

"I keep telling you I'm from the *nice* part of Detroit, asshole. I bet Afghanistan is making you miss your family, though." I smiled.

"What?" He looked confused.

"On account of your family tree not having any branches, you white-trash fuck." Most of the squad giggled in the darkness.

"Fuck you, Kassabian," he said a little louder than he should have.

After a long but uneventful patrol, we walked back through the gates of Spartan Base and right back into a guard tower. Because both squads were back for at least a little bit, our shift lengths shrank by a little. Cali and I were so tired we no longer had the ability to carry on a conversation.

I was chain smoking and dipping in an attempt to stay awake. At one point I keeled over because I had fallen asleep on my feet and just tipped over. Thankfully, two exhausted soldiers from First Squad came up to replace us, and we slowly shuffled off to bed.

After only a few hours, Gunny came out of the command building holding a piece of paper. "Hey, go start getting the trucks ready. We have to go secure an area for some soldiers from the Tenth Mountain." He could tell from the look in our eyes we wanted to kill him. "Sorry, guys," he said before he turned around and walked off.

When our convoy slowly rolled out of the gate, we were all on the verge of passing out. Rip-It energy drink cans rattled around under our feet. At that point, massive doses of caffeine and nicotine were the only thing keeping us going.

Cali was dozing off at the wheel, and Grandpa and I were loudly singing country music to fight back sleep. The mission was a blur to me. There is an excellent chance I just passed out and didn't notice.

We rolled back to the gate after about six more hours and started shuffling back to bed.

"Hey, where are you guys going? It's your shift on guard!" Thad yelled at us.

"Man, fuck that. We've been awake for over a day!" Perro cursed.

"Second Squad in the towers!" Gunny yelled.

I spun around and dragged myself to the tower, Cali close behind me. This time, there was no fighting it. We both fell asleep on and off throughout our entire shift in the tower.

Grandpa kept bringing us energy drinks and whatever nicotine products he had on hand to try to help us, but it was no use. Nothing short of smoking meth could have fought off the level of exhaustion we felt. At one point, we took turns stripping our gear off and lying down on the floor of the tower and sleeping while the other one watched for NCOs.

Strange things start happening when you're operating on no sleep whatsoever. You feel high, but not in a good way. Like that point of a party when you're incredibly drunk, but you want nothing more than to be sober. You see things, and when you're standing guard in a warzone the last thing you want to do is hallucinate.

I could have sworn I saw a squad of Taliban fighters advancing on my position. I dove toward the M240 machine gun that was mounted on the tower and pulled the charging handle back as hard as I could. When I looked up, the streets were empty. There was not a single Taliban fighter in sight. I didn't bother waking Cali up for that.

I was standing in my tower staring off into the market when a fire caught my eye. A roaring fire was tearing through the ramshackle tin shacks. I panicked and kicked Cali awake. "Dude, wake up, the fucking city is on fire!" I screamed.

Cali rolled over, grabbed his rifle, and jumped to his feet. He peered out into the dark market and gave me a confused look.

"What the fuck are you talking about?" he asked.

I rubbed my eyes, and the fire was gone. Just the same old shitty unburned market.

"I...uh..." I stammered. "God, I'm so high from lack of sleep." I shook my head.

On another occasion, Nan and Oldies were in a tower together, just as sleep-deprived as the rest of us, and Oldies swore he could see a group of Taliban hiding in a ditch. Nan fired a flare into the air to illuminate the area. It wouldn't have been a big deal if anyone knew he was going to do it.

Everyone else on tower guard at the time saw a random flare light up the night sky and freaked out. It lit up all our positions like a goddamn sunrise and we ducked behind the low tower walls. In our fragile, delirious states, we nearly started a firefight with absolutely nobody.

"Do you see anything?" Cali screamed at me as everything turned a faint shade of green from the flare.

"Fuck, man, I don't know!" I yelled back staring over my rifle.

"Should we start shooting?" Cali asked.

"If you do, I will."

"Let's wait for someone else to start first."

"Don't fucking fire!" The radio screamed at us. It was Gunny. "Don't fucking fire unless you see something!" At that point, Gunny's voice was certainly the only thing that stopped us from shooting. We would have rather shot at nothing than missed our chance at getting a piece of the Taliban. Of course, we weren't sure. We were just waiting for someone else to start the show.

The days all started bleeding together. The first three weeks at Spartan Base, we never once slept more than two hours at a time. Between random missions, planned missions, guard tower duty, and supply runs, there simply wasn't time. We became masters of falling asleep in any position at any time if we were given more than, say, five minutes without something to do.

More than once I caught people falling asleep while taking a dump. The only reason I was so rude as to wake them up was because they were taking up the only toilet that still had a door attached. More than once, it was me slipping off to dreamland with my pants around my ankles.

Lack of sleep and frustration with the entire situation made us turn on each other. At one point, Slim and I had to be separated after we went at each other's throats over a cup of coffee. Nan's sanity took a steep dive when his undiagnosed brain injury, stemming from the grenade attack, was combined with sleep deprivation.

Eventually, Nan started randomly stabbing people with a small pocket knife, myself included. Another time, while Cali and I were giving him shit for being terrible at catch, he found a hand grenade and pulled the pin.

I have had a lot of things happen to me over the years: being blown up, shot at, but I can tell you this was probably the most scared I have ever been. Nan's crazed eyes and insane laughter—kind of like a Midwestern version of the Joker—while he held a primed grenade in his hand scared the living shit out of me. Hand grenades aren't the most well put-together piece of weaponry the army has. They're made by the lowest bidder, and their firing pins are renowned for being unreliable.

"Hey man, just put the pin back in that fucker. This isn't funny," I tried to talk him down from whatever plan was swirling around in his damaged head. He wasn't fazed by my pleas.

"I mean, you guys are so much better at catching than me, right?" Nan laughed.

"Nope! Not even in the slightest. You are the goddamn grand champion of catching. Now, just put the goddamn pin back in that thing!" I pleaded. I thought about making a run for the door of the bay.

"Come on, man!" Cali added, his voice ringing with terror.

"Man, you guys are such *pussies!*" Nan smiled at us and started putting the pin back in the grenade. Or at least he was trying to. He fumbled with the pin nearly dropping the still-armed grenade, but he managed to wiggle the pin most of the way back in. "I think it's good," Nan remarked.

"You know, this is something I'm going to need you to be pretty fucking sure about," I said with probably too much fear in my voice.

As a precaution, Cali fished some duct tape out of a bag, and we wrapped the grenade in it, forcing the arming spoon to stay on.

"What do we do with it? I'm not putting it back in my gear," Nan said.

"You figure it out, asshole," Cali spat.

"Okay, I'll just throw it into the market." Nan shrugged and started walking toward the bay door.

"Whoa! You are *not* throwing a live grenade into a crowded market!" I stepped in front of him with my hands up. "Think of how long that bullshit mission would be, man!"

"Shit, we'd be standing out there for hours," Nan sighed.

I couldn't help it. I started laughing, and Cali followed suit.

"Can we just put it back in the ammo tent? No one will notice," Nan offered.

"How did that become our best option?" I shook my head.

"When the fucking psycho decided he would pull the pin on a grenade, maybe?" Cali said.

"You guys are drama queens." Nan smiled. He walked out of the bay and climbed into the ammo storage tent. He placed the taped-up grenade in an ammo box in the back of the cache and shut the top. "There, I fixed it."

We all walked away and tried to forget the day that Nan almost murdered us as a practical joke.

The one refuge we had between the never-ending shifts and the missions was talking to our loved ones. But like some cruel joke from the gods, that too was soon taken away from us. A supply convoy stopped by Spartan Base one day to drop off a replacement generator and their truck's long antennas tore down our low-hanging internet cable.

As the cable snapped it dragged the satellite from on top of the command building and broke it into pieces as it slammed to the ground. Suddenly, I felt bad for all the power lines I'd torn down as I'd driven through the city. More people were pissed about the sudden lack of new porn than about not being able to talk to their family.

"Aw, shit, Joe, your model friend is going to lose interest." Slim laughed as we stood over the destroyed satellite dish.

"She was clearly only talking to me for my winning personality," I said. "This could really only help me."

"Must be for the money," Slim said sarcastically.

After losing internet, Gunny saw the platoon's morale imploding in record time, so he cut the guard towers to one soldier each during the day. It wasn't much, but it would give us a little bit more time to try to sleep. Maybe we could actually take care of ourselves. During the perpetual cycle of missions and guard shifts, no one shaved, bathed, or washed their clothes. We all smelled as shitty as we felt.

I used my first free hour to wash my clothes in an empty paint bucket I'd found. Spartan Base had no washers or dryers. Our still-broken shower trailer meant that after I finished washing my clothes, I had to fill the same bucket up again to wash myself.

I stripped down naked and dumped the bucket over myself, scrubbed up with a bright pink loofa, refilled the bucket, and dumped it back over my head. I felt like a new man. I tried to ignore the half-dozen Afghans watching me.

Boredom was painful. It made the hours feel like days and the days feel like weeks. We became masters of passing the time doing random bullshit. We played a game called "Marry, Fuck, Kill." One person would name three people, and everyone would have to pick one that they would marry, one they would fuck, and one they would kill.

It's a pretty straightforward game. At least for the first few hours you play. Eventually, you run out of real women. You go to cartoon characters. At one point I had to choose between Lassie, Betty Boop, and that lamp that was shaped like a leg from *A Christmas Story*. I married Lassie.

Nan, Guapo, Walrus, and I also invented a new game that could be played in the shower bay. It was a variant of football, baseball, and pure idiocy. One person would be the pitcher, but instead of a baseball, they would throw a football. They would chuck the ball to the batter, who was armed with an aluminum softball bat we'd found lying around.

The batter would smash the football as hard as he could, sending the oblong pigskin bouncing off the walls, ceiling, or whatever else got in the way. The score was determined by committee. Whoever was watching the game would scream loudly whether they thought the hit was a single, double, or triple. The score was based on how much damage the ball caused as it smashed off of things. Nan dubbed our new stupid game "Footsketball."

The shower bay and command room were only separated by a thin piece of plywood. So every single time we played Footsketball someone from the command cell would barge into the shower bay and scream at us to be quiet. I couldn't blame them for being pissed because Footsketball was a loud affair. It was a veritable ruckus with the screaming of curse words, racial slurs and insults, and the football wreaking havoc as it slammed off of things.

Eventually, Gunny outlawed our glorious new sport, and we resorted to playing tackle football out in the gravel motor pool.

I tried to put all of this out of my head. If I sat around and dwelled on how miserable life at Spartan Base was, I probably would have driven myself insane. Or pulled an armed grenade on someone the way Nan had. I tried to focus on the fact that I was supposed to be jetting off to Florida in a few weeks.

CHAPTER 17

THE BATTLE FOR GRIZZLY BASE

GRIZZLY BASE WAS BEING SHUT down, and the rest of our company was being moved into the cramped confines of Spartan Base. We were leaving Grizzly Base to the ANCOP guys. Which really meant we were abandoning the area to the Taliban.

We knew the drawdown in that area would get the Taliban's attention. They were always watching us and could clearly see that troop numbers inside the base were shrinking. That made Grizzly Base a huge, poorly defended target.

Our convoy was rumbling through the gates of Spartan Base after one of our incredibly dull mounted patrols when a voice crackled to life over the radio.

"Spartan Base, this is Grizzly Base. We have troops in contact at our location, requesting QRF (Quick Reaction Force)." The voice was cool, calm, and collected.

What he meant was someone was attacking them, and they wouldn't be able to stand on their own. Before we could respond over the radio, he said: "Send Second Squad." In the middle of a fight for their lives, they explicitly requested us, and only us, to come save them.

Our trucks spun around and hauled ass out of the gate. Blasting through Kandahar City traffic, we sideswiped a few unfortunate cars and made Afghan police dive out of our way. No one was stopping for anything. Cali did all this to the smooth stylings of Avril Lavigne's 2002 hit "Sk8ter Boi" playing on Grandpa's iPod.

We expected to see some massive battle when we rolled up to Grizzly Base, but instead we saw absolutely nothing. But we could clearly hear gunfire coming from down the road around the local Afghan police checkpoint. It seemed like Grizzly was perfectly fine.

"Grizzly Base this is Spartan two-two," Slim called over the radio. "What's your situation?"

"The attack moved down the street," they said. "Toward the Afghan police checkpoint. Move in that direction and give them support."

"Roger," Slim said with an unmistakable tinge of happiness in his voice. The idea of a firefight always got Slim going.

Our convoy continued down the road past Grizzly Base toward the small Afghan police checkpoint. The road leading to the checkpoint was a single-track dirt path that was just big enough to fit our trucks on with steep drop-offs on either side.

We slowly pulled onto the road, moving at a crawl so we could keep our trucks on the road. We came to the checkpoint, which was really nothing more than a pink lawn chair and some traffic cones. The Afghan police were nowhere to be found. "What the hell?" Grandpa said. "Where did they go?"

"They didn't have time for this whole war business," Cali said, laughing and making finger quotation marks.

Machine guns roared to life from the village on our left. Their bright green and yellow tracer rounds cut through the air like laser beams. The checkpoint's lawn chair was disintegrated by the burst of gunfire, turning into a spray of splintered pink plastic.

"Back the fucking trucks up!" Slim yelled over the radio.

"We can't! We don't have enough room!" Grandpa radioed back. We were stuck. We were also handicapped. The Taliban were shooting at us from inside a village. They knew we couldn't bring our heavy mounted weapons to them because of our restrictive Rules of Engagement.

Rules of Engagement are the rules put forth by our commanders that outline how we can fight the enemy. One major rule was absolutely no heavy weapons in heavily populated areas without permission. Permission that was practically impossible to get.

"Dismount!" Slim ordered. Drivers and team leaders were to get out and fight on foot while we tried to get permission to use the big guns.

When Cali and Grandpa climbed out of the truck, another group of Taliban that was hiding in the fields behind them opened fire. Immediately Grandpa's team was pinned down around the truck.

"Shit! Contact rear!" Cali called out. Grandpa and Cali turned and engaged them. The dirt road exploded all around them with the impact of enemy gunfire.

"Contact front!" Slim called out over the radio. Walrus, Slim, and Perro were pinned down at the front of the convoy. They took cover behind an old concrete road barrier. It cracked and broke away with every bullet impact. When the barrier exploded next to Walrus's head, he dropped. His helmet fell off and rolled away.

"Fuck! Medic!" Slim called out and dragged Walrus behind the wall. Sal rushed from the back of the truck and grabbed him.

"Shit! Let go, man, I'm good!" Walrus pushed him away and picked his rifle back up. The tone of his voice was equal parts anger and shock. Once again, lackluster Taliban marksmanship had saved Walrus from being shot in the face.

"Grizzly Base this is Spartan two-two! Troops in contact! Requesting air support!" Slim called over the radio but got nothing. A bright red light cut through the air, everyone hit the dirt.

"RPG!" Grandpa screamed. Everyone waited for the inevitable impact of a rocket-propelled grenade, but it didn't come. We sat up and saw the red light fizzle into nothingness. It was a flare.

"It was just a fucking flare!" Cali screamed between gunshots. Empty brass casings gathered in little piles by his feet. Bullets slammed off his beloved Lexi's armor next to his head.

"Grandpa! How are you guys doing back there?" Slim asked from behind the ever-shrinking barrier at the front of the convoy.

"We're hanging in there," Grandpa responded. "You guys alright?"

"Oh, just fucking great," came the sarcastic answer. You could hear the snaps and cracks of incoming gunfire in the background of Slim's transmission.

Green, yellow, and red lights kept firing up into the night sky. The soldiers in Grizzly Base's guard towers were shooting off flares into the sky in a failed attempt to illuminate the Taliban hidden in the fields. It didn't work, though it did light up the stranded squad on the road perfectly.

"*God dammit!* Stop shooting off fucking flares!" Slim screamed into his radio. "You're illuminating our fucking position!" He yelled so loud that the microphone transmitted mostly static. "Where is our fucking *air support?*" The concrete barrier the guys at the front were hiding behind was getting precariously small. Everyone's ammo was getting dangerously low. "What's the air support's ETA?" Slim asked Grizzly Base.

The air was suddenly full of the angry chopping sound of helicopter blades. The helicopters weren't in sight yet, but their mere sound made the Taliban's fire die away faster than it had started.

"Spartan two-two this is Long Knife," came the voice flying overhead. "We are on site, how are you guys doing down there?"

"I think we've been better, sir!" Slim answered. "We had contacts to the west from the village and the south in those fields. You see 'em?"

"Roger Spartan two-two. I have eyes on six armed adult-aged males making their way through the village. I am not cleared to engage. Sorry, guys." Even the pilot was handcuffed by the Rules of Engagement. He could clearly see who had just attacked us, but because they were hiding in the village, he couldn't do anything about it and the Taliban knew it. He just hovered overhead harmlessly.

"God dammit!" Slim cursed. "Grizzly Base, this is Spartan two-two requesting permission to assault the Taliban position that Long Knife spotted."

"Negative, Spartan two-two. Return to base."

Slim was speechless for a second. "But..." Slim started. He wasn't even talking into his radio or to anyone in particular. He was just venting the confusion and aggravation we were all feeling. "I..."

"It's over, man," Grandpa said, shaking his head.

"Roger," Slim finally answered. "Returning to base."

Everyone felt a mixture of relief and anger. Relief that we were all still alive and in one piece. Pissed because Grizzly Base wouldn't let us chase down those assholes and kill them. They were only a hundred feet away hiding out in a village, and no one could touch them.

We had two helicopters full of rockets and machine guns hovering overhead, four heavily armored trucks loaded out with heavy weapons and grenade launchers, and a squad of incredibly angry soldiers and we couldn't touch them. It was maddening.

That was our war.

We slowly backed our trucks out of the death trap we had gotten ourselves into a few minutes before. The process required two people standing on either end of the truck and slowly guiding the driver back down the road, one truck at a time, until they were all back on the main road. The whole process took half an hour.

We swore up and down we would never use that piece of shit road ever again. A promise the Afghan police apparently kept as well. They never manned that checkpoint again.

CHAPTER 18

THE HOOLIGANS SAVE A LIFE

OUR SQUAD HAD BUILT UP one hell of a reputation for being violent assholes. We were proud of that reputation. We hadn't started out that way, though. Before Slim became our squad leader, we were little more than the bastard team that regularly screwed everything up.

During field training, we failed almost every test thrown at us. We completely lacked the motivation to do anything and generally didn't care to improve it. Soldiers like us needed firm leadership to put us in line. Slim was that leader.

Slim was more than firm, though. He was an unrelenting psychopath who would fly off the handle at the littlest thing. He would scream, yell, and throw things. He would get so angry whatever the hell he was screaming wouldn't even make sense. He threatened to beat and kill us if we stepped out of line. Honestly, I kind of believed him. Under Slim's watchful, crazy eyes, we fell into line. We started acting like him, too.

I once told Slim he treated us like trained pit bulls. "You beat us, mistreat us, barely feed us, and every once in a while you let us off the chain to attack someone," I said.

It wasn't entirely a joke. Harsh treatment and corporal punishment had been linked to utter viciousness during wartime. A lot of historians chalk up the terrible brutality of the Japanese Imperial Army during World War II to their mistreatment during training. Not that Slim was a Japanese military historian or anything. The only book I ever saw him even start reading was the biography of George W. Bush. Insanity and sadism are timeless, though.

The reason I mention the squad's upbringing is that one of the main missions for allied forces in Afghanistan is the so-called "Hearts and Minds" campaign. These missions are the ones you see on CNN when a high-ranking officer cuts a big stupid ribbon for an Afghan school or hospital that cost an obscene amount of American taxpayer dollars to build.

They look pretty for the camera but never accomplish anything. Most of the time, whatever we build ends up never being used. Other times, the Taliban just moves in and turns it into the local command post. Then the Air Force bombs it, returning the area to its natural state.

It became clear to our commanders early in our deployment that Second Squad was absolutely terrible at Hearts and Minds missions. They pretty much forbade us from going on them. Instead, they held us in reserve to raid houses or go kicking in doors searching for weapons. They used violence to fight violence.

But patrolling a war zone wasn't all kicking in doors and capturing Taliban commanders. Most of the time it was mindless patrols, either on foot or in our trucks. We called them Presence Patrols. Reminding people that those assholes who'd invaded their country ten years before were, in fact, still there.

Tons of random things happened on these patrols. We found IEDs, got ambushed, and arrested people who were smuggling weapons into our area. But most of the time, nothing at all happened. Just one boring walk after another.

On one of these pointless patrols, we were packed into our trucks and driving around in circles. We spent so much time patrolling the cramped confines of Kandahar City that we started to neglect the surrounding villages. So, of course, Gunny sent us out on an hours-long patrol to the area instead.

The outlying villages were the picture of poverty and misery. Ditches full of human waste and garbage lined every dusty dirt road. Most of the houses were made of crumbling mud bricks and had tin roofs. Almost nobody had running water or electricity. The way the Afghan tribal system worked meant that normally at least three generations of a family lived under one tiny, dilapidated roof.

Most of the roads were single-lane dirt tracks barely big enough for regular cars. It made driving our hulking, armored beasts nearly impossible—made even worse by the new rules we were made to follow that forced us to allow Afghans to pass us while we drove down the roads. Before this rule, which was meant to make us seem nicer to the Afghans, we could force traffic to stay well behind us to ensure a suicide car bomb wouldn't get close to the convoy.

"This is fucking stupid," Cali complained. He was gripping the wheel so hard his knuckles turned white.

"Hearts and Minds, man," Grandpa said sarcastically.

"We have them by the balls, their hearts and minds will follow," I joked. It was something an old team leader of mine used to say.

"Where are these guys even in a rush to go to? It's not like they have fucking jobs," Cali said.

It was probably true. Every single job project the Afghan government tried—all of which were bankrolled by the U.S.—failed miserably. The number one employment sector in Afghan was growing opium.

Before I could utter a smart-ass remark, one of the many cars that were zipping around us sped off at around fifty miles per hour and slammed right into a sheep that was crossing the road. The sheep cartwheeled through the air in a white blur and crumpled onto the side of the road. The car sped off as if nothing had happened.

"Holy *fuck*, did you guys see that?" Slim laughed over the radio.

"Poor sheep never saw it coming," I said.

"Guys, that wasn't a fucking sheep!" a medic named Pico screamed over the radio. Pico was filling in as our medic while Sal was on leave. "Pull the fucking truck up!" As our truck got closer, we saw the road was totally covered in blood and broken glass. On the side of the road lay a man wearing what had been a traditional white robe, now completely soaked with dark red blood. He wasn't moving.

Before anyone could give any orders, Pico was out of the truck and sprinting toward the man. We quickly rushed after him to make sure he was safe.

Pico saw the man was still breathing and stabilized his neck. "He needs a medevac!" Pico yelled at Slim, who was trying to tell Spartan Base what exactly was going on.

"Spartan Base, this is Spartan two-two requesting dust-off," Slim said calmly over the radio.

Dust-off was the universal term for a medical evacuation by helicopter. Slim turned to Pico and shook his head. The army wasn't going to lift a finger for an Afghan civilian.

"Fuck!" Pico yelled. "He needs to get to a hospital *now*. Give me something, Slim."

A large crowd of locals slowly began to surround us to see what we were doing. They looked on with concern as someone they undoubtedly knew barely clung to life in the hands of an American medic. A few Afghan police in pickup trucks pulled up to the scene to see why there was a massive crowd gathered.

"Hamid!" Slim yelled at our interpreter. "Tell those mother fuckers this guy needs to go to the hospital now or he's going to die."

Hamid dutifully translated. The Afghan police made a dismissing gesture with their hands and shook their heads.

"They say if you give them one hundred dollars they will transport him," Hamid said with remorse.

"They want a fucking *bribe* to do their fucking *job*?" Slim screamed. He was getting to the point his voice was cracking, and his Florida accent started to come out.

"Tell them we will give them fuel!" Grandpa yelled. Fuel was nearly as rare as an Afghan who owned a toothbrush.

Hamid translated, and the Afghan police jumped out of the truck and ran over to the dying man.

"Tell them that they have to keep his neck stable and not to jostle him around too much," Pico tried to explain to Hamid.

Before Hamid could translate, the police roughly dragged the man to the truck and chucked him into the bed as if he were luggage.

Cali grabbed a fuel jug off the back of our truck and gave it to the policeman who stayed sitting in the bed of the truck with the now probably dead man. The little green pickup truck sped off, kicking up dust and sending several civilians diving out of the way.

"Who the fuck doesn't try to save one of their own?" Pico shook his head.

"They're cops, for fuck's sake!" Cali snapped. Cali always talked about becoming a cop when he got out of the military. It wasn't because he was on a power trip or anything. Cali really believed in the criminal justice system. He saw the law as a black and white thing and truly wanted to "serve and protect."

The surrounding Afghans came forward and hugged Pico. A few of them gave him the traditional kiss on the cheek. They shook the rest of our hands and smiled. I couldn't help feeling bad for them as they turned and walked back to their slum. The very people that were supposed to be there to protect them, the Afghan police, wouldn't even lift a finger to bring one of them to the hospital unless they were bribed. They were helpless to care for themselves and were caught in the middle of a three-way civil and international war, and utterly powerless to effect change in any area of their lives.

I could see Slim leaning against his truck watching a child try to kick dust over the dark blood puddle that stained the dirt road where the man had been mowed down by the careless driver. He walked over and helped the kid, using his large combat boots to smear over and dilute the blood. It was the most caring thing I had seen Slim do for a local during the entire deployment. Even though it only lasted a few seconds, it showed me that my friend and squad leader still had some humanity left in him.

CHAPTER 19

KANDAHAR AIRFIELD, KUWAIT, AND FLORIDA

BUGSY, GRANDPA, AND I WERE sitting around on the steps of the command building chain smoking and shirking whatever duty we were supposed to be doing when Gunny burst out of the command room.

"Hey, you two go on leave next week, right?" Gunny asked Bugsy and me.

"Yeah, why?" I asked.

"There's a convoy going toward Kandahar Airfield in an hour, I'm putting you two on it. Go pack." Gunny ordered.

"A week early?" I questioned.

"Don't question that shit, man, you get to hang around the airfield for a week and then go home. That's like a whole bonus week of leave!" Grandpa laughed, slapping me on my shoulder. He was right. The airfield had running water, real beds, internet, cable, you name it, and those lucky assholes had it. Bugsy and I quickly rushed to our living areas and started packing.

I wasn't even really looking at what I was packing. I just shoved it blindly into a duffle bag. I had no civilian clothes anyway, so I only needed the uniform on my back and maybe some shorts. I was done with just enough time to give my weapons and ammo to Grandpa before I jumped into one of the trucks.

Eastwood's platoon drove us slowly down Highway One toward the airfield. Highway One was the only semi-modern highway in all of Afghanistan. It was one of NATO's first big reconstruction projects in the country. The highway made one giant loop around the entire country, passing through every major city. It looked just like any four-lane highway back in the U.S. It even had traffic lines that were dutifully painted on by hand.

The problem with only having one highway in an entire country filled with angry, murderous, terrorist groups was that it made for one hell of an easy target. The surface of the road was pockmarked with bomb craters and the burnt-out hulks of cargo trucks. Our convoy weaved around the craters, some of which were big enough to swallow our truck whole. It was the middle of the night so the road was abandoned. We were all on edge.

Thankfully we rolled through the airfield gates without incident. The airfield was such a big place, we still had about twenty minutes of driving to get to where we needed to go once inside its walls. Eastwood's soldiers dropped us off at a small huddle of green tents and drove away.

Bugsy and I found our way into an office that had a sign outside that read "Slum Lord." Inside was an Air Force guy who was so fat the buttons of his uniform were straining to hold together. The overweight Air Force guy assigned us our own tent in the corner of the compound.

The compound was recently a British army living area. Signs were posted everywhere telling me to "watch my mate's back" and not to "have a bit too much ale at the pub" when we went home.

When the Brits left, the U.S. military turned it into their transient center for people going on leave. Thankfully, the Brits left behind about twenty shower trailers and several huge generators.

We dropped our bags off in our tent and were surprised to find shitty green cots instead of beds. Most of the cots were cracked or breaking. The fabric in the middle was torn and sagging. It was like finally going to Paris only to discover the whole place smelled like shit.

Bugsy and I shuffled to the showers. It had been the only thing on our minds since we arrived. I couldn't remember the last time I had had a proper shower with actual hot water. I climbed inside the tiny shower stall. I had to kneel down a little bit to fit inside leaving the showerhead at about neck level.

There wasn't a knob or anything that worked the water flow. Instead, it was a push button that would dispense hot water in ten-second bursts. I managed to wedge my body wash bottle at just the right angle to force the button to stay down and nearly scald me with hot water. It felt glorious.

I'm not sure how long I was in there, but it was long enough for a huge line of angry people to form outside. I finally got out and got dressed. I walked back across the compound and into our tent. Bugsy was already passed out on his cot snoring away. I climbed inside my sleeping bag and was asleep in seconds. I slept deeper and longer than I had since I'd left American soil.

I sat up in my cot; drool plastered across my unshaven face and saw it was still dark outside. Bugsy and I weren't alone in the tent anymore; two more bodies filled the cots around us. Everyone was asleep. I looked down at my watch. It was around three in the morning. This confused me because I could have sworn we had gotten into our tents around four in the morning.

"Fuck, man, what day is it?" Bugsy asked, still half asleep.

"Thursday," I said still a little confused. "I think we slept a whole day."

"That explains why I am so goddamn hungry," Bugsy said rifling through his discarded pants looking for his cigarettes. "Let's go get some food."

"The chow hall is closed," I pointed out.

"Nah, man," Bugsy said shaking his head. "They have a whole boardwalk area that never closes. They sell burgers and pizza and shit," he informed me while clenching a cigarette between his teeth. Bugsy had spent a few days at the airfield learning to use some bomb detection robot that we had broken within a few days of receiving. He had learned his way around the airfield. "They have nightclubs and shit over there man. It's crazy."

"Nightclubs?"

"Yep. There's still no booze or anything, but a bunch of Air Force POGs dance around to shitty music and grind up on each other." POG is a derogatory term used by combat soldiers to insult the guys who don't do any fighting. An old tank commander of mine explained to me it used to mean "Persons Other than Grunts," but has since evolved to mean pretty much anyone whose job in the military isn't combat related.

We got dressed and started to head toward the tent's exit when we were stopped by a thunderous explosion that shook the ground. The air was full of a horrible shrieking noise that we both knew pretty well. The Taliban were launching rockets in the airfield's general direction.

"That was a little close," Bugsy giggled.

"That would be our luck—having a rocket land on us while we waited to go home on leave." I shook my head. We decided to wait on our cross-base trip to the boardwalk until the rockets stopped falling. We stepped outside and watched the bright orange lights from the rocket's motors streak overhead. On impact they lit up the horizon, landing on some unseen target off in the distance.

"That had better not be the fucking pizza place exploding," Bugsy said.

"I hope it was the nightclub," I countered.

Before long, the rockets died out and we started walking again. Normally on the airfield they had a bus service that stopped at every little compound and shuttled people to the areas of heavy traffic. But because it was so early, they weren't running yet. The boardwalk was about three miles from our compound through the never-ceasing, terrible-smelling dust haze that always shrouded the airfield.

The airfield always stank of a mixture of burning rubber and human waste. Burning rubber from all the burn pits that lined the airfield's outer walls, and human waste from the massive shit pond that had been built in the middle of the base. It was hard to discern which was worse.

The burn pits coughed out choking black smoke that never ceased being pumped into the air. All the airfield's garbage was brought to these pits and set on fire by criminally underpaid Afghan laborers.

The one kind of waste that wasn't burned was stored. Sometime during the early stages of our occupation here they had to figure out what they were going to do with thousands of soldiers' shit and piss. One guy had the bright idea of digging a massive hole in the ground right in the middle of where everyone lived and dumping it all in there.

Since then, it had only grown in size and odor. Command had posted a sign at the banks of the shit lake that read, "Do not enter, extreme health hazard," which might be the most unnecessary sign in human history. Shortly after that sign popped up, someone posted another sign next to it that read "No lifeguard on duty," and hung a little ring buoy from the signpost.

Somehow Bugsy and I made it past the shit lake without passing out or vomiting. We came up on the boardwalk. It was a haphazard gathering of buildings built around a large wooden deck. In the middle of the vast area was a full soccer field, turfed with bright green fake grass.

Loud salsa music pumped through the night and bright neon Christmas lights hung from the edges of all the buildings. People were dancing all over the place, grinding and freak dancing on each other.

"Mother of God," I gasped.

"I told you, man," Bugsy said. I noticed a lot of the women were decked out in full makeup and were wearing the army-issued physical training uniform—a shorts and T-shirt combo we wore when we worked out. They had the shorts hiked up as far as they would go, exposing a fair amount of ass cheek.

I hadn't seen so many women in months, and I couldn't help staring as I tried to take it all in. I couldn't even smell the shit lake anymore. The only thing I smelled was the combination of about one hundred different perfumes and body washes all clashing with each other.

"Look at all those bitches," I stammered.

"Do you want to go try to dance with one of them?" Bugsy asked, laughing.

"Are you kidding me?" I squinted at him. "I don't know how to dance. I'm too white for that." I lit a cigarette. "Besides, I probably don't even know what to do with a woman anymore."

"Don't tell the model that," Bugsy said, reaching into my cigarette pack.

"Oh don't worry, I fully plan on disappointing that poor girl." I blew out a puff of smoke.

We walked into the boardwalk area and pushed past the grinding throngs of humanity. We passed a Fridays, a Burger King, and a Dairy Queen—all of which were packed. Bugsy was taking me to a tiny pizza place that was tucked away in the corner of the boardwalk. It was strangely empty.

A tiny weather-beaten old Filipino woman shuffled to our table and took our orders. I ordered a large pepperoni pizza entirely for myself, and Bugsy ordered a large sausage and pineapple pizza. Before long they were rushed out to us, piping hot and smelling so amazing it nearly left me speechless. Then I actually looked down at my pizza.

"What the fuck?" I cried. "These aren't fucking pepperonis!" Instead of slices of pepperoni on the pizza I had paid fifteen dollars for, it was topped with slices of hotdogs. "This is goddamn heresy!"

"Quit being dramatic and eat your hotdog pizza," Bugsy said between mouthfuls. I shut up and ate it. Even though my pizza made me think of a ten-year-old's version of mac and cheese, it was probably the best thing I had eaten in six months. I downed the whole pizza in less than ten minutes and washed it down with a can of Fanta.

With our stomachs slightly distended from the massive amount of pizza we'd just eaten, we started making the hike back to our camp. The irritating salsa music was still pumping throughout the boardwalk and soldiers, marines, airmen, seamen, and civilians were all still grinding all over each other. We pushed our way through the sweating roiling mass of overly sexualized servicemen and women and made for the exit when the familiar sound of a robotic British woman piped from several huge loudspeakers.

"Rocket attack," she said in a monotone, almost bored voice. Like the robot voice had been busy doing something else and was irritatingly interrupted to tell us about our impending death.

The crowds around us vanished, all making a dead sprint for the bunkers that were in the middle of the boardwalk area.

Bugsy and I stood there watching the herds of people running for their lives. We couldn't even hear the rockets flying overhead, no shrieks, screams, or whistles. The rockets were nowhere close to landing on us. We ignored them and just kept walking down the boardwalk. We made it out to the road when a military police SUV pulled up and shined a flashlight out of the window and into our faces.

"Hey! Don't you hear the sirens? Get to the bunkers!" one of the MPs yelled at us.

Bugsy, always the smartass, looked at the dark night sky and shrugged. "I don't see any rockets," he said.

"Just some assholes in a Toyota," I laughed.

"Get your asses back to the bunkers!" the MP yelled angrily. We turned around and walked back toward the boardwalk, making sure to give the MPs the finger as we walked off.

The bunkers were so full of people, about half the boardwalk's population was just sitting around them in the dirt. We sat down with them and waited for another siren to come over the loudspeakers to let us know that the rockets that never actually threatened us were gone.

We made the long hike back to the camp, collapsed back into our cots, and fell asleep.

It turned out being stuck at the airfield was a curse rather than a blessing. Time crawled by as we waited for our flight out of Afghanistan. We went back and ate at the pizza place nearly every day, bought tons of bootleg DVDs of varying quality from the kiosks on the boardwalk, and daydreamed about all the things we were going to do once we got to Florida.

Finally, mercifully, we got shoved onto a cargo plane with about one hundred other people and flown to Kuwait. Kuwait serves as a massive transient point for soldiers going to various warzones throughout the Middle East. Occasionally, it's a springboard for an invasion or two. We were now at a different military airfield called Ali al Salem.

Ali al Salem was located in the middle of the barren Kuwaiti desert. Compared to Afghanistan, it was a paradise. All the tents had comfortable, real mattresses laid upon real bunk beds. Sure, the tents had a pretty bad rat problem, but getting bitten by a rat was better than getting bitten by a rocket.

Our first stop after finding a tent was the chow hall. It was open twenty-four hours a day and put no limit on how much you could eat. In Afghanistan, we were under pretty strict rations. All our food came in brown boxes called Unitized Group Ration or UGR-As. The UGR-As were mostly boil-in-a-bag kind of meals that were only a few steps up from an MRE. They were issued to outposts based on how much someone in some high command thought that specific number of soldiers should eat. The portion sizes were laughable and even though one of our cooks had a college degree from a legitimate traditional French cooking school, it all tasted like cardboard.

Bugsy and I attacked the Kuwaiti chow hall like we were starving inmates escaping a gulag. On my first plate, I had a little bit of breakfast, lunch, and dinner while Bugsy's was mostly pie and ice cream. People were giving us strange looks as we went back for our third, fourth, and fifth plates of food. Eventually, a fat black guy in civilian clothes approached our table looking pissed.

"Excuse me, soldier, what the hell is on your face?" he hissed at me angrily.

I looked at Bugsy and pointed to my face. "Do I have food on my face?" I asked him.

"He means you haven't shaved, dude," Bugsy pointed out.

"Oh, I'm sorry, sir, I didn't mean to offend you with my unshaven appearance. I just got off the plane from Afghanistan and was hungry." What I said must have come out sounding a whole lot more sarcastic than I originally intended, because that made the fat black guy look even more pissed.

"*Sir?*" he screamed at me.

I squinted as little droplets of spit flew into my face.

"I am a goddamn *Sergeant Major!*" he kept screaming. "How about you stand at parade rest when you speak to me?"

Parade rest is a position the military makes you stand in when talking to a non-commissioned officer. You stand with your legs about shoulder-width apart and your hands clasped behind your back just above your ass with your head and eyes straightforward.

Bugsy and I slowly climbed to our feet and assumed the position of parade rest.

"I'm sorry, Sergeant Major, we didn't know your rank," Bugsy pointed out.

The sergeant major fished around in his pocket and pulled out his ID card. It had his picture and his status printed on it. "You didn't know?

It's right *here!*" He shoved his ID in our faces as if we were somehow supposed to have seen it while it was buried in his pocket.

Bugsy and I shot each other confused looks.

"Now get out of my fucking chow hall and shave your goddamn faces!" he screamed.

"Roger, Sergeant Major," I answered. There was never any point in attempting to correct *any* senior NCO about *anything*. We just left our food on the table and walked out of the chow hall.

That was when we ran into another soldier from our unit, Corporal Flip. He was standing outside the chow hall looking depressed. "Did that fat bastard kick you guys out too?" Flip asked.

"Yeah, Kassabian didn't shave so we forfeited our right to nourishment. Why did he kick you out?" Bugsy asked.

"He said my hair was too long," Flip whined, brushing his long black hair out of his eyes.

"We just aren't pretty enough for food," I laughed. We gave up and went back to our tents to sleep until our flight out of Kuwait took off in a few hours.

We were shoved into a convoy of Greyhound buses and sped off into the night through the Kuwaiti desert. Our bus convoy was surrounded by heavily armed Kuwaiti police trucks with lights flashing. I tried to go to sleep, but the constant honking from pissed off motorists that the police forced off the road kept me awake.

If there was one thing I learned about Kuwait during that drive to the airport, it was that there were more European supercars on that road than probably anywhere else in the world.

Our buses pulled right onto the airport's tarmac next to a massive Boeing 747 that already had its engines roaring. It was pretty clear the Kuwaiti government wanted us out of there as fast as humanly possible. We all filed into the big plane and took our seats; poor little Bugsy was smashed in between Flip and me in the center section.

We all reached into our carry-on bags and pulled out boxes of cold medicine. It wasn't our first time enduring the horrible eighteen-hour flight in the cramped confines of a government-chartered jet. The best way to do it, we knew, was to eat an entire box of cough and cold medicine at the beginning of the flight. It put you into something just short of a coma, and when you woke up, you were somewhere in America.

I soon blacked out in a pseudoephedrine haze and had the kind of vivid dreams you have after ingesting an entire box of over-the-counter cough medicine. Images of theoretical model girlfriends and gallons of booze danced through my head. I was awakened by the plane bouncing off the runway.

"Where the hell are we?" I managed, trying to clean away the sleep in my eyes.

"Atlanta, I think," Bugsy answered, still half-drunk from the mixture of sleep and cough medicine. It was our final immigration check, and we got our government-funded tickets to our last destination.

Now, you would reasonably expect than an immigration check for returning soldiers would be incredibly easy. We don't travel on passports, and it's pretty clear where we've just come from. But that's assuming the soldier hasn't lost the little slip of paper given to him in Kuwait—the one that says he is a soldier returning to America on leave. You would have to be really stupid to do that.

So, of course, I'd lost my little slip of paper.

An astonishingly overweight TSA agent detained me by the immigration gate until I could prove I was, in fact, a U.S. soldier. There I stood in full camouflage, unshaven, and stinking like a Middle East hellhole, and he wanted more proof.

"I bet if you test my hands they'll come back positive for explosives," I said. Obviously, this was meant to be evidence that I had just come from a war zone, not that I was a terrorist.

The TSA agent looked mortified. He talked to someone over his radio and turned back to me. "Let me see your ID," he said, looking annoyed.

I fished around in my pocket and pulled out my Department of Defense ID card.

"Okay, you're good to go," he mumbled and officially let me into the United States of America. I rolled my eyes because one of the first things I'd done when he first detained me was to show him my ID card and he said it wasn't good enough. I picked up my bag and sprinted past the TSA agent.

I was supposed to be on the same flight as Bugsy. A flight that was taking off in five minutes. You would be surprised how quickly people get out of the way of a crazed-looking soldier running as fast as he can through crowds of people. I parted that sea of people like Moses.

I made it through the tunnel right before they closed it and sat down next to Bugsy in the cramped plane. We were still a little loopy from cough medicine but were too excited to fall asleep. He had his wife and baby girl waiting for him at the airport, and I had Brooke—the girl who was apparently dying to meet me.

We had hit it off over the internet over the last few months, and she was going to meet me at the airport with Bugsy's wife. I kept having Bugsy reassure me that she was real, that this wasn't a giant joke at my expense. Honestly, if it were anyone other than Bugsy, I wouldn't have trusted them.

As our little plane descended into Florida, a beautiful coast came into view. Rows of palm trees and sandy beaches, the sun glinting off the blue ocean. It was the best thing I'd seen in six months.

"Holy shit, look at this place, man!" I gasped.

"I know," Bugsy rolled his eyes. "I grew up here."

"Why did you ever join the army?" I shook my head. "If I got to look at this every day, I never would have left home!" I was from Metro Detroit. The only thing to see around there was homeless people, potholes, and drunk autoworkers.

"I never said I was from this part of Tampa," Bugsy said, laughing.

Our plane bounced as it hit the runway and I pressed my face against the window with a huge child-like grin on my face. After what felt like an eternity, our plane made it to the terminal and the doors opened. We were sitting in the back of the plane and forced our way out of the door first.

Standing at the gate was Bugsy's wife Alissa, a short woman with librarian glasses, several piercings, and olive skin. A tiny human was clinging to her hand. Before we deployed, his daughter didn't yet stand or walk. Now there she was standing in front of us, and she took off running toward her father.

Behind Alissa was a short girl with bright blonde hair. She swept her bangs aside when she saw me, flashing icy blue eyes. She smiled. I stood there frozen like an idiot. I wasn't really sure what to do next. Was I supposed to hug her? We didn't technically know each other. Not in the real sense.

Luckily she broke the ice. She walked up and wrapped her arms around me. I suddenly remembered I was wearing the same tattered, nasty uniform that I left Spartan Base in and hadn't showered in about two days. She didn't seem to notice or care. I was overtaken by her perfume, and I tried and failed to find words.

"Hey," Brooke said softly. She smiled a little smile that showed her nearly perfect teeth.

"Hey," I managed to get out. "Nice to finally meet you."

"Yeah." She laughed a little. I felt like a giggling schoolboy. I just stood there smiling like an idiot. I felt giddy and had butterflies churning through my stomach.

"Since you guys don't have clothes, we are going to go to the mall, is that cool?" Alissa asked. I just nodded. Brooke and I were too busy staring at each other like idiots to say anything.

We piled into Alissa's car and headed off to the local mall. We made small talk, but I wasn't really paying attention. I was far too busy staring at the woman who was holding my hand and looking out the window at the beautiful Tampa Bay scenery.

Bugsy's daughter babbled away next to me in her car seat. I kept putting her snacks back into the car seat's cup holders after she'd thrown them at me.

Once inside the mall, I was taken aback by the massive crowd of people. I hadn't seen so many people in one place in a long time. I stopped in my tracks taking it all in. My heart started slamming into my chest, and I had trouble breathing. My eyes darted everywhere, looking at every person that passed up and down.

I tried to look into every single bag they were holding, I suddenly felt incredibly naked and unarmed. I looked over at Bugsy, and he was doing the same thing. We were both having panic attacks. We were having fucking panic attacks in a mall.

"It's okay," Brooke cooed, urging me forward into the mall. She reassured me by squeezing my hand in hers as I forced myself to walk forward.

After a few minutes, I managed to put on a face of total calm. Brooke wasn't aware that underneath my calm exterior there was abject terror. It would be hard to explain to her that she waited for some war hero to come home, and he was scared shitless of the local mall.

Bugsy was trying to do the same thing on his end. Putting on a façade for his wife while he was screaming inside.

We happened to be in the yuppie mall of Tampa. I had never even heard of most of the stores. I wasn't really sure on where to start looking for clothes.

"What store do you want to start at?" I asked Bugsy.

"Not a clue. I just kind of figured the women would pick the clothes out for us." He shrugged. We wandered into a few different stores, and Brooke picked out a few pairs of pants and shirts for me.

I paid some obscene amount of money before walking out. I ducked into the nearby bathroom and changed out of my tattered uniform. I looked in the scuffed up bathroom mirror and sized myself up in my new civilian clothes.

My skin, which was normally pasty-white, had a dark tan from months of the unbearable Afghan summer. My cheeks were sunken from endless patrolling and uncontrollable sweating. New wrinkles had set in above my eyes and each side of my mouth. I was balding. It wasn't the face I had left America with.

I walked back out into the mall to meet Brooke, who gave me another hug and told me how I looked like a human again. We held hands and walked back to the car. We started making our way to Bugsy's mother-in-law's house. As we drove across several bridges out of Tampa and into the suburbs, my eyes were glued to the road.

Every box or garbage bag we passed made my heart skip a beat. Every time a trailing car got too close to us, I was suddenly nervous. At that second there was no difference between the route we took in Kandahar and that highway in Florida. Everything was a threat.

I didn't notice I was breathing hard or sweating, but Brooke did. She put her hand on my thigh and smiled at me. I sat back in my seat and tried not to focus on the war zone I had created in my head.

We arrived at a small house in the Tampa suburbs. I had to say goodbye to Brooke. Unfortunately, she wasn't able to get the whole day off and had to go back to work. We hugged and I lingered a bit too long looking into her eyes. I tried to work up the courage to kiss her, but it never came. She never leaned in toward me, either. I got her phone number, and she headed back to work.

We were all supposed to go out that night and, for Bugsy and me, get drunk for the first time in half a year. I laid down on the couch and fell asleep quicker than I thought possible. I was awakened later in the day by Bugsy. I quickly rolled over and checked my phone to see if Brooke tried to call or text me, but there were no notifications.

"So what did you want to do tonight?" Bugsy asked.

"Dumb question," I laughed. "We're getting shitfaced."

"Just making sure. You hear from Brooke?" he asked.

"Nah, I'm assuming she's busy at work or something."

"Shitty," Bugsy said, setting down a six pack of beer. "Let's start pre-gaming." We cracked a few beers between us and started drinking.

Drinking is completely banned in war zones for the U.S. military. This made my tolerance go from being able to drink a bottle of whiskey in one sitting—a skill honed by my years in the army—to being a little buzzed from a couple of beers. We kept drinking as we waited for Brooke to get off work and for Alissa to get ready to go out.

"Brooke's going to meet us at the bar," Alissa said dusting on another layer of makeup.

We jumped in Alissa's car and headed off to the bar. It was a small place that had cornhole and beer pong games going on. Throngs of people were sitting around enjoying the warm Tampa night air.

Bugsy and I started doing shots, which was probably a bad idea as we were already a little drunk. I was trying to steady my nerves for when Brooke showed up. I had been such a nervous wreck when I met her the first time that I was afraid I'd made a huge ass of myself. After a few shots, Bugsy and I signed up for beer pong.

There was a large March Madness style bracket set up on the wall with team names written in. Bugsy and I were "The Stepfathers." We explained to our opponents it was because they hated us and we'd fucked their moms. No one else seemed to find it as funny as Bugsy and I did.

We won our first few games. I was talking so much drunken trash that people just started throwing the ball at my face rather than the cups. Bugsy, looking like the Penguin with a cigarette at the end of a long filter clenched between his teeth, was cackling like a madman next to me. We kept winning and kept drinking and at some point Bugsy had to run outside to puke. That was my last clear memory. At some point, Alissa managed to put us into a car and get us back to the house.

I woke up soaking wet and naked on the couch. There was water all over the place. It drenched the couch I was lying on and was pooled on the kitchen floor where my clothes sat in a heap. My head felt as if it had been split open by a jackhammer and my mouth tasted like whiskey and vomit.

I climbed into the shower to wash off the night and tried to mop up some of the mystery water. I put the couch cushions outside to dry in the warm air and checked my phone. Brooke hadn't returned any calls or texts, and she'd never shown up at the bar.

As I sat there in my only other pair of shorts trying to nurse my exploding brain I couldn't help feeling that I had been stood up. I sent her another text message.

"Is everything okay?" I wasn't really sure what to say. I had never been in that situation before. Surprisingly, this time she texted me back.

"I'm sorry. I just can't do this anymore," she replied.

"Can't do what?" I typed back. I was pretty confused. What couldn't she do anymore? We hadn't done anything in the first place. She never answered, and I never heard another word from her. I was crushed.

Did I scare her off when I first awkwardly got off the plane and had no idea how to talk to her? Or when I broke down into a panic attack in the mall or on the road? What the fuck was so wrong with me that I could take a girl who was infatuated with me for months and terrify her in the span of just a few hours?

I didn't know how to process the whole thing. From the time I had enlisted in the army at seventeen, I had been on a constantly rotating deployment cycle. I had no meaningful connections with other people. Like most soldiers, the only way I knew how to express my emotions was through heavy drinking and outbursts of anger.

I walked to the corner store and started hitting the bottle. Bugsy joined in shortly. The stress of family life, even in that short amount of time, was driving him insane.

It's nearly impossible to step off that plane from a war zone and slip right back into whatever role you had before. Bugsy was having a hard time falling back into the role of father and husband. He was sitting on the curb with me taking swigs from a bottle of cheap whiskey.

We didn't need to say anything to each other to know what was going through each of our heads. For the majority of the trip,we didn't sleep, eat, or socialize with anyone. We just sat next to each other in silence drinking or chain smoking. We were both totally lost.

Alissa managed to get us to go out for Halloween. We went to get costumes at the last second so all the good ones were already taken. Bugsy dressed up like Hunter S. Thompson, circa *Fear and Loathing in Las Vegas*. Alissa dressed up like a slutty cab driver, and I dressed up as Jesus.

We started drinking at the house and eventually went out to a bar that was on the ocean shore in downtown Tampa. Bugsy got shit-faced drunk, entered a costume contest, and won. He even beat some girl who dressed up as Jasmine from *Aladdin* and had taken her shirt off onstage.

I hit the bar and drew a lot of attention in my crown of thorns and robes. Girls kept coming up and stealing my crown of thorns. I would have to stumble after them drunkenly to take it back. The night came to an end with Bugsy and me vomiting on the beach under the evening stars and collapsing into the sand.

"I fucking hate this place," I slurred.

"Tampa? I thought you liked it here," Bugsy said sitting up and spitting out a mouthful of sand.

"No, America," I said. "All these assholes pass through life without a care, but they still bitch and complain about every little thing."

"You mean like you're doing now?" Bugsy laughed to himself.

"Fuck you. We just came from a country where there's no clean water, hospitals, schools, and mother fuckers randomly throw acid on girls for showing their ankles. Yesterday I heard someone bitch about getting their soy whatever-the-fuck latte a few minutes late."

"They're pussies. You can't hate them for being pussies, it's just who they are."

"Stop making sense; I'm drunk and angry," I whined punching the sand. He laughed and handed me a cigarette. I lit it and angrily rolled it back and forth in my teeth. We sat there in silence until Alissa came outside and yelled at us.

We got up, brushed ourselves off, and got back into the car. No one said anything on our way back to the house. I was still drunk and pissed. Alissa was fighting back the various emotions that come with having to say goodbye to her husband yet again the next day. I think Bugsy passed out.

When the time came for us to depart, the Bugsy family and I slowly walked through the airport to our gate in silence. I stood in front of the gate awkwardly as they said their goodbyes to each other. Alissa hugged me and asked me to keep Bugsy safe, to which there is nothing you can say. Bugsy and I turned around and walked down the tunnel not looking back. We sat in our seats and watched as Tampa slowly vanished from our view.

CHAPTER 20

THE SUICIDAL PERSON'S GUIDE TO BOMB DISPOSAL

KANDAHAR IS LITTERED WITH EXPLOSIVES. Thanks to its history of constant war, occupation by foreign nations, and good old fashioned civil conflict, there is never a shortage of military grade munitions for the person who wants to find some.

The Soviet army planted hundreds of millions of landmines and dropped millions of pounds of bombs in a futile attempt to defeat the Mujahideen in the 1980s. The vast majority of those landmines were never triggered, and due to fantastic Soviet engineering, a lot of those bombs simply buried themselves into the dirt rather than explode. But for a fighter too lazy to grab a shovel and go unearth some military grade explosives, it was plenty easy to make some of their own.

Afghanistan doesn't have much of a legal economy to speak of. What it does have is a thriving poppy farming industry that has made them the number-one producer of opium poppies in the world. That meant it was normal to see tons of fertilizer bags piled around everywhere we went. It was incredibly easy for a Taliban operative to mix some of this fertilizer with some kerosene to create an ammonium nitrate fuel oil explosive, or ANFO, in the comfort of their own home.

It took a particular kind of fertilizer to make ANFO. Knowing this, the Afghan president Hamid Karzai made it illegal to own. He waved his hands and figured that would solve the problem. Unfortunately, no one ever figured out a way to replace the millions of tons of old fertilizer that was lying around. And farmers needed to farm. So they just ignored the presidential order and no one ever enforced it.

The Taliban would take whatever choice explosive they were using, pack it into a box, bag, or sometimes into a vest they would wear, and place it somewhere to attempt to blow up allied soldiers. Every once in a while, their bomb would fail, and we would recover it. Back in the day, we would just shoot at the unexploded IEDs on the corner of the road and try to make them explode.

Someone above me in the chain of command realized we could use those bombs to try to find the bomb makers. So the new rule became to call EOD. If they thought they could safely transport the IED, they took it with them to a forensic lab and went all CSI on it.

They'd pull fingerprints, building schematics, and note what region the parts came from. Using all that information, they would dispatch soldiers to go looking for the masterminds behind the bombs. These orders were killing more U.S. soldiers than anything else.

Which brings me to a mission we were sent out on one incredibly hot day in the middle of nowhere on the outskirts of Kandahar City. All the bombs recovered by EOD are processed by forensic units. They were then brought to one central location at the local Afghan Police Provincial Headquarters. It was staffed by both Afghans and Americans. The Afghans hadn't figured out how to keep their trucks running, let alone plan and execute their own missions.

We arrived at the small, cramped, and dusty compound and set out to find the EOD soldier in charge of the mission. Slim, Nan, and I walked into a small tent that was supposed to be acting as EOD's headquarters. We were confronted by several confused Croatian soldiers who were sitting around in lawn chairs.

"We are looking for Sergeant Day," Slim said, anxious to get on with the mission. The Croatian soldiers exchanged glances with each other and gave us blank stares.

"E-O-D?" Nan said doing that weird thing people do when talking to people who don't speak the same language. He said it more slowly and more loudly.

"Oh!" The Croatians looked like they understood.

A big guy with a shiny bald head pointed to a patch on his arm that clearly said EOD.

"I am EOD!" he said in a thick accent.

"Umm…" Nan started.

"You clearly speak the most Croatian of any of us," I said.

"Shut up," Nan snapped at me. He turned back to the Croatians. "You have…mission…with…us?"

"Goddamn, you speak Croatian so badly I could swear it was retarded English," I said.

The Croatians looked confused again. We were at a loss about what to do.

An American soldier burst into the tent behind us. He looked a little surprised to see us standing in there. "You must be our escorts," he said without introducing himself, though I could read his nametag. It said "Day."

"Yeah," Slim answered.

"Sorry about that, we were getting our truck ready. You want to come give us a hand?" Day wasn't really asking as he'd already turned around and walked out of the tent. The Croatians rushed out after him and we followed.

The EOD soldiers had an old beat-up flatbed truck pulled up next to a storage container. The storage container was full of unmarked white bags. Some of the EOD guys were tossing them onto the back of the truck.

"We are loading up all of our ordinance in the back of the truck, then we'll head out. There's a lot of it, though, so we might need your help," Day said, pointing to the massive storage container.

"What is it?" Slim asked.

"Explosives, dude." Day gave him a look that just screamed *no shit*.

We fell into the chain of people who were handing the explosive cargo down the line and into the truck. Every bag I was given leaked small, white pellets out of various holes. Each bag weighed easily forty pounds, and there were hundreds of them.

It took hours to load all the white bags in the blistering heat. I was originally taken aback when the Croatian soldiers started lighting cigarettes. They were surrounded by literally thousands of pounds of explosives. I made the universal symbol for a cigarette to bum from the nearest Croatian soldier. He smiled and handed me one. "This sucks…Marlboro…dick!" he said with a big smile on his face. I honestly had no idea what that meant, but I thought it was hilarious and started laughing. He started laughing too, probably just as confused as I was. In his jovial laughter, his cigarette dropped from his lips and plummeted toward the ground.

All around us were millions of tiny white pellets. Tiny white pellets of ANFO. Everything slowed down into a Hollywood style bullet-time effect as the cigarette bounced onto the pile of ANFO pellets. I saw my incredibly disappointing life flash before my eyes.

Nothing happened. Everyone saw the look of absolute terror on my face and started laughing. The Croatian soldier who gave me the cigarette smiled at me. He made an explosion sound with his mouth and feigned injury. All of the EOD guys knew the explosives were more or less safe and knew that unless they were wired up to actually explode, nothing was going to happen. I smiled and tried to laugh it off.

After the countless unmarked bags of ANFO came the standard military hardware. Land mines, artillery shells, mortar rounds, grenades. You name it, and it was probably in that pile somewhere. Even though the explosives had been around since the days of the Soviet invasion, absolutely no care was taken into loading them up on the truck.

The first time I saw a Croatian with a lit cigarette throw a mortar round while doing his best Tom Brady impression I was a little surprised. Afterward, with soldiers from various nations and various units throwing unstable explosives through the air, I inexplicably calmed down. I assumed the experts knew what they were doing. Even if they didn't, I wouldn't feel a thing from the resulting explosion anyway.

With all the explosives loaded up on the truck, we all gathered around for the briefing of what came next.

"We have a detonation site a few miles out, one of our trucks will take the lead," Sergeant Day said. We normally had a detailed briefing before every single mission. We would go over the exact route we would be taking, what our plans were if we got attacked, and how we planned to respond. Day didn't have any of those things.

Slim asked the question we were all wondering. "What if we get in contact along the way?"

Day laughed. "I understand your concerns if we are attacked. But if this truck gets hit," he said, pointing to the pile of explosives in the back of the truck, "the resulting explosion will vaporize everyone in the convoy. So there isn't really a need for a backup plan."

Not one of us had anything to say to that.

Day was speaking the truth. There were easily several thousand pounds of explosives in the truck's bed. If we were attacked, Kandahar City would resemble Nagasaki. The world might be a better place for it.

Our convoy slowly pulled out of the headquarters' cramped confines. A large EOD vehicle known as a Buffalo led the way. If our MATVs were armored semi-trucks, then a Buffalo was an armored school bus. The thing was huge, sat about eight people, and had a giant robotically controlled arm that hung off the side. EOD could use it to probe possible roadside bombs while in the relative safety of their giant armored bus.

I had always heard rumors that in over ten years of war, not a single soldier had been killed while riding in a Buffalo. Seeing it up close, I could understand why that was possible.

The shuddering, rickety, explosives-laden cargo truck followed behind it being driven by Croatian soldiers. Our squad's vehicles pulled up the rear.

Watching the massive Buffalo—which had to be the biggest vehicle to ever grace the road in Afghanistan—maneuver through the congested roads of Kandahar was pretty impressive. Meanwhile in our truck, Cali kept sideswiping cars and mowing over unattended motorcycles that were even slightly in his way.

"Oh come on, dude, that one wasn't even in your way!" Grandpa yelled into his headset.

"It was coming right for us!" Cali joked through a mouthful of dip.

"I hate you guys." Grandpa shook his head and changed the music on his iPod from Justin Bieber to some awful country singer I didn't recognize.

"What is this shit, man? Like living in Afghanistan isn't depressing enough, now we've got to listen to how this cowboy's dog died and his wife fucked his tractor," I complained.

"You have the worst musical taste of any human being I've ever met," Grandpa shot back. "It's nothing but whiny suburban kids screaming about how much they hate their parents." He, of course, was insulting my taste in metalcore music. As much as I liked it, I couldn't argue; it was pretty bad.

"At least I know none of my favorite artists banged one of their relatives," I laughed.

"Don't hate on them because they have game, Joe," Grandpa said and spat a wad of dip spit into an empty bottle.

"That still doesn't explain all the Bieber, dude," I said.

"It was my little girl's iPod before we deployed. Reminds me of her," Grandpa said with a smile.

"Ugh, that's so fucking heartwarming I can't even judge you for it. Asshole." I feigned disgust.

"Doesn't mean *I* can't," Cali said sidelong.

We turned into what could only be described as suburbia hell. It was a strange site. It was styled in the western grid pattern of nicely paved streets with neat little white concrete sidewalks lining them. There were even streetlights, though no electricity would ever flow to them. It was as if someone started building one of those manufactured suburban neighborhoods, but stopped just short of starting to build the houses themselves.

"Does this remind you of home?" Grandpa joked, looking at me.

"Aren't you from Chicago?" I asked. "Or are there not enough gunshots to make you reminisce?"

"Nah, man." He shook his head. "Streets are too nice."

"Doesn't it make you wish the U.S. Army would invade your city and help build all this beautiful shit?" I laughed.

We drove slowly down the street gawking at the piece of abandoned Americana. It was slowly being reclaimed by Afghanistan. People started setting up tin shacks on the empty house plots, donkeys wandered the streets, and trash and human waste had started piling up at the street corners. It would probably have some stupid name like "Freedom Hills" or "Orchard Estates" if it were ever finished.

Thankfully, we made it out of the twisting innards of downtown Kandahar unscathed and started cruising through the countryside. Before long, the lead truck turned right and led us into a barren valley. Our trucks kicked up a blinding dust cloud and I could barely see out of my window.

"You okay, Cali?" Grandpa asked with concern.

"Me? Yeah, I'm all right," Cali answered calmly.

"You can see through this shit?" I asked.

"*Oh.*" He was surprised that was what we were talking about. "No, man, I can't see a damn thing."

I couldn't help laughing nervously as Grandpa shifted uncomfortably in his seat.

"Hollaback Girl" by Gwen Stefani came on the iPod.

"How old is your little girl?" I asked.

"Nine." Grandpa smiled, pointing to a picture he had taped to the windshield. A little girl in a red dress was smiling while sitting on a swing.

"Tell her that her taste in music fucking sucks."

About halfway into the valley our convoy ground to a halt. The EOD guys hopped out of their mammoth truck and gathered behind the cargo truck full of explosives. We clambered out of our trucks and followed them.

"All right, guys, this is where we're setting up," Day said. "Unload the ANFO first into a neat little pile." We all nodded and got to work. We formed a chain passing the leaking bags from one person to another. When a bag got to the last person, they piled it in the little square that Day had laid out.

The heat was oppressive, even for southern Afghanistan. The dusty valley we were in amplified the heat like an oven. Without giving orders, Slim took off his body armor and tossed it into the dirt. We all quickly followed suit and it suddenly felt like the weight of the world had been removed from my shoulders.

The ANFO bags quickly piled up into a neat square, and we all sat down in the dirt trying in vain to hide underneath the scant shade of our trucks. We tried to replace the puddles of sweat we lost by desperately chugging water. The beating sun had put my water a few degrees south of boiling and scorched my mouth.

"Good job, boys!" Day smiled. "Now we're going to pile all the bombs and mortars in the middle."

We all groaned, stood back up, and got back to work. We unloaded all the rusty, dented, and probably unstable munitions down the chain and onto the ground. We were so tired at that point that several of us dropped shells or mortars and watched them bounce off the ground with no reaction. Finally, all the munitions were loaded in a pile within the pile of ANFO bags.

The sun was mercifully starting to sink in the sky, and the temperature finally dipped below the climate of the Sun's surface. I plopped down in the dirt next to one of the Croatian guys and put in a dip.

The Croatian soldier stuck his hand out like he wanted some. I shrugged and gave him some. I would have explained to him that the first time I dipped I got the worst heartburn of my life and puked all over the place, but I had a feeling he wouldn't understand. He took a massive pinch from my can and stuck it in his lip.

The EOD guys grabbed what looked like a huge roll of Fruit by the Foot from the back of their truck. It was a large, industrial roll of thick, bright green tape. They started unspooling it all around the pile we created.

"The fuck is that?" Cali asked, hiding under the MATV bumper in the shade.

"Data sheets," Day quipped. He saw the clueless look on our faces. "It's plastic explosive."

"There weren't enough explosives before?" Cali asked.

"Sometimes that old shit doesn't like to go off like it should. This tends to help it along the way," Day said. "And it makes a sweet fireball."

"Sweet fireballs are important," I agreed.

After the data sheets had all been laid out, they started unspooling wires and cords in every direction.

Before we could ask, Day filled us in. "Detonation cord," he said shortly. "It's explosive cord that will trigger the explosion. We are going to spool it all the way out to the safety zone."

"Safety zone?" I asked.

"Yeah, we're supposed to be about a mile away when this amount of shit goes off." Day lit a cigarette. "But then you don't get to see any cool shit, so we're going about five hundred meters back."

"Sergeant, I don't mean any disrespect, but that is significantly less than a mile," I tried to point out helpfully.

"Hey, which one of us is the explosives expert?" Day smiled, blowing smoke through his nose.

"You, apparently." I shrugged. With the cord unspooled, we picked our body armor and weapons back up and climbed into our trucks. The sun had set behind the mountains, and the clear star-lit sky shone overhead.

We drove out to the mouth of the valley and parked our vehicles. Slim had won a game of rock-paper-scissors between himself, Day, Kitty, and Perro and won the right to set off the explosion. He got out of his truck and climbed into the EOD guy's Buffalo.

"Okay, guys, is everyone buttoned up in their trucks? All hatches closed?" Day asked over the radio.

"Yep," Grandpa responded.

"Roger," Kitty answered.

"Da," answered a heavily accented voice.

"Fire in the hole. Fire in the hole. Fire in the hole," Day repeated.

An angry red fireball erupted into the night sky lighting up the valley like high noon. It was oddly silent for the first few seconds until the blast wave hit our trucks.

It sounded like a freight train passed right by my head. Our truck shook on its axles. Pebbles and rocks smashed into our windows leaving tiny cracks all over. The entire valley was blanketed in dust and debris, and we couldn't see anything. It went back to pitch darkness just as quickly as it had lit up.

"Holy shit!" Grandpa screamed, laughing.

"My fucking windshield!" Cali cried. Sometimes I could swear he loved that truck more than his wife.

The dust cleared, and the valley was once again enveloped in darkness. The Buffalo circled around and started driving back toward the city and we followed suit.

"That was fun, boys," Slim laughed over the radio. "Maybe next time, don't wait a year to blow some shit up."

"A year?" Day laughed in response. "That was from last month in our district alone."

Inside our trucks we all exchanged looks. All *that* was from one month in the district we had been living in for the better part of six months?

It was unnerving to think about how much of what we'd just blown up was initially meant for us. Just one of those bags of ANFO would have turned one of our trucks into scrap metal and all of us into little more than a memory.

CHAPTER 21

CALI AND THE MEMPHIS BLUES

TO PUT IT BLUNTLY, AFGHANISTAN is not a clean country. It has no sanitation systems, sewage systems, trash pickup, and practically no understanding of basic germ theory. Trash and human waste piles up everywhere, and the whole country smells like something out of your worst nightmare. Combine all that with almost no healthcare of any kind, and it leads to outbreaks of horrific illness and disease.

That's where our lily-white, pampered asses come in. Once upon a time, white folks came to North America and almost wiped out the natives because we carried new and unheard-of diseases. Since then, we have gotten fat, lazy, and overly medicated. We have fully functioning sewage and sanitation systems and an almost-working healthcare system depending on how much money you have. Our pristine insides were in no way prepared for the beating they were going to take while in Afghanistan.

The army tried its best to prepare us. We were injected with so many vaccines that I lost count. I was protected against diseases that I hadn't even heard of. Most of what I recognized were from the damn history books. They weren't things I thought people had to deal with anymore. Diphtheria, cholera, smallpox—the vaccine that left a massive scar on my shoulder—just to name a few. There were other shots, too, but after a while they all just blended together.

We all figured that after that barrage of first world medicine, we were bulletproof against anything Afghanistan could throw at our immune systems.

We weren't even close to being right.

Within the first few weeks of deployment, Memphis went down. It started with diarrhea and quickly led to vomiting. Both of those things eventually became uncontrollable. The big country boy was laid out in his cot, puking off the side and shitting in his pants.

Gong, being a decent and caring medic, did his best to clean up after him and keep a steady flow of IV fluids going into him so he didn't die of dehydration.

Once Memphis caught whatever it was that he caught, it started a never-ending cycle. It tore through our platoon one man at a time. Normally it would floor a person for a week or two before passing on. Because he was our unlucky patient zero, we dubbed the sickness The Memphis Blues in honor of his uncontrolled diarrhea. No one was safe from The Blues.

I was hit by it a week or so after Memphis went down. My case ended up being way worse than his. Gong insisted that I stay in bed and keep up with my fluids, but I insisted I was fine. I wouldn't take a day off from patrolling or working out in our makeshift gym. This ended up being my downfall.

One day while out in the burning sun I was lifting weights and going at it as hard as a sexually frustrated young man locked up in a war zone can go. I loaded up plate after plate on the barbell preparing to deadlift. I bent over, grabbed the bar, and lifted with all my power. I grunted, strained, and yelled. The bar inched up very slowly, scraping against my shins as it went. My lift quickly turned bad.

I got lightheaded, dropped the bar, and very nearly passed out. I fell to my knees with bright colors flashing in my eyes. I tasted copper in my mouth, and my head pounded. Then something I never thought would happen to me as a grown man happened: I shit my pants.

It wasn't something I could consciously stop from happening. It just happened. No one was around so I tried to struggle my way to the port-o-johns. I was so lightheaded I could barely walk. I ended up crawling across the ground, shit streaming along behind me until I made my way to the toilets.

After that, I decided to listen to Gong and stay on my cot. Not that I had much of a choice. After my failed lifting session, my condition quickly went downhill. As soon as I tried to drink or eat anything, it would rocket its way out of my body one way or another. After a few days, I gave up trying to nourish myself in any way and waited for the release of a shit-covered death.

Gong hooked me up to two different IVs and kept prodding me to eat something. He was like my fat little Asian deployment mother telling me I was just skin and bones. He wasn't wrong. Within the first week of being felled by the Memphis Blues, I had already lost nearly fifteen pounds.

Trays of uneaten food piled up around my cot as Gong failed to convince me that I needed to eat to survive. I didn't move other than to retch into an ammo box someone had given me to act as a bucket or to attempt to race to the port-o-johns to fire burning liquid out of my ass.

I lapsed in and out of consciousness, and no one other than Gong bothered to check in on me. Over a week passed and I wasn't getting any better. Gong started to get a little concerned and talked about sending me back to Kandahar Air Field to see a doctor.

Things like a soldier's general health really don't matter when you have a war to fight.

After about a week and a half, Slim kicked me awake and stood over me. "Wake up, fucker, we have a patrol."

I slowly opened my eyes. They were so dehydrated I swear I could hear them crack as my eyelids slid over my eyes.

"I...what?" I croaked through a terminal case of cottonmouth.

"It's been a week, you should be fine."

"All right...let me just get my clothes on." I struggled to sit up. That little amount of effort caused my head to spin on its axis. My stomach lurched, but I fought my way to my feet. I staggered and stumbled around trying to put pants on for the first time in what seemed like forever. Gong had to help me put on my combat gear. He handed me my rifle. Gong had tried to talk Slim out of making me go, but it was useless. I dragged my feet out to meet the platoon and prepare for our patrol. Everyone recoiled when they saw me.

"Jesus, he looks like a fucking zombie." Cali cringed.

"Good enough to fuck your mother," I spat back.

"See?" Slim slapped my shoulder. The force was almost sufficient to take me down. "He's good. Let's get going."

It was dark out, and the rough Afghan terrain was only lit by the moon and stars. Several Afghan policemen joined us, and we ventured out into the night. I lagged at the back of our column with a few of the Afghans. This was hardly the best place to be when I was perfectly healthy and alert; right then it was damn near suicide. I wasn't looking anywhere other than down at my feet, trying my hardest to just keep moving. The Afghans noticed my struggle.

"You okay, friend?" one of the Afghans asked me in broken English.

I was bent over with my hands on my knees. My rifle hung uselessly from its sling in the dirt. "Yeah, friend, I'm fucking grand," I barely got out. The words were barely off my tongue before vomit rushed up my throat and out of my mouth. The burning bile splashed across the Afghan's boots, and he shrieked and jumped back. "Sorry, bro," I coughed and wiped my mouth with my sleeve.

Slim must have heard the commotion in the back of the patrol because it didn't take him long to run back there with us. Slim took one look at me bent over and vomiting all over our Afghan brother-in-arms and mustered up all his compassion. "The fuck is wrong with you now?" he complained.

"I think my insides are dying," I moaned. More bile bubbled up in the back of my throat.

"I swear you're a massive pussy sometimes."

"Yep, that's me, huge pussy." I puked again.

Finally, Slim had some mercy on me and turned the patrol around before I collapsed. Gong helped me to bed and stuck some more needles into my arm. The patrol walked back out of the gates without me. I was sidelined for another week before I recovered.

Probably the funniest case of The Blues was Sal's. Unfortunately, Sal, being a medic, was someone we simply couldn't do without. So throughout his whole sickness, he had to slog alongside us on patrol. One night while attempting to raid a target's house, he stood up next to me with a start.

"I gotta shit, bro," he moaned and rushed off into the bushes. I heard him crashing off through the brush like an animal for a few minutes and then he settled down. I couldn't see him in the pitch darkness, but someone above could.

Above us hovered a Kiowa Warrior recon helicopter outfitted with heat and night vision. I heard someone's voice over the radio.

"Spartan two-two, this is Long Knife." It was the helicopter.

"This is Spartan two-two," Slim said.

"Be advised, there is an armed...pants-less man in the bushes about fifty meters to your squad's rear."

I could hear the voice on the radio fighting back laughter. He had used his multi-million-dollar piece of weaponry to see our poor, sick medic shitting his brains out in the bushes behind us.

But the worst case of The Blues by far went to Cali. In his case, the symptoms started while we were out on patrol and he suddenly started having to stop every few minutes to run off into the bushes to shit. Later that night, he couldn't get off of his cot without projectile vomiting like the girl in *The Exorcist*.

Sal was watching over Cali's deteriorating condition in our shared tent. Cali was lying in a pool of his own sweat and vomit, mostly dead to the world.

"He going to die?" I asked.

"Not really sure if he's alive right now," Sal joked. "His vomiting is getting worse, I think I'm going to have to give him some medicine other than saline."

"What...am I getting?" Cali croaked through a dry throat.

"Something to help your stomach feel better." Sal smiled and nodded at him. We helped Cali to his feet, me holding an IV bag over his head while Sal gave him support. We walked him across the little base and into the aid station.

Sal's aid station was little more than a wooden shack with a cot in it. He sat Cali down on the cot, took the IV from my hands, and placed it on a stand. Sal popped the top off a little bottle of medicine and drew it into a syringe. He rolled Cali over and stuck the long needle into his ass cheek.

Cali was so out of it that he didn't even flinch.

"What was that?" I asked.

"It'll help his nausea. But it has a slight side effect," Sal said.

"Like what?"

"Well, it'll make him act like he's drunk as hell. Normally not a big deal, but since we're in the middle of Kandahar, if he goes wandering off into the night he'll get his head sawn off. We're gonna have to watch him."

"Good point."

We picked Cali back up and walked him to his cot. We carefully laid him down and set his IV back up. He didn't seem drunk. He was just tired and out of it the way I was when I was fighting The Blues.

But it didn't take long for the effects of Sal's butt shot to take effect. Cali started giggling to himself and rolling back and forth on his cot. It was as if he wasn't sick at all anymore.

The laughing stopped as quickly as it had begun. "I gotta puke," Cali moaned. He rolled out of his cot, tearing the IV from his arm and leaving it dangling and dripping blood all over the place. Cali crawled hand over hand to the entrance of the tent and puked into the rocks. I remembered I was supposed to be helping and assisting him, but instead was watching and laughing at him. I started to feel guilty until I saw Sal doing the same thing.

"I shit..." Cali said, drooling puke out of his mouth.

"What?" I asked.

"I shit myself. I fucking shit myself."

"Wonderful." Sal shook his head.

"I have to shit again," Cali informed us. He pulled himself to his feet and drunkenly wandered off into the night. Sal and I chased after him as he staggered to the line of faded blue port-o-johns. Cali nearly tore the door off the hinges of the nearest one and climbed inside. The door slammed shut, and we could hear him banging around inside. The port-o-john shook and moved around.

"The hell is he doing in there?" Sal asked.

"No idea. You think he's okay?"

Almost as if he was trying to answer our questions, the port-o-john shook violently, and we heard a splash. "Ah! Mother fucker!" we heard Cali scream from inside.

Sal and I shot each other confused looks and ran to the door. Cali had locked it from inside,so we had to force the door open. It was surprisingly sturdy for being a plastic latch. Finally, it snapped under our assault, and we got to see what was going on inside.

Cali was standing inside the toilet of the port-o-john, more than waist deep in that mysterious blue liquid that swam with human waste.

"How the fuck did you manage that, dude?" I fought back laughter.

Sal wasn't fighting back a damn thing. He was laughing so hard he wasn't even making noise anymore. In between fits of laughter, we managed to pull Cali out of the shitter. He was covered in bright blue liquid; it almost looked like paint. Almost.

"What do we do with this dude?" I asked Sal. We were trying our hardest to help him along, but not let his lower half touch us.

"He needs a damn shower," Sal said.

"After the shitter incident, if we put him in a shower, he's going to end up drowning himself," I pointed out.

"Godammit. We're going to have to bathe him. He can't walk around covered in shit and blue juice. He'll get Hep C or something," Sal lamented.

"I hate you right now," I muttered to Cali. We slowly walked to our single working shower stall. It would only produce ice-cold water, but it was good enough to wash the shit and disease off Cali.

We walked Cali up the rickety steps that led to the shower. We sat him down inside and stepped back.

"Get naked, you gross ass," Sal said, trying to look away.

I did the same.

Cali fumbled with his clothes, and after a whole lot of fighting, got them off.

Sal squeezed past Cali, who was trying his hardest to stay on his feet, and turned the shower on.

I picked up a bottle of liquid body wash and sprayed it at Cali. "Rub that shit around," I said trying my hardest to look anywhere other than at my naked friend.

Cali was hardly the last person to catch The Blues, but he was by far the worst case. As far as I know, I was the only one ever to vomit on an Afghan cop, and he was the only one to take a swim in the port-o-potties. Sal never tried to treat anyone with anything more than IV fluids after that. I guess having to physically shower one of your best friends changes a man.

I never offered to help Sal in his aid station again.

CHAPTER 22

FUEL BOMBS AND
THE MYSTERY GRENADE

THE ARMY HAS SOME SHITTY ideas when it comes to having fun: mandatory unit functions like Christmas parties, barbecues, and various other things they can think of to force you into spending time with people you generally dislike. Kind of like a holiday at your in-laws. Only with guns and little bottles of dip spit lying all over the place.

When you're deployed, they really can't make you spend any more time with the people that, in all probability, you hate more than the Taliban. So, of course, they encourage you to go out to the gun range. The only problem was, we didn't have one. We would have to find one.

Camp Spartan was the size of a basketball court. It didn't have a washing machine let alone the facilities to build a gun range. So we did the most American thing we could think of: found on a map a random mountainside that looked uninhabited. We decided that it was going to be our range.

I was never a huge fan of going out to the range. It required loading up hundreds to thousands of rounds of ammo, waiting hours upon hours in the hot sun for your turn to shoot, and then spending even more time cleaning your weapon than you ever did firing it. That hatred probably had a lot to do with why I wasn't a splendid marksman.

I was always able to qualify on the army's marksmanship test, but only just. I had never fired a gun until I enlisted at seventeen. Before then, they were some mystical thing I got to play with in video games or something that killed bad guys in action movies.

Once I actually got to use one, I didn't think it was as awesome as all the movies made it seem. The army never convinced me that shooting guns was fun. I always just saw it as part of my job. Kind of like how I had to stand around in pointless formations or tuck my pants into my boots.

We set out through the city with the backs of our trucks loaded down with thousands of rounds of ammunition. Because of the MATV's horrible design with no covered trunk area, it was all bouncing around completely unsecured.

We drove out of the city, off the roads, and into the winding mountain trails. The roads were crumbling, narrow, and in a lot of places totally unfit for the vehicles we were driving.

"Why do you look like someone killed your dog?" Slim turned and asked me.

"Our one day since we've been in this country that we don't have a mission planned, we have to go out and shoot for no reason," I complained.

"Sorry, am I cutting into your valuable jerk-off time?" Slim smiled.

"You know damn well you're cutting into the whole squad's." I feigned outrage.

Our mission tempo had been insane since we'd gotten to Spartan Base. Everyone was running around like maniacs trying to keep the simmering, boiling, cauldron of rage that was Kandahar under control and we were failing miserably. To get a day off was incredibly rare. So Slim, of course, volunteered us to go out and shoot at a damn mountainside.

"Cheer up, asshole! It's fun!" Slim smiled.

"People keep telling me that," I said under my breath.

"Look at the bright side, we get to fire off the mystery grenade!"

The legend of the mystery grenade started when we moved out of the Reserve. Slim found a strange unmarked white grenade in a busted up box when we were moving. Normally, there are only a few types of grenades we can fire from our mounted grenade launchers. We knew what they all looked like even without the markings. But none of us had seen anything like the mystery grenade before.

We asked around Grizzly Base and Dealer Base, but no one recognized it. We used our limited internet abilities to try to find it online but failed. We really had no idea what it did.

Slim had carried it in his truck ever since he found it.

"Consider my day brightened." I smiled.

We pulled up to a desolate mountainside that, despite minutes of diligent planning, clearly had a village on the other side of it. No one seemed to care, and we started unloading boxes of ammunition. We gathered around behind Slim's truck, and Gunny started giving us some quick rules for our impromptu range.

"Don't be stupid. You guys know how to use your weapons," he said and wandered off. Gunny was always a man of few words, but that was surprising. Back when he was our company operations NCO, he was a serious hardass.

He was strictly by the book and would absolutely never falter from it. Even once he became our platoon sergeant, he would never bend the rules. He used to yell at me for not wearing kneepads to my tower guard shifts. Yet here he was, surrounded by thousands of rounds of ammunition and explosives, and he was telling us to just do whatever we wanted. As long as we didn't accidently kill ourselves.

I loaded up my M240B machine gun. It was a big, hulking machine gun that we would both mount on our trucks and carry with us on patrol. It was one of the only weapons that I would qualify regularly with at an above average level. It was also one of the only weapons in the army I really had fun with while shooting.

Grandpa, Slim, and Perro all began to fire off grenades from their launchers. They impacted the dirt about one hundred meters away with a dull thump and a puff of dust and smoke. Hand grenades were probably the most disappointing weapon I ever used.

Being an ignorant kid who played a lot of *Call of Duty,* I thought they made some big impressive explosion and a fireball. In reality, they were kind of loud and just kicked up some dust. They would kill and wound everyone within a few feet, but they just weren't impressive to watch in action.

Cali started firing off rounds from his rifle, and Guapo followed suit. There wasn't really any method to anything anyone was doing. They were just randomly firing off guns at a mountainside. We didn't even have any targets set up. That quickly got boring for everyone so Slim got an idea. I knew from experience that was never a good thing.

"I bet you can't fire the two-forty from your shoulder," he wagered.

The M240B is supposed to be fired lying down or when the gun is mounted on a vehicle. I was the biggest guy in our entire platoon and one of the largest in the company. This was mostly a byproduct of having no social life and spending all my time either lifting weights in a gym or punching people in bars.

"Dude, I won't just shoot it standing up. I'll fire it while running forward," I said.

"You won't do it!" Perro called out.

I picked up the heavy weapon and waited for everyone else to stop firing. I pulled back its stubby little charging handle. I shouldered the big bastard and let her rip.

It kicked like a damn mule, and I lowered my shoulder and ran forward as fast as I could. The machine gun slammed against my shoulder the whole way. I didn't stop firing until my belt ran dry and the entire barrel was burning. It coughed out acrid smoke. My body still vibrated for a few seconds after my gun went silent.

"Suck it!" I cheered back at them. "I think I even hit the mountain once or twice." I laughed. I was careful carrying the weapon back to the trucks as the barrel had become red hot. Gunny was laughing along with us. Slim took that as permission to come up with even worse ideas. Slim jumped into the back of one of our trucks and pulled out a five-gallon fuel can. It had recently been filled to the brim just in case we had to bribe any Afghan police.

Slim ran out toward the mountain, dropped the can of fuel on the ground, and ran back. "Let's blow this mother fucker up!" He laughed.

"I don't think that'll work like that, man," I said.

"It will if we use tracers," Slim said. He had obviously thought this through a little bit. A tracer round is a special round that is tipped with a tiny pyrotechnic charge so that when fired you can see it glow as it flies through the air. Everyone loaded up magazines full of tracer rounds and prepared to fire at the little tan fuel can sitting out in the distance.

Slim started taking pot shots at the can. He hit it and sent it spinning around on one of its corners. Nothing happened.

"I told you, man. This shit isn't like an action movie," I chided Slim.

We were all kind of disappointed, but not too surprised. We showed our disappointment the only way soldiers know how: by unloading on the poor defenseless little fuel can. The ground around the can exploded with gunfire as we shot without aiming. The can was hit and danced around in every which direction. Then it happened: the fuel can exploded in flames.

We all cheered and shot at it even more. The fireball kept climbing into the air. Our firing tore the can into shreds, and the fireball vanished as fast as it came.

We were quickly running out of dangerous ways to entertain ourselves, so Slim pulled out the mystery grenade.

I felt nervous. It wasn't the same kind of nervous I had felt before getting shot at, or the same nervous feeling you get before taking a test. It was different, like that feeling you get as you make a move on a girl. It could either be incredibly awesome or totally disappointing.

Slim loaded the grenade into his launcher. He held his rifle at about waist height and fired the grenade into the distance. We waited with thundering hearts and abated breath. It felt like forever for that little white bastard to sail through the air and hit something. There was a quiet *poof* noise, and white smoke drifted into the air. After all that waiting and suspense, it was a fucking smoke grenade.

"Are you fucking serious? That was more disappointing than a Korean hooker," Slim yelled at the smoke.

"You need to find better hookers," Perro nodded.

"Well, ain't that a bitch." I shook my head.

Before I saw what was happening, Slim loaded another grenade into his launcher. His aim crept dangerously close to the ground right in front of us. He fired. The grenade landed maybe fifteen feet out in front of us and exploded. The shock wave shook me to my bones. I felt the shrapnel and rocks from the explosion whistle past my ears. Everyone ducked and ran for cover a bit too late.

"What the fuck was *that*, asshole?" I screamed at Slim. My ears were ringing and my heart racing from nearly being murdered via grenade by my own squad leader.

"I was trying to skip the grenade across the ground." Slim looked surprised that it didn't work.

"It arms after ten feet, you mother fucker!" Grandpa yelled at him.

"More impressive than the mystery grenade." Slim smiled.

"Though less impressive than your mom," I joked. The guy almost killed me, but the asshole was still one of my best friends.

We all laughed it off, even Gunny. Our hard-bitten platoon sergeant didn't seem to care that four of his soldiers almost accidently killed themselves. Slim had broken the only real rule that Gunny had laid out for us.

After our near-death experience, we decided to call it a day. We never told anyone else about the mystery grenade. Or about how grenades do not skip across the ground like stones on water when fired out of a grenade launcher. Like that was something we had to do fucking research on.

Surprisingly, Gunny never brought any of that up again. It was probably because he knew he was an accessory to most of what we did and he would get in almost as much trouble as the rest of us. Gunny may not have gotten any of us in trouble, but that was the last random mountainside gun range for the Hooligans.

CHAPTER 23

GRANPA LEAVES, WINTER COMES

WINTER IN AFGHANISTAN IS A funny thing. Even though most American soldiers, citizens, and politicians think of it as a Middle Eastern nation baking under the gulf sun, it isn't. Afghanistan is a mostly mountainous country that covers both central and south Asia. What I am getting at is that its location makes winter fucking terrible. I had previously spent a winter in northeastern Afghanistan during which an avalanche wiped out the small village of Salang.

Though it does get cold, it's not completely miserable. The main difference being that while the northeast was much colder, the base we lived in was much nicer. We did most of our patrols warmly packed into armored vehicles. Down in Kandahar, the city that was the birthplace of the Taliban, we had to go on constant foot patrols. We walked through its winding alleyways and markets regardless of the weather.

Winter in Kandahar wasn't marked by driving snowstorms as it was in the north. It was characterized by constant rain and brutal winds that made us all completely hate our lives. The frigid wind easily ate through our cutting-edge winter clothes and burned our skin. Our operation's tempo never once changed due to the weather.

The ironic part of all this is that the war is known to have two seasons. During the summer, the Taliban launch all-out attacks on the Afghan Security Forces and the NATO soldiers stationed there. In the winter, they vanish. The winter in Afghanistan is too brutal for the tribesmen in flip-flops to operate.

To start the worst season of the year, Second Squad, unfortunately, lost one of its best leaders. Grandpa was sent home for a chronic back problem that had all but crippled him. His back had been a constant issue ever since he was blown up in an IED attack years before while fighting in Iraq. He tried to stick it out for as long as he could. He did an incredibly good job at keeping it a secret.

Only Cali and I had any idea how bad it was. He could barely get out of bed in the morning by the time winter set in. One night while on Sergeant of the Guard duty, he couldn't get out of the chair he was sitting in. Unfortunately this time, instead of one of us finding him stranded, Gunny did.

Gunny was a good man but didn't bend his moral compass for any reason. He saw a person in pain that needed help. He didn't see an incredibly effective combat leader whose soldiers absolutely loved him. It didn't take long for Grandpa to be shoved into an outgoing convoy toward an airbase.

Before he left, Cali and I got to say our goodbyes. Cali and I were both nearly in tears watching him pack his things.

"You know I love you guys, right? I wouldn't leave you if it were up to me," Grandpa said, his voice slightly quivering. He didn't mean that like we were best friends, he meant it because he saw us like family, just as we saw him. He always treated Cali and me as if we were his children. He was the closest thing I had to a father figure since I'd left home to join the army.

A few months after we had arrived in Afghanistan, my maternal grandfather died. He was one of the best men I'd ever known and someone I was very close to. He was one of the few people in my life who really supported my joining the military. When Gunny told me the news that my grandfather had died, I was shattered and ducked away behind a guard tower to cry to myself.

It didn't take Grandpa long to find me. I thought he was going to give me the bullshit "He's in a better place now" speech. He knew I was an atheist and hated that shit. Instead, he sat down next to me and put his arm around my shoulder. He didn't say anything, and he didn't have to.

Grandpa was generally a good and kind man, a great husband, and a model father. I wasn't really sure how I would make it through the rest of the deployment without him.

My previous deployment to Afghanistan had resulted in us sitting on our asses in our patrol base during in the winter. We had been able to huddle around and enjoy a functioning heater that time. We weren't so lucky this time around. Our operational tempo actually increased as the temperature plummeted.

Our unit managed to get its hands on an unmanned drone called a Raven that could be launched by throwing it into the air. It would beam back live video feed to a screen as it flew around in little circles. They tasked a soldier called Bama who had just joined our squad with controlling the little robot. It was a task he absolutely hated.

Bama was a die-hard Alabama Crimson Tide football fan. The guy even hung a massive flag from his bunk in the shower bay. Even though he came from the dirtiest of the dirty south, he was one of the most understanding and kind people I had ever met. He would routinely mock rednecks and other people from Alabama. He was married with children and had recently been shifted over from First Squad so he could be a team leader in Grandpa's absence.

Soon a never-ending battle between Bama and the Raven started. Afghanistan in the winter is an incredibly windy place, and a Raven is nothing more than a small, remote-controlled plane with a camera attached. You can see why that would be a problem.

Bama needed about one hundred feet to get a running start and chuck the little bastard into the sky. The only place with enough room to launch the Raven was the motor pool.

The motor pool was also full of heavily armored trucks and surrounded by a twenty-foot-tall concrete wall. Bama would pick up the little plastic plane and take off at a sprint and launch it into the air. Because of the wall and all our trucks, he had to throw it nearly straight up, which resulted in it crashing down to earth like a goddamn meteor every single time.

Eventually, we received permission from the Afghan police (who lived next door) to use their roof as a launch pad. Of course, the biggest problem with that was we were in the middle of Kandahar City. We were surrounded by ten-story buildings that stood directly in the little Raven's flight path.

"You think this is going to work?" I asked Bama.

"It can't be any worse than throwing it into the side of our trucks, can it?" he replied.

Bama picked up the Raven, started its pitiful little prop engine, and took off running. He heaved the contraption into the air. It buzzed, sputtered, and took glorious flight. It slammed right through a large, ornate window on the sixth floor of a neighboring building. The sound of broken glass filled the night.

"Fuck!" Bama cursed in his thick southern accent.

"Holy shit! You broke that guy's window!" I cried.

"You think he'll make me pay for it?" Bama joked.

The radio Bama carried crackled to life.

"What's the situation with the Raven?" It was Gunny. He was constantly worried the Taliban were using the winter to prepare for some world-ending attack. So he kept sending the Raven out in futile attempts to catch them.

"It, umm...crashed," Bama replied.

"Roger, where did it land?" Gunny asked. The Raven would give us exact grid coordinates for where it crashed so we could hunt it down.

"Um, you know that building with the big, red window to the east of Spartan Base?"

"Yes..."

"I think it's in that guy's living room."

"Are you serious?" Gunny said slowly in his gravelly voice.

"Well, to be fair, it could be some kind of breakfast nook or something. We can't confirm it's in his living room," Bama said.

I couldn't help myself anymore and started laughing. Bama was pissed. Not because it crashed, but because it always made him look bad. Everyone knew the Raven was a piece of shit, but they heaped the blame on him whenever it failed.

Gunny ran over to the Afghan police compound and told them what happened. The police ran to the man's house and retrieved our Radio Shack reject.

That was the first of many times Bama would assault that same man's house with a multi-million-dollar spy drone. It got so bad that eventually the man who lived in the house would just bring the drone back to our camp, laughing.

We all took turns attempting to throw the Raven into the air. Without fail, we were all terrible at it. I never hit the man's house, but I did throw it as hard as I could into the concrete retaining wall and broke it in half. I wasn't allowed to play with Bama's toy after that one.

Winter made everyday activities absolutely terrible. Tower guard—usually just an annoying duty that would interrupt your sleep for the night—turned into an hours-long exercise of trying to stay warm. For obvious tactical reasons, the towers were built up and out of the way from everything else. That meant they were the most exposed to the wind. We were given small metal burners that we could use to stay warm, but that would conceal an open flame so we wouldn't stick out like sore thumbs at night.

The large problem was that firewood is as rare as diamonds in a barren, mountainous country with no forests. We burned anything and everything at night to keep warm. Ration bags, garbage, you name it. Of course, breathing in burning waste fumes was the least of our worries when people began burning the very towers we were standing in. At some point, people started prying away pieces of the wooden tower frame and burning it for warmth. It left huge gaps in the very walls that were supposed to be protecting us.

Gunny lost his shit when he discovered large chunks of missing guard tower during one of his many inspections. But because the point had been made that we were dying out there, he ordered tons of wooden pallets for the express purpose of burning them. We didn't think twice about the dangers of breathing in the toxic fumes.

Of all the things we did that winter, breaking U.S. Central Command's rules and directives was probably the worst. Central Command is the one U.S. operation command center over the entire Global War on Terror. It was in control of the Iraq War and the Afghan War at the same time. It was in charge of coming up with all rules, policies, and overarching battle plans. Two of the biggest impact rules they laid out were complete bans on pornography and alcohol while in a war zone.

It goes without saying that everyone broke the first rule. Everyone traded porn like baseball cards. The weirder, the better. Most people used it more to freak each other out rather than for any erotic purpose. No one was ever punished for having porn.

The second rule—the total ban on any form of alcohol—was strictly enforced. It was so rigidly pressed that I can honestly say in almost seven years of service I never once saw anyone drinking while deployed. We were scared shitless of doing it because we knew we would be demoted in a heartbeat.

That would change one freezing night when Perro got a care package from home.

He cracked it open and pulled out several bottles of whiskey and Jaeger.

Slim and I stood next to him, speechless.

"It keeps you warm, man," Perro smiled.

"They will seriously fuck us up if they catch us, dude!" Slim said. The fear was obvious in his voice. That scared me. Slim was a guy who had attempted to skip a live grenade across the ground, stolen a car while on a patrol, and was once in a Mexican standoff with an entire platoon of Afghan army commandos. Yet somehow drinking whiskey while in Afghanistan was an absolute no-no.

"We haven't gotten in trouble for anything else we've done. Why would this be any different?" Perro replied. It was true; our squad was pretty much untouchable for reasons we didn't understand.

"Fuck it," I said.

"I can't argue with that," Slim responded.

So Perro brewed a pot of coffee, and we poured probably a bit too much whiskey into it. We sat around and had a drink on the cold tile floor of his shower stall. The warmth of the cheap dime-store whiskey flooded my system. I no longer cared that I lived in a freezing bathhouse with thirteen other men. That plastic jug of booze made the world feel like a better place for about five seconds.

"We should have a drink at the top of OP Townhouse," Perro joked.

Townhouse was the name of one of the observation points we had in the city. It was the tallest building in the area. We had command of our little slice of the city while we were up there.

"Let's do it," I laughed. "How fun would a fire fight be when you're shit-house drunk?"

"Y'all mother fuckers are insane." Slim shook his head.

If your idea was so crazy that Slim shot it down, you knew you were out of line. We all crawled back to our shower stalls to put on a few layers of clothes before we went out on our night patrol. The mercury had dipped into the low single digits, but Gunny was insistent that we keep patrolling the frozen nothingness of Kandahar City: a place so fucking miserable in winter that even the Taliban wanted nothing to do with it.

We trudged out of Spartan Base and into the driving, freezing, and unrelenting wind. Even though I was wearing three different layers, it cut right through me. Somewhere along the line, Cali and Nan joined up with us. The five of us hiked down the eerily abandoned streets to OP Townhouse.

Townhouse was actually an Afghan police base. They never bothered to go outside anymore. A few weeks beforehand someone on a scooter had driven by and shot one of their men while they were standing on the corner. Ever since then they stayed their asses securely inside. We walked up three flights of stairs and came out on the roof.

The roof was littered with garbage and scattered pieces of wood. It was the perfect vantage point to stand watch over everything in sight. So, of course, the Afghans used it as a place to throw their trash. We knocked a few holes in the partition wall to use as gun ports to over-watch the city. The Afghans were only curious about why we happened to be so on guard, not why we were destroying their building.

Cali piled up the wooden debris and some of the garbage in the middle of the roof and lit it on fire.

"Dude, everyone in the city is going to know we're here," Nan said fairly pissed off.

"They already know we're here." Cali shrugged and basked in the fire's warm glow.

"He has a point," Slim laughed. "And honestly, I kind of wish someone would attack us. I'm bored as hell."

Perro slid up next to Slim and pulled the bottle of Jaeger out of his backpack. "Did someone say 'bored?'" he smiled.

"Oh shit, this just turned into a party." Cali smiled.

"This looks like a supremely bad idea." Nan shook his head.

I looked at him, slightly shocked.

"Whoa, that doesn't mean I don't want any," Nan clarified.

We all sat down around the fire and placed our weapons on the ground. No one was on guard anymore. Even a few of the Afghans joined us.

Slim sat down at the head of the fire and cracked the little green bottle. "Fuck it," he said, taking a drink.

We all laughed and passed it around. I absolutely hated Jaeger but took a swig anyway. It tasted like black licorice that someone else had already chewed up and spit out. I gagged and passed it down the line.

Before long we were all pretty drunk, even though we barely had anything to drink. You would be surprised how quickly your tolerance vanishes when you don't get to drink for months at a time.

It didn't take long for the bottle to be emptied. Slim stood up and flung it off the roof. We heard a distant shattering sound when it connected with something.

We all took off our armor and relaxed. Warm, with a belly full of liquor, and the glow of a shitty, choking garbage fire.

Cali giggled and fired off a flare into the night sky, lighting up the darkness with a green hue.

"I love you mother fuckers," Slim said. "Best fucking squad on earth."

"I just wish we had someone to kill," Nan sighed. "This no-war winter is getting old."

"And no one to play catch with, you must be bummed." I laughed.

"Oh, fuck you, man," Nan said.

Before long we got bored and started chucking burning wood and garbage off the roof onto the streets below until there was no more bonfire left. We all laughed to ourselves, strapped our body armor back on, and walked home.

It would hardly be the last time we would do something stupid on top of Townhouse. We would routinely take naps on the floor surrounded by Afghan garbage. We made a huge mistake in doing all of that. Writing off the Taliban as gone for the winter was single-handedly the worst thing we could have done. There was a good chance that at least one of the Afghan police were Taliban members or sympathizers, and they were watching us make complete idiots of ourselves.

As a squad, we weren't exactly the most professional or morally strong characters on Earth, but we were certainly the most violent and hard-bitten in the area. There was an excellent reason we called ourselves the Hooligans. Our operations taught the Taliban that we weren't to be fucked with and gave us room to operate without any problems.

There is a saying in the army: "Don't be a soft target." It means that if you make yourself look like a badass, people generally won't want to mess with you. If you act like a pushover, you'll find yourself in someone's crosshairs sooner rather than later.

That was Slim's whole philosophy. To make ourselves look like the last squad you would want to engage in combat. Though it turns out if you act like a raging asshole all the time, someone will eventually come along and punch you in the mouth. It doesn't matter how big of a badass you *think* you are.

CHAPTER 24

BLOOD AND RAIN

THE ROUGH AFGHANISTAN WINTER BROUGHT driving rainstorms. It turned the fine dust-like sand into a slurry of relentless sucking mud. The clay worked its way into every single nook and cranny of everything you owned. Slim would scream at us constantly for not keeping our areas clean because we eventually gave up and submitted to our new, muddy overlord.

Unfortunately, this time of year also had us saying goodbye to another person from our squad. Sal wasn't technically in our unit but was on loan from a medical unit on Kandahar Airfield. His unit requested we give him back because they had taken over responsibility for the main emergency room on the airfield.

It was hard watching someone who had become one of my best friends go. It was even harder watching the best medic I'd ever worked with leave. I always knew that if I got hurt and it was something serious, having Sal nearby gave me the best possible chance of pulling through.

Sal and I hugged it out before he climbed into an outgoing truck that would take him back to the airfield. Sal was a different guy when he left than when he first arrived. His hair was thinning, he had deep-set wrinkles creasing his face, and he had the ever-present blackness surrounding his eyes from sleep deprivation.

"It's going to be hard dealing with all of those hot meals and showers." I laughed at him.

"Fuck you, man. You know I don't want to go back." He shook his head. The last thing he wanted to do was go back and work in a hospital. He honestly wanted to stay at that shitty outpost in the middle of the war zone with us. He was part of the Hooligan family, even if he didn't start that way.

"I know." We hugged again, and he got on the truck.

The move back to the airfield was also his first step on his way home to his wife and kid. He had deployed a few months before us with his unit, so he was only a few months away from leaving. It made me feel better that my friend would be able to ride out the rest of his time in the safety of the airfield.

In his place we received two new soldiers. One was a short, fat little Thai medic named Kham who had a perpetual shit-eating grin plastered across his face. Alongside him was a tall blonde girl named Pip. She was brand new to the army and looked terrified of everything. She had that annoying overeagerness that every new soldier had.

Kham had never deployed before and came from a background of intelligence and privilege. He talked about how he drove a BMW and drank Voss bottled water while riding out his army contract stateside. He ended up getting snatched up as a replacement a few months before the end of his service.

Slim was not friendly to new people. "This little fucker is yours, Joe," Slim snapped at me when Kham showed up outside the shower bay, bags in hand. "Make sure he doesn't kill himself by accident before we get some use out of him."

I sat up on my cot and nodded at Slim without paying much attention.

Kham dropped his bags and gave a little laugh. "Is he always like that?" Apparently Slim's tough-guy act failed to impress the little medic.

"Mostly, yeah." I shrugged.

"Great, I found the squad leader with something to prove. Fuck, I always end up in that guy's squad."

"No, he doesn't have anything to prove," I corrected. "He's just insane."

"Is that better?" Kham asked.

"No," I laughed. I noticed Kham didn't have a weapon. "Where's your rifle?" I asked.

"They never gave me one," Kham said.

"Wait, what?" You always deployed with your own weapons. We certainly didn't have any extras lying around.

"They said you guys would give me one when I got here," Kham said.

"Do you see any extra weapons lying around this shit hole?" I asked. I was beyond frustrated with our Rear Detachment or Rear D.

Rear D is the unit in charge of setting things up for us when we got back home, training, deploying replacements, and most important, outfitting said fucking replacements. Every single Rear D I had ever had in my career had been fairly useless. Though they had at least given soldiers weapons before sending them into a war zone.

"Rear D is a fucking joke," Kham said. "They never even sent me to my pre-deployment medical training."

I didn't have anything to say to that. I just reached over and put a wad of dip in my lip. I got up, leaving the new medic behind, and walked into the TOC (Tactical Operations Center). There I saw Gunny and Slim seated behind a desk studying maps. "I have a problem with the new medic," I said sitting down next to them.

"I know Sal was your friend, Kassabian, but he isn't coming back," Gunny said sharply.

"No, Sergeant, not that. Rear D didn't give him a weapon," I muttered.

"You're fucking with me, right?" Slim laughed.

Gunny shot him an angry look for daring to laugh. "I'll handle it," he said matter-of-factly.

I looked at Slim, and he shrugged at our platoon sergeant's words. "Yes, Sergeant," I said and quickly exited the TOC. I had no idea where Gunny was going to get another rifle, though I had no doubt he would find one.

I retreated out of the rain back into the shower stall where Machete and Cali were mopping the tile floor for about the ninth time that day. I walked in and re-tracked in a fine slurry of mud and pebbles that stuck to everything. Cali dropped his mop in defeat and sat down. In the back corner of the shower stalls, Guapo and Walrus listened to some god-awful rap song.

Cali sat down next to me in my stall. He reached into my pocket without any words, took out my dip can and stole a pinch. "I hate the fucking winter," Cali said. "It's nothing but rain and mud."

"And cold as hell," I added. "I wish someone would attack us."

"Me too." Cali spat into the mop bucket. "We need to give the Taliban winter clothes so they can hang with us year 'round."

"For only one dollar a day, you too can support international terror," I mocked. "A whole bunch of bearded cave people running around in Patagonia jackets and Danner boots."

We both laughed.

"We really need more reliable internet." Cali shook his head.

"Why? Running out of porn?" I asked.

"No, I don't think that's possible. Walrus has been listening to the same five fucking songs for weeks," Cali said.

"Fuck off!" Walrus yelled at us from the back. "It's better than that cousin-fucking country bullshit you listen to!"

Cali tossed a bottle full of dip spit toward the back of the room.

"Lil Wayne's music sounds like two fax machines fucking!" I yelled at him.

"And he looks like a Gremlin with a coke problem!" Guapo's laugh filled the shower stalls. It was more of a high-pitched cackle than a laugh. One of those laughs that forces an entire room of people to laugh along with it.

The shower bay door slammed open and Gunny's soaking wet form stepped through. He was holding a rifle and six magazines full of ammunition. "Kham," he said calmly.

Kham peeked out of his stall, headphones around his head.

"This is your rifle," Gunny said, thrusting it at him.

Kham took it . "There are many like it, but this one is mine?" he asked.

Gunny grimaced at the little medic's joke.

"I mean, thank you, Sergeant!"

Gunny spun around and walked back out of the bay.

"What's his problem?" Kham asked us.

"He only feels anger," Cali said.

"And hatred," I added. "Slim swears he saw him smile once, but we don't believe him."

"This place keeps getting better," Kham sighed.

"It *does* get better," Nan piped in from his cot.

"When?" Kham asked.

"After I got my brain injury, everything started to come around," Nan replied.

That evening, we all gathered around in the shower bay like any other night. Slim had a large map on the wall and a roster of names written next to it. Each truck commander had three or four names scribbled down next to his in various positions. My name was next to Slim's as a "dismount," or extra soldier who rides in the back of the truck.

"We are going out with a few ANPs, visiting some checkpoints and making sure their stupid asses didn't freeze to death yet and to make sure they're still working," Slim said. "Should be there and back in a few hours."

When he was finished, no one had any questions or comments. Another meandering winter mission with a seemingly random objective. There wasn't much of a real concern that the ANPs would vanish. Winter was one of the few times of year they actually went to work. The threat of a Taliban attack was almost nonexistent.

I wrapped my face in a scarf and trudged outside to the trucks. It was one of the few dry nights of the winter so far. The wind was still biting, though.

I climbed into the back of Slim's truck. For some reason, at the last minute Slim decided he wanted to be a gunner on the mission.

Gunny decided he was going to roll out with us and took overall command of the squad away from Slim.

An ANP climbed in our truck. He filled in the empty seat we had. He didn't look happy for having been made to go with us. Oldies climbed behind the steering wheel and before long we were out of the gate and driving off into the night.

Even with the cutting wind, the streets were packed with people shuffling around the bazaars and markets. Scooters zoomed by, piled high with people. Some of them were still wearing flip-flops and man-dresses.

"I don't think they realize it's cold as shit out," Slim said, hiding behind the turret shield to protect himself from the wind.

"I get it," I laughed. "In Michigan, if it's over thirty degrees, it's pretty much shorts weather. This probably isn't that cold to them yet."

"That's because you Yankee fucks have brain damage from all the factory fumes," Slim quipped.

"I'd rather have that than a family tree that doesn't branch, you white trash bitch."

"How's your dad's Ford job treating him?" Slim joked.

"My dad's dead, you asshole!" I yelled.

Our convoy pulled up outside our first stop of the night. We all climbed out, minus Slim, who stayed up on his turret. We automatically started setting up a traffic control point to slow the volume of traffic and start searches. I ended up near the front of the control point with Oldies, Perro, and our ANP. Gunny, Walrus, Guapo, and Bama took up the rear of the control point, and it was their job to actually check on the ANPs in the checkpoint.

Perro and I started slowly searching cars and people to pass the time. Gunny was incredibly long-winded whenever he visited ANP checkpoints. He was one of the few people who really thought the ANPs could be turned into an effective fighting force against the Taliban because, as he said, "Someone turned Machete into a soldier–anything is possible." He was one of the few true believers in the cause.

"Shit, could he go any slower?" Slim complained from on high, perched up in his turret.

"At least you have heat, you dick," Perro yelled at him.

"Don't you hate it when people do their job?" I asked sarcastically.

"Go to hell, Joe. Go grab me an energy drink," Slim called out to me.

I sighed, walked over and climbed up the side of the truck to grab some cash from him. Afghan energy drinks were strange. Even if they carried the same name as their American equivalent, they were never the same. They generally came in short, stubby cans and their telltale logos always looked odd. All the writing was in Chinese. The Afghan merchants tried to pass them off as the real thing anyway.

I turned to walk back to Perro when two massive explosions tore through the night. Their blasts lit up the sky, and for a few seconds, I could clearly see down the road toward the rear of the convoy.

"The fuck was that?" Slim yelled over his radio. No one answered.

"Medic!" a voice cried in the night. "Medic!"

I looked over at Perro, and he looked at me. "Let's go!" I yelled at him, and we took off running down the road into the night. I was wearing over fifty pounds of combat gear, but it felt light as a feather as we sprinted.

Muzzle flashes ripped to life from the rooftops on the sides of the road. Bullets smashed into the road around Perro and me. We could hear the cracks and whistles of the bullets as they passed by our heads. I heard the ANP cry out in pain somewhere beside me. My body was telling me to get behind something. Hide from the incoming fire. Protect yourself. I didn't care. Someone out there wanted to hurt my brothers and it was going to take a whole lot more than some fucking bullets to stop me from helping them.

"Contact left!" Perro screamed. He fired his shotgun over my shoulder at the rooftops. I raised my rifle and started hammering out rounds at the unseen enemy. I wasn't aiming. I was running as hard and fast as I could to get to whoever was hurt.

I dropped the empty magazine from my rifle when it ran dry and slammed in another one. I fired and fired. It suddenly felt like every Taliban fighter in Kandahar was on top of us. Muzzle flashes were all along the rooftops like a string of Christmas lights.

Another explosion ripped through the night, lighting up the street like dawn. We didn't slow down. A face appeared over the roof ledge. It had a thick brown beard. An AK-47 was in the man's hands, pointed directly at me.

Perro's shotgun boomed again and in a spray of dust and debris the bearded man vanished. I don't know if Perro killed him, but we didn't get shot at from that angle again.

The first thing I saw was Gunny. He was sitting in a pool of his own blood and leaning against the tire of his truck. Gunny was as stoic and calm as ever. The polar opposite of me. "We are going to have to evac' to Camp Nathan Smith," he said.

"Where're you hit?" I asked him. Blood was all over his face, arms, and legs. It was impossible to tell where it was all coming from.

Perro blasted off another shotgun round at something in the night. Rounds were impacting all around us, but Gunny didn't seem to notice or care. Crew-served heavy machine guns ripped into the night. They sent torrents of lead at the rooftops. Their tracers cut through the night air like laser beams.

I was pushed aside by someone. I looked over to see Kham unslinging his medical bag and start working on Gunny. "I got him, look to the others," Kham said calmly.

"Others?" I asked.

"Walrus, Bama, and Guapo are all hit. Not as bad, though. Go cover them."

I didn't say anything I just ran toward the back of the truck. As I crossed an alleyway, a burst of gunfire tore up the road at my feet. I stumbled back and nearly fell over, I fired a few shots and took cover behind the truck. I reached into a pouch on my vest and pulled out a hand grenade. I ripped the pin out, took a few steps toward the alley, and chucked that little thing has hard as I could. It exploded down the lane with a dull thump. The gunfire from the alley stopped.

"Get the fucking wounded in the trucks!" Gunny called out. He was being propped up by Kham.

Bama, Guapo, and Walrus were all helped back into the trucks. Perro and I started the run back to the head of the convoy. Random gunfire snapped out at Perro and me as we ran back. It was a lot less accurate that time around.

Slim had switched with Oldies, jumping out of the truck to try to direct the fighting on the ground. Oldies fired his machine gun at multiple enemies in the darkness.

"Let's fucking go! You're driving!" Slim yelled at me.

The truck was combat locked. As a rule, we locked our doors from the inside when we were conducting traffic control points to ensure no one tried to pop a door open and throw a grenade inside. It required a wrench to unlock from the outside. Oldies tossed one down to me.

Bullets rained down on Slim and me as we tried to get into the truck. I crawled underneath the truck to slide Slim the wrench. He quickly unlocked his door and slid it back to me. I crawled back out and was met by a burst of gunfire that hit the driver's side door all around me. One of Oldies's bursts must have finally met its mark. After a long rip of gunfire at the rooftops, all firing at me stopped. I jumped into the truck and stomped on the gas.

I sped off so fast I never even turned the truck's headlights on. Slim was on the radio screaming status updates back to the TOC. He leaned over, smacked me, and pointed to his eyes. The signal to turn on the damn headlights. I felt at the control switches next to the steering wheel blindly and fumbled with them until the lights turned on. I'm not sure how fast the Oshkosh MATV was rated to go, but I know I had the needle buried.

The engine screamed, and the surroundings whipped past us faster than I could recognize them.

"Next right!" Slim yelled. An Afghan police checkpoint was up ahead. Concertina wire was pulled across the road blocking it off. Several Afghan police milled about with rifles slung on their backs not paying attention to the convoy that was flying toward them.

I laid on the truck's horn, but the police didn't move. I wasn't going to slow down. I had no idea how severely wounded everyone was, and nothing was going to stop me from getting them the help they needed.

"Run it!" Slim yelled. The police dove out of the way at the last second. The concertina wire caught on the hood of the truck and snapped in half, sending shards of razor-sharp metal flying into the air. I ripped the steering wheel to the right, and barely managed to keep the truck upright as it bounced around the corner and smacked into an unmanned fruit stall.

I could see the lights from Camp Nathan Smith down the street. Slim had radioed ahead to tell the camp we had multiple wounded soldiers so they could be ready. No one had told the Afghan police outside the camp to clear the road. We blew through two more checkpoints. I took the bumper off one of their trucks and sent several more police diving for safety.

The camp's gate was closed. A rickety, metal pole swung down to lock in place and was manned by two Afghans. The Afghans at the gate saw us plow through the other checkpoints and quickly started pulling the gate up. It bounced off our antennas as we rushed through. We pulled our convoy across the threshold and were met by a large crowd of people.

We jumped out of the truck and were immediately assaulted by an incredibly loud siren yelling in a British accent, "Mass casualty event! Mass casualty event! All medical personnel report to your stations!"

Slim and I ran back to the second truck in the convoy where Gunny was sitting. We had to push through crowds of medical personnel that had rushed to our trucks. They were standing around holding bags of gear and not doing anything. I violently shoved a few out of my way.

Gunny had opened the passenger door and was trying to climb out under his own strength. I helped him down using his good arm; the other was completely soaked in blood. I glanced inside the truck and saw that the area he sat in looked like a horror show. Blood was everywhere.

Two people carrying a backboard and a medical bag rushed up to Gunny and me. "Put him on the backboard!" One of them yelled at me.

"Fuck you, I'm walking," Gunny growled.

"Then let us help you," the same one said. He tried to grab Gunny's shredded arm, and Gunny kicked him away.

"Don't fucking touch me," he snapped at them. Out of the entire situation, that was the only time I heard Gunny lose his cool. We hobbled on through the crowd and toward the aid station, leaving a trail of blood behind us.

The aid station was crowded with people. Several people were waiting outside wearing camo-patterned scrubs, and I handed Gunny over to them. They laid Gunny down on a stretcher in a row beside Bama, Walrus, and Guapo. The medics pushed me out of the aid station and slammed the door. Slim, Perro, and I paced around outside the station absolutely furious that they wouldn't let us in to see our wounded friends.

"This is fucking bullshit!" Slim screamed at the medics. "What is going on?"

"Let us the fuck in!" I yelled. We heard someone in the aid station call for a helicopter evacuation.

"Tell us what's happening!" Slim yelled, rushing the door. Several medics forced him back. Perro and I joined in trying to push past them to see what was happening with our friends.

A large black guy wearing the rank of a first sergeant appeared behind the line of medics. "At ease, Sergeant!" he yelled at Slim. "You cannot come in here!"

"Fuck off, you fat prick!" I yelled back. "We need to see them!"

"Excuse me, Specialist?" he shot back at me.

"Move your fat ass!" Slim yelled at him and stiff-armed the first sergeant in the chest.

The first sergeant stumbled back, and we had an opening. We tried to rush inside the aid station.

"What the hell is going on?" asked the calm voice of Rocky, who had arrived at the camp at some point. We stopped what we were doing and slowly turned to look at him.

"They won't let us in to see our brothers!" Slim half screamed, half whined.

"*Excuse* me?" Rocky marched up to the aid station. "Get out of my way!" he ordered. The medics parted like the Red Sea.

We started pushing our way inside when Rocky turned back to me. "Go back to the convoy and check on the younger soldiers. Make sure they aren't going crazy."

"Yes, sir," I said. I hesitantly turned and left the aid station and started walking back to our trucks. I was stopped by a large civilian wearing a shirt that said "Paramedic" across the front. He patted me on the shoulder and handed me a pack of Marlboro cigarettes and a lighter.

"Thank you," I said, nodding at him.

"You need more than me," he said in an implacable eastern-European accent.

I reached into the pack and placed a cigarette between my lips, I flicked the lighter and took a deep drag. A cold rain started hitting my skin and before long it turned into a downpour. It chilled me to the bone.

I made it back to the convoy and found some of our younger soldiers frantically cleaning blood off the wounded guys' weapons. I saw the young girl, Pip, scrubbing away at someone's rifle. She wasn't saying anything.

"Make sure the weapons are serviceable and ammo's reloaded," I said, smoke trailing out of my mouth.

"Joe, are you hurt?" Oldies asked me. He pointed down at my pants. I hadn't noticed, but I was soaked in blood. I noticed Kham had rejoined the squad. The normally energetic medic sat away from the rest of the soldiers, smoking in silence.

"None of it is mine." I shook my head. "Make sure we're ready to go back out and fuck these dudes up." I was so angry I was shaking. The rain finally soaked my cigarette through, and it fizzled out in my lips. I wanted to get back in our trucks. I wanted to go back out to that street. I wanted to just start shooting people. I didn't care who. I just wanted them to feel the way I felt. I wanted to hurt someone they loved.

The unmistakable sound of a helicopter's whirling blades filled the air and I watched the body of a Blackhawk take off. I noticed the large, red cross that was plastered on its side.

Slim, Rocky, and Perro reappeared by the trucks.

We all stopped what we were doing and turned to face them.

"Mount up, we are going back to Spartan," Rocky said calmly. He was doing his best not to let everything that happened show on his face. He tried to be a rock his soldiers could rally around during the hard times.

"Sir, we aren't going back out?" I asked.

"No, Joe," he shook his head. "Your squad doesn't have enough soldiers to run all of its trucks effectively, let alone carry out combat operations."

"We'll get them next time," Slim said, rage boiling in his words. His eyes told me he was feeling the same way I was.

"How are they?" I asked.

"Gunny and Walrus are the most serious," Slim said. "But everyone is going to be fine."

I breathed a sigh of relief.

We had to borrow a few soldiers from First Platoon to drive our vehicles back to Spartan. I climbed into the commander's seat of Bama's truck. His blood was caked to the cloth seat, Blue Force Tracker screen, and windshield. I tried to remind myself my friend was going to be okay as I sat down in abundant pools of his dried blood.

We arrived back at Spartan without having spoken a word. We were greeted by every living person on Spartan. They wanted us to know they were there for us. Several people approached me and wrapped me in big hugs. I saw Eastwood wrap his arms around Slim and say something into his ear. Everyone wanted to know what happened, but I couldn't bring myself to put any of it into words.

I lit a cigarette and paced back and forth. I watched several soldiers clean the blood out of the trucks with water bottles and scrub brushes. Red water splashed onto the rocks and the truck's running boards.

Ginger walked out of the TOC and met Slim, Perro, and me. "How are you guys doing?" he asked in a kind voice.

"Could be worse." Perro made the slight joke, though none of us laughed.

"Gather up the squad in the shower bay, Rocky and I would like to talk to you guys," Ginger ordered in a soft voice.

The squad gathered around in the shower bay a few minutes later. None of us were talking. I don't think anyone had anything to say for the first time since we had been deployed. Rocky and Ginger walked into the bay. We all clambered to stand at attention—the prescribed way to stand when an officer enters the room.

"Cut it out." Rocky waved at us. He never liked formalities. We all slowly sat back down. "You boys did good out there tonight," he started. "We gave just as good as we got and I'm proud of you. Get some rest." Rocky turned and walked out of the shower bay. Ginger followed at his heels.

We all filed into our shower stalls and dropped our gear off. It felt like a million pounds fell off of my back as my pack slammed into the tile floor. I retreated to Slim's shower stall and found him sitting with Perro.

Perro was huddled around a small coffeemaker, adding grounds to a pearl-white filter. None of us were going to bother to try to sleep. We sat in silence, listening to the coffeemaker bubble and percolate. We weren't sitting there for the conversation, but for the company.

CHAPTER 25

THE HOOLIGANS NEARLY GET KICKED OUT OF A HOSPITAL

A FEW WEEKS HAD PASSED since we'd been ambushed. The squad was itching for a fight. The problem was we couldn't get in one even if we tried. Since the ambush, our squad was limited to guarding towers and filling in for other squads that were short of men because our numbers were so small. We didn't have the men to load our trucks or to perform a patrol of any kind. We were trapped on Spartan Base, and it was driving us insane.

Thankfully, Ginger put together a convoy to take us to Kandahar Airfield to visit our wounded brothers. At least what was left of them.

Gunny's injuries were so extensive that he was put on a flight to Germany and then on to the States. According to Guapo and Bama, as Gunny was wheeled out of the hospital and onto the tarmac, he fought with the medics trying to take him away and screamed: "I'll be back, boys! I'll be fucking back!" If anything the guys had said was true, it would never happen. Gunny had suffered neurological damage to his hand from shrapnel and would most likely require extensive surgery.

I didn't care if it was true or not, but I wanted to believe he would be back.

That left Walrus, Guapo, and Bama sitting in a cushy hospital at Kandahar Airfield with no supervision and raising absolute hell. The hospital staff had sent Rocky several warnings that if his soldiers didn't start behaving, they were going to send them back to the States.

Which, knowing Walrus, may have been his goal in the first place. We all laughed when we heard about what they were doing. Stealing food and drinks, shamelessly hitting on all the women, smoking indoors, and spitting dip all over the floors. I think it actually made Slim proud.

Our convoy pulled through KAF and journeyed deep into the strange pseudo-city to try to find the hospital. It was the only brick and mortar building that I remember seeing on the airfield. It was painted a blinding white and named after some dead soldier from years before. It could have almost passed for a stateside hospital.

We all piled into the hospital and surprised a woman who was manning a desk at the front door. "What unit are y'all in?" she asked, looking up from her magazine as if we were rude for making her do her job.

We told her what unit we were in, and who we were there to visit.

"Oh. That makes sense," she said in a smug voice while eyeing us up and down. "Third floor. Room two-twenty."

We didn't have to look hard for them. Ear-splitting Lil Wayne music was pumping from one of the rooms. The door was wide open and we could hear Guapo's unmistakable high-pitched cackle. When we stepped through the open door we found Walrus and Guapo watching porn on a laptop and Bama sitting by himself across the room reading a book.

The room was probably the nicest one I'd ever seen overseas, even if a thick cloud of cigarette smoke hung in the air. It was probably better than the barracks room I had back in Texas.

"About time, assholes!" Walrus yelled when he saw us. He limped to his feet and hugged Slim and me.

"How are you guys feeling?" Slim asked.

"Bored as shit," Bama said, lowering his book.

"I don't think they like us here," Guapo cackled.

"Bro, you guys are about to get kicked out of this place." Slim stifled a laugh.

"How the fuck do you almost get kicked out of a hospital?" I asked, shaking my head.

"Man, these guys suck," Walrus sneered. "They're just pissed because we tried to bring bitches in here."

"And they put a bunch of wounded guys on the third floor. I'm not limping my ass downstairs if I need to smoke," Bama said.

Slim cut to the chase. "What are the doctor's telling you?"

"Nothing good," Bama said. "My limp isn't going to get any better, but they aren't sending me home."

"So you're going to be gimping your country ass around the battlefield?" I asked.

"They're talking about sending me home," Walrus said. "I guess I fucked up my back somehow."

"Explosions will do that," Slim pointed out. "At least you'll get to be there when your son is born."

Walrus was one of the only people in the company who had actually deployed with his significant other. She was in another platoon, but that didn't stop them from banging whenever they got the chance. Walrus's son was probably conceived on a rickety bunk bed somewhere on Spartan. His wife was sent home soon after they found out they were expecting.

"Stop making sense, Slim, I don't want to leave you guys," Walrus said.

"You guys are high," I laughed. "If someone was offering me a ticket home, I'd be out of here so goddamn fast all you'd see was a smoke trail."

"You love it here." Slim slapped me on the shoulder.

"I know, but if I say it out loud, I get depressed."

We hugged it out one more time and had to leave. Unfortunately, we weren't able to bring any of them back with us that day. A few weeks later Guapo and Bama would rejoin us at Spartan. Unfortunately, Walrus was on the next plane back to the U.S. with a serious back injury and shrapnel wounds all over his body. As much as it hurt to see him go, it made me happy to know my friend was going to be safe.

CHAPTER 26

THE HOOLOGANS WITHOUT SLIM

WITH GUNNY SIDELINED BACK IN the States with severe injuries, the leadership of Second Platoon fell to Slim. As happy as I was to see my good friend get elevated to a higher position, I was scared to see where that would leave us. Slim was the heart and soul of our squad, and without him we were just misbehaved soldiers with drinking problems. Slim gave us our identity. Without him, we were doomed.

"I hear they're going to disband us. Make us fall in with First Squad," Nan said. The way he was smoking his cigarette made me think he was angry at it.

"That would never happen," I snapped at him.

"Yeah?" Nan gesticulated wildly with his arms. "Who else could be our squad leader?"

He made a good point. Outside of myself, only Perro and Kitty were technically leaders. And I had already been demoted. None of us were ready to lead an entire squad. With Grandpa being forced to go home early, we had no one with any real leadership experience. Suddenly Nan's bullshit made sense.

"If they disband us, who are they going to have do their dirty work?" Cali asked.

"Maybe we don't want any more dirty work." Guapo shook his head, his wounds still fresh in his body.

"Man, fuck that," I said.

"I don't give a fuck who they put in charge of us," Perro said cleaning his rifle. "We are still going to be the goddamn Hooligans."

We all tried to boost ourselves up about what would happen next. We talked about a rumor that I was going to get a battlefield promotion to sergeant for capturing the third most wanted man in Kandahar. As cool as I thought it would be, I didn't believe it for a second.

A battlefield promotion is a promotion to the next rank that went around all of the usual paperwork and bullshit that came with trying to further your military career. A battlefield promotion came via a direct order from a general. Normally, these were based on battlefield merit or courage or something. Literally nothing I did fell under those two categories. I kicked in that guy's door totally by chance and didn't fire a shot. None of that took courage or battlefield merit. The promotion never came. But a squad leader did.

Tooth, an older guy from First Squad, became our squad leader. He earned his nickname by having a large majority of his teeth knocked out by an exploding fire extinguisher early in his Army career. Tooth was a nice guy, though he was the only person who could give Memphis a run for his money when it came to being the most redneck soldier in the platoon. He didn't have any squad leader experience but had been in the army for about a decade. Tooth got along with the Hooligans and none of us were worried about him taking over. While we were obviously going to miss Slim's uncontrolled insanity, we thought we were in good hands.

Our first mission came upon us without warning. Bama had crashed his stupid drone into a field, and we rallied together to go grab it. God forbid the Taliban steal his retarded RC plane.

Bama apologized to us as we climbed into our trucks and drove out in the middle of the night. Nothing felt right driving out without Slim leading the circus he'd created.

We flew down the road as fast as we could while Tooth frantically called over the radio for us to slow down.

"You hear something?" Cali asked me.

"I think he said to go faster," I said. We drove on, ignoring his orders, and quickly approached the area where Bama's plane went down. It was a dry, cracked, and barren field. No doubt someone's bountiful harvest.

One shack stood in the middle of the field, crumbling and falling apart. An angry old man stood outside screaming obscenities at us as we pulled our massive trucks onto his farmland. The man stood outside my door and screamed at me as I got out.

"You must be mistaking me for someone who gives a fuck," I said to him. Not that he understood anything I said. He screamed something back at me.

Machete palmed the man's face and pushed him back through the open door of his shack. He drew out a massive, foot-long machete—his namesake—from the back of his vest and pointed it in the man's face. "Fuck you, mother fucker!" Machete screamed at the man.

"Hey, Joe, you think you should call him off?" Cali asked me.

"I'm curious to see where this is going," I said.

Machete kept waiving that blade around like a goddamn madman and screaming curses at the old guy.

"You yell at my boss again, I'll skin your ass and wear you like a cape!"

Cali and I laughed at the stupid shit Machete was spouting.

Tooth came running over to where our truck was parked. "Where is your third guy, Kassabian?" he yelled at me. He looked equal parts confused and scared. I smiled and pointed over to where Machete was threatening the local farmer with a large-bladed weapon.

"What? Why the fuck does he have a machete?"

"He thought it might come in handy," I said simply.

"And so far, he's kind of right," Cali said.

We all absolutely hated Machete as a soldier. He never showered, even when getting a shower was a possibility. He had somehow managed to get even fatter while in Afghanistan and consistently fell asleep while on duty. But we would be goddamned if we let some guy from First Squad talk shit about him. That was *our* job.

"Slim never had a problem with it," I said.

"Well, Slim isn't your goddamn squad leader anymore!" Tooth yelled at me. "Now get your people spread out and secure this fucking field!"

"It's like a mile wide, dude," Cali smiled a little and splayed his arms out to show how broad the area was. "We can't secure the area with three people."

"Do it!" Tooth ordered. We shrugged and meandered off into the distance. We knelt down in a ditch and stared off into the pitch-black night. Everyone wandered around trying to find all of the pieces of Bama's plane.

I flipped down my night vision, and the countryside turned a sickly shade of green. I put a dip in my lip and waited. I heard footsteps behind me and spun around in the night to see Tooth running toward me.

"Is everything all right?" I asked. I double-checked my radio to ensure it was on and working properly. It was. I could hear every other team in the squad talking to each other.

"Yeah," Tooth exhaled. His years as a smoker caught up too quickly. "Spread your team out down the western edge of the farm."

"Um, okay," I said. "Is your radio working?" I asked.

"Yeah, why?" he looked confused about why I would ask.

"You ran like a quarter of a mile over here to tell me that."

"Yeah," Tooth replied. As if nothing sounded weird about that. There was no reason to run around the dark countryside wearing almost half your body weight in combat gear unless someone was actively trying to kill you. Tooth apparently didn't agree. He turned around and ran back the way he'd come.

"The fuck is he doing?" Cali asked.

"Maybe he needs some PT," I said and chuckled.

We sat in the dark for what seemed like hours. We didn't hear any update over the radio. I started nodding off and had to stand up. In the distance, I saw the lights from a few of the trucks turn on in the darkness. I grabbed my radio, wondering what was happening. "Hey, what's going on?" I asked no one in particular.

"We found the pieces, and we're getting ready to roll out," Tooth answered.

I wanted to scream at him for being willing to leave without us. He was just going to leave us hanging out in that ditch. But devolving into profanity probably wasn't the best first impression to give a new squad leader. I feigned calm. "Roger, we're moving back to the trucks," I said between gritted teeth.

We hoofed it back to the truck and climbed inside. We rumbled off into the night back toward Spartan but took a different route than we originally planned.

"Are we going across the Bridge of Doom?" Cali asked. The Bridge of Doom was a tiny mud bridge that crossed a massive ravine in the middle of a village. You had to perfectly position your vehicle on the bridge to fit, and even then your tires would hang over the edges by a few inches. We never crossed it at night. One wrong move and everyone in your truck would plummet to their death.

"Oh God, I think so," I said. I immediately became scared. Rolling over in a vehicle was one of my biggest fears.

When I was eighteen and training at Fort Knox, the truck I was riding in rolled over three times and landed upside down. I wasn't hurt, but the experience shook me to my core. Driving around in Afghanistan, that fear was always in the back of my mind. Right then, it came screaming to the forefront of my brain and I suddenly became aware that I was gripping my rifle so hard my hands hurt.

"Why are we going this way?" Perro asked the question we were all thinking.

"We have to switch up our routes," Tooth answered. To an extent, he made sense. We never took the same route twice while out on a mission. If your travel habits became predictable, you became a target for a Taliban ambush. Rather than cross the Bridge of Doom at night, we usually took a different, much longer route back to Spartan.

We turned into the small bordering village. The buildings were so close, our mirrors almost scratched at the mud walls of the houses. We lined up at the mouth of the Bridge of Doom. The bridge was so rickety only one truck could cross at a time, and even then you prayed to all major and minor deities for it to hold.

Perro's truck, driven by a scout named Kermit, was the first to cross. It hadn't crawled across the bridge ten feet before they all nearly fell to their deaths.

The left front tire fell off the edge of the bridge and the truck's axle slammed down onto the surface. The bridge shook, and rocks fell into the river below.

"Ah! *Fuck!*" Perro screamed over the radio. His voice was so loud it came across the radio as mostly feedback and static. I was about fifty percent sure I was about to watch four of my friends die. I lit a cigarette and stared hard into my night vision goggles.

In a normal situation, we would hook up tow cables to the stuck vehicle and pull it out. There was absolutely no way that bridge would hold two trucks at the same time. They would have to get themselves out. Or so we hoped.

Perro jumped out of the truck and ran behind it, lighting up the area with a flashlight and checking behind the truck to make sure the bridge itself didn't break apart.

"Gun it back and to the left," Perro ordered Kermit. Kermit slammed on the gas. The truck hopped back onto the bridge and stopped so fast that the truck rocked and shook with the force. Perro climbed around the side of the truck and back into his seat. They crawled forward again. That time without incident.

Cali gunned our truck across the bridge at about three times the speed he should have. With that, we were safe on the other side. We drove back the rest of the way in silence. I tried to ignore that our new leader had almost left us in a ditch. It was a little harder to forget that he made us cross a bridge we should never have been on.

Tooth was a new leader, and I gave him the benefit of the doubt. He was a good guy with good intentions. His biggest flaw was that he wasn't Slim. And he would never be one of us.

CHAPTER 27

KEEPING YOUR COOL

A FEW WEEKS HAD PASSED, and we came around to Tooth as our squad leader. But he wasn't the iron fist of Slim that we needed, and when given an inch, we took a mile. When we were given a mile, we sprinted off into the horizon. We all slowly but surely became depressed about our new lot in life. We were no longer the ultra-violent squad that everyone wanted on call. We were just another unit in the company.

Even though Slim was in charge of the entire platoon, he spent most of his time hanging around and going on patrol with us. He constantly undermined Tooth and retook command of his former squad. Eventually, Tooth realized he wasn't really in charge of the squad.

We were still stewing over the fact that we hadn't been able to get revenge for our wounded comrades. Since that rainy night we were mangled on that godforsaken road, the Taliban had completely left us alone. We hadn't even found an IED waiting for us. It was as if they knew they'd won, claimed the prize, and gone home.

That didn't stop us from lashing out at everyone and everything. Every single traffic control point we set up was an opportunity to ruthlessly search every passerby. Every car had every single occupant ripped out of it so it could be torn apart. We tore seats out and took knives to the insides of the floor and ceiling liners. We didn't find a damn thing.

"I don't get it," Cali mumbled while shredding someone's driver seat with a knife. "It's fighting season, and we are in Kandahar. Where the hell are all the Taliban?"

"Who knows," I said with a shrug. "Gathering their numbers, waiting to overrun us at Spartan?"

"Then where the hell are all the weapons?" he asked, kicking shreds of torn fabric around.

"You ever think we just suck at our jobs?" Perro laughed as he went through the car's trunk.

"I *know* I suck at my job," I said.

Our unforgiving searching methods made us no friends. Traditionally, if women were in the cars, we weren't allowed to pull them out and search the car. That wasn't a directive of ISAF, but of our local Afghan police. It made sense; there was really no faster way to make the populace hate you in Afghanistan than to mess with their women. But we stopped caring about their feelings when they started to blow our friends up.

We weren't grabbing the women and yanking them out of the cars. We were just opening the doors for them to indicate they should step out. We would never touch them or search them personally, even though we wanted to. On several occasions, the men would try to physically stop us from opening their back doors. That never ended well for them.

As much as we wanted to search them, we were never allowed to. There were dozens of intelligence reports about Taliban hiding as women, only to jump out and take a shot at a soldier. Or for men to use their own wives and family as conduits for weapons smuggling, knowing we wouldn't touch them. Higher Command thought the Afghans' feelings were more important than our safety.

I opened up the back door of a little rusted Corolla and motioned for a woman who was clad head to toe in a blue burka to step out. An older man shoved me square in the chest as hard as he could. I was a well-built, two-hundred-and-thirty-five-pound man wearing about fifty pounds of combat gear. I didn't budge. I cocked my arm back and punched him as hard as I could in the middle of his chest. He crumpled like a piece of paper.

"Kassabian!" Tooth yelled at me. His already red face was suddenly so flushed he could have passed as a tomato.

"What?" I yelled. His voice snapped me back to reality. I had blacked out and caved in the guy's chest. I wanted to smash him across the skull with my rifle until his eyes went dark and he twitched. I wanted to stomp his face in with my size-thirteen combat boot. I wanted to kill him.

Nan put his hand on my shoulder, reassuring me. It calmed me back down.

"Asshole tried to grab his gun!" Nan yelled back at Tooth. It was a blatant lie, but it seemed to be enough for Tooth. He walked away and left us alone.

I had never lost it like that before. I stood there trying to gather my thoughts as the guy writhed around on the ground in front of me. I knelt down and grabbed him, pulled him to his feet, and shoved him back into his car. "Get the fuck out of here," I growled at him. He motioned wildly with his hands. He screamed at me in words I didn't understand. I noticed two streams of tears that had cut through the caked layers of dust he had on his face. It made me feel better about myself. Finally, he drove off, kicking dirt up as he went.

We were walking back to Spartan when Cali walked up next to me. "You all right man? I think you punched through that guy's chest."

"Yeah," I lied. "Asshole shouldn't have touched me." For all the things the Hooligans did as a group, we almost never straight-up assaulted people.

"Next time, you should just shoot 'em," Cali said spitting out a massive wad of dip spit.

"Noted," I said curtly.

We made it back to Spartan where Tooth sent me to talk to Slim. Clearly he was upset with my random act of violence but was unable to speak with me himself. I sat down in Slim's tiny room where I noticed he had George W. Bush's autobiography cracked open on his bed. "Is everything okay, man?" Slim asked.

"I should ask you the same thing." I motioned to the book on his bed.

"Hey, it's a good read."

"You know there's no way he could ever actually write a whole book, right?"

Slim cracked a smile.

"Shit, he probably couldn't even read one," I added.

"I was kind of hoping it was a picture book." Slim laughed. "Hey, man, I know how we used to run things, but try not to knock anyone out with Tooth around. He might actually report it," he said with a small smile.

Slim not addressing how seriously messed up it was for me to randomly punch out a villager didn't make me feel any better. I think the worst part was I didn't even feel bad about doing it. As far as I was concerned, I was still trying to pay back Kandahar for fucking up my friends.

I wasn't the only one welling up with anger, aggression, and uncontrollable violence. One day while out on patrol, a rare and beautiful thing happened: the Afghan police did their jobs. They came back into Spartan with a young man hogtied and blindfolded in the back of their pickup truck and walked into the TOC.

Hamid, our interpreter, told us they captured someone on a scooter and wanted to talk to us. Slim, Ginger, and I exchanged confused glances. It was rare they ever captured anyone. Typically, they just robbed them and sent them on their merry way. Either that or executed them on the side of the road.

Ginger went outside to talk to them. In a few seconds, he came back into the TOC. His red face looked like it was going to pop. "They captured someone on a scooter who had grenades on them," he said, trying to keep himself calm and failing miserably.

The same thought immediately crossed all of our minds: *this is one of the assholes who attacked us*. We rushed out of the TOC and crossed into the Afghan police side of the base.

Word had spread to the rest of the Hooligans, and they were running out of the shower stalls half-dressed and armed. We came upon the Taliban fighter. He was frail and skinny and had the patchy beard of an awkward teenager. He was clearly terrified. Tears streamed down his dirty face and mixed with the blood from several wounds that were undoubtedly inflicted on him by the police during his capture.

"Hamid!" Ginger growled.

Hamid, who was clearly uncomfortable with the situation, pushed through the growing crowd of U.S. soldiers and Afghan police. "Yes, sir?" he asked.

"Ask this piece of shit if he was the one who ambushed us," Ginger commanded.

Hamid dutifully and quickly translated Ginger's words into Pashto. The young fighter suddenly looked petrified. He wildly shook his head and spouted off terrified Pashto so quickly he was stumbling over his own words.

Our translator turned to us. "He says he is no Taliban." Hamid smiled. It was his little tell that let us know he thought the guy was lying.

"Then why the fuck did he have a bag of grenades?" Ginger grabbed the young fighter by his man-dress. He lifted the man to his feet so he could stare into his eyes.

Hamid translated.

Another hysterical outburst of words I couldn't understand.

"He says they were not his," Hamid said, once again with a smile on his face.

"Oh, right, he just went to get rice and ended up with a bag of explosives. I hate when that happens," Ginger said. I could tell from the tone of his voice the civil part of this conversation was about to end.

Ginger grabbed the guy by his throat. Ginger's knuckles were turning white with strain as he crushed the guy's windpipe. The Afghan's eyes bulged. He kicked and flailed. He thought that that was it—he was going to die. I hoped he was right.

Ginger let go, shaking his hand out. The Afghan slumped against the wall gasping for breath. Perro kicked him in the stomach and Cali slapped him. The Afghan tried protecting himself as I stepped behind him and grabbed him, pinning his arms behind his back. He struggled as hard as he could, but he didn't have a chance to break away from my grip.

The surrounding soldiers closed in and rained blows on him. Eventually, they got tired and walked away. I dropped the man in the dirt, where he landed with a thud.

The Afghan police continued the beating where we left off. We didn't stick around to watch. The Afghan police's reputation for brutality was well known.

I sat on a small bench across from the TOC and fumbled with a cigarette pack. My hands were shaking so violently, I could hardly light it. I knew what we'd done was wrong, but I didn't care. I would have shot him on the spot if I thought I could have gotten away with it.

I wanted that guy to hurt. I wanted him to feel the pain that our friends felt. I wanted him to bleed for what he did. The fact that he probably had nothing to do with the attack didn't matter to me anymore.

I shook so intensely, I dropped my cigarette into the dirt. I didn't bother to try to pick it up. I just dropped my head into my hands. I felt someone sit down next to me. In my periphery, I saw that it was Nan. He didn't say a word, he just sat there.

None of us were coping with the stresses of our circumstances well. Everyone had taken up smoking, dipping, and drinking bootleg liquor.

My main addiction was the gym. Before Sal left us for hospital life on KAF, we would spend what few free hours we had in the gym. Sometimes going several times a day. We accrued massive stockpiles of supplements through shady online dealers. As far as we knew, they were all legal. We became massive, hulking beasts that everyone else literally sat back and watched.

More than once between sets of whatever it was we were lifting, we would have a gathering of people watching us. Afghan police and other U.S. soldiers would sit back and watch as we punished ourselves in our tiny, mostly handmade outdoor gym. Every single barbell was bent at an insane angle, mostly due to Sal.

After he was sent away, I had no one else who could hang with the horrible torture I would put myself through. After he left, I would just put my headphones on, listen to the angriest music I could find, and wreck myself under the burning Afghan sun. Eventually, I got so big none of my uniforms fit, and my body armor started making it hard to breathe.

It was one of the few non-violent and non-drug-fueled releases I had. It was more cathartic than spending quality time with the massive squad-wide porn collection, which was where most other people spent their time. At night, you could see an eerie glow coming from the port-o-potties. They were lit up like disgusting candles by everyone's laptop screens. Most people didn't even bother plugging in headphones anymore. It became routine when you went to go take a shit to be surrounded by that flat, meat-packing sound of male self-love.

No matter the release, we were all boiling cauldrons of uncontained rage and violence waiting to explode. Whether it was from the stress of the constant threat of a quick and violent death, or the unfinished business of paying the Taliban back for what they had done to the men who were very much our family, once that time bomb went off it would be hard to contain. We could only hope to direct it in the right direction.

One night, our squad was sitting around our trucks on a standard QRF rotation. Normally this just meant we fell asleep in our trucks waiting for the radio to scream to life and give us something to do. Almost nothing ever happened when we were on QRF.

I was just dozing off when the radio crackled. I was hovering in that halfway point between being asleep and being awake so I didn't immediately understand what was being said.

Oldies reached over and slapped me on the shoulder. "Third Platoon got hit!" His speech problem meant he couldn't pronounce the R in "third."

"What?" I said, still not entirely conscious.

"They threw a grenade at Danny!" Oldies yelled.

"Second Squad, we are rolling out!" Tooth screamed over the radio.

I rubbed the sleep from my eyes and put a dip in my lip.

The truck rumbled to life as Slim jumped into the front passenger seat. "You fuckers ain't leaving without me." He smiled, looking back at me.

"Think it's the same boys that fucked *us* up?" I asked him.

"Who knows, man? I'm looking to peel some scalps back regardless," Slim said.

The Taliban in our area knew which squad, platoon, and company were which. They knew who to hit and who not to hit. Deep down inside I hoped this was the same group that hit us. Anyone who ever said the Taliban were stupid never had to fight them.

"Let's fucking do this," I said.

Our convoy stopped in a small, nondescript village. The tiny dirt-track road we were parked on was centered between two open-air sewer ditches. Third Platoon was already spread out and searching the area for their attackers. I couldn't see the truck that had the grenade thrown at it. I hoped Danny was okay.

Danny was a short, energetic Mexican kid whom I'd known for years. He was actually one of my soldiers when I was first stationed at Fort Hood and he had deployed with me before. I couldn't wait to get my hands on someone—anyone—who had anything to do with the attack.

"IED!" Tooth screamed.

Slim, Oldies, and I froze in place. Tooth ran back up to the narrow road our trucks were parked on.

"Where?" Slim asked.

"Down in that guy's front yard." Tooth pointed to a small compound that had a perfect view of the road.

"Joe, Nan, go check it out," Slim ordered.

I nodded. Nan and I were frequently picked for that sort of duty. Not because Slim didn't like us, but because we didn't much care for our own safety.

We climbed down into a small sewer ditch and up and over to the other side to the compound where Tooth had seen the IED.

Almost squarely in some guy's front yard, maybe twenty feet from his front door, was a pile of dirt with wires running over to a junked-out car.

"That certainly looks like an IED to me," I said, fighting with a lighter in the night breeze.

"Maybe that's what they want us to think," Nan responded, looking at the dirt pile sideways. He advanced on the dirt pile and gave it a stiff kick. He turned around and walked back to where I was still standing. "Yep, it's an IED."

"What makes you so sure now?" I smiled a little.

"Car is full of jugs of yellow shit." He shrugged.

"Shouldn't you be dead or something?" I asked.

"Yeah, probably. Maybe we got the IED B squad today." He reached into his pocket and pulled out a pack of disgusting menthol-flavored cigarettes. We slowly made our way back to the trucks and met up with Slim.

"So?" Slim asked.

"If it's not an IED, they certainly went to a lot of trouble building a fake one," Nan pointed out. "Probably tried to lure us all out here with that bullshit grenade attack and were planning on fucking us up with that big bastard down there."

"You're probably right," Slim said, nodding.

"I don't think we have anything to worry about. I kicked the shit out of it, and it didn't explode." Nan blew out a cloud of smoke.

"You *what*?" Tooth gasped in shock.

"Don't worry, it's standard procedure." I laughed, but I was only half-joking.

"Thanks, boys, I'll call EOD and we can finish up clearing out this village." Slim turned and grabbed his radio. "You're going to have to take Hamid and clean out those houses in case EOD blows the thing in place."

"Roger," I nodded. Nan and I walked back down toward the bomb. "Isn't this a good way to die? Keep wandering down the same road to a known explosive?"

"Yes. Joe, you forget EOD is worth much more than you or I. A year-long school where they learn to take apart the most complicated bombs...any idea how much that costs?"

"Good point."

"What did they teach you to do? Fire a rifle and listen to commands?"

"They taught me how to drive a tank once," I pointed out. I walked up to the ramshackle door of the compound and pounded on it with my fist. The whole thing rattled and shook. The door struggled to stay on its hinges.

A man with a patchy beard answered the door, looking confused.

"Have you heard about our Savior Lord Jesus Christ?" Nan asked, a cigarette dangling from his lips.

"Or about the benefits of washing yourself daily?" I smiled broadly.

Hamid shrugged and translated what we were saying. The man smiled and shook his head. He was still confused as to why we were standing at his door.

"Tell him his family needs to pack their shit because we found a bomb in their front yard," Nan told Hamid, who quickly translated to the man. The man's eyes widened, and he shook his head at us, spouting off words I couldn't understand.

Hamid smiled and turned to us. "He says there is no bomb."

"Then what the fuck is going on with his car over there?" I asked.

"Fuck this guy. Do you still have that contact paper?" Nan asked me. We carried pieces of paper with us that we could wipe on people's hands and then spray a chemical on it. If they had been in contact with any explosive material or gunpowder residue the paper and chemical mixture would change color.

We almost never used it, and I wasn't really sure why. I fished it out of my bag and handed it to Nan. Without a word, Nan grabbed the man's hand and rubbed the paper all over it.

Nan pulled out a small spray bottle and sprayed a liquid on the paper. By that point, another old man and a younger man had gathered in the doorway to see what all the ruckus was about. The first old man was trying to wave us off. He was attempting to be in control of the situation in the way old men in Afghanistan do. He yelled in Pashto and pointed at me.

"Hey, Old Man River, shut the fuck up or I'll break your jaw," I said, sticking my finger in his face. The younger man slapped my hand away, and I shoved him to the ground. "Hamid! Tell that asshole if he touches me again, I'll fucking kill him."

Hamid nodded and screamed at the group of people; they quickly settled down.

Nan tapped me on the shoulder and showed me the paper. It had changed from a light tan to a deep blue. The fucker had been handling explosives. Nan dropped the paper and grabbed the man out of the doorway and threw him to the ground. He pinned him there with his boot. For someone who looked more like a book nerd than a warrior, Nan could handle himself.

"You lying fucker!" Nan kicked him in the ribs. The man screamed out. He yelled unknown words at us.

Hamid translated. "He says he's not Taliban." He smiled, stifling a laugh with his sleeve.

"Maybe he has a bomb in his yard for self-defense," I joked.

Nan bent down and ripped the guy back up to his feet and slammed him against the house. Slim, Cali, and Tooth made their way over to the man's compound; they were obviously surprised to see us assaulting people.

"What's going on?" Slim asked.

"Piece of shit has explosive materials all over his hands!" Nan cursed.

"Oh, *yeah?*" Slim's attitude immediately changed from jovial to furious. He advanced on the man. "You want to kill Americans, you piece of shit?" Slim grabbed the man from Nan's hands and got in his face.

The second old man and the younger man from inside the house tried to rush out, screaming and yelling.

I stepped forward raising my rifle and slammed the barrel of it into the younger man's chest, sending him collapsing to the ground holding himself. I cross-checked the old man with my rifle, slamming him into the wall and making him slump down to the ground. Confronted by the level of brutality we were using on these people, Tooth turned and walked back to the trucks without another word.

"Stay the fuck down!" I screamed at them pointing my rifle at them both. Slim pulled out a pair of plastic zip cuffs and roughly secured the man's arms behind his back. The man sat up and spat a loogie at Slim. It sailed wide left, and I kicked the man in the back and slammed his face into the dirt. I kept him pinned there with my boot.

"Where's EOD?" Nan asked.

"Just got here," Slim answered. "They're going to disconnect it and bring it with them." He motioned to the squirming man pinned under my boot. "Good catch, by the way, boys."

"You think these assholes had something to do with the attack on Danny?" I asked.

"Probably," Slim nodded. "We're going to hand him over to the Afghans and let them handle this shit."

"Good," I said. As we reached down to grab our new prisoner, two men with massive beards and baseball caps entered the compound.

"Where's the IED?" one of the bearded EOD guys asked.

"Attached to the car right there," I pointed. "Wires go into the ground."

"Thanks," the bearded guy responded. He said something hushed into his headset, and he and his partner walked past us without another word.

I dragged the kicking, cursing prisoner out of the compound by his zip-cuffed wrists and tossed him on the ground in front of an Afghan police truck that was waiting next to our own.

An amused-looking Afghan police captain climbed out of the truck and looked down at the cuffed man writhing around in the dirt.

Hamid translated something to him, and the captain shook his head.

"Tell him he can take the gas can off the back of our truck," Slim answered.

Hamid translated to the Afghan captain. The captain smiled and ran off to grab the can that was strapped to the back of Slim's truck. It had become so commonplace to bribe the Afghans that we didn't even wait for the bribe request anymore. We would just give them shit and hope they would do their jobs.

As with most attacks on U.S. forces, we left the scene without capturing who was responsible. In a country full of people who wanted to see your blood spilled, it was hard to single any one person out. Thankfully, Danny turned out to be mostly fine with only a slight concussion—same as Nan back when he was hit.

Even though we captured someone who probably had something to do with the attack, it didn't feel like we actually accomplished anything. It never really did. Unless we captured Mullah Omar himself, nothing we did on the ground would ever really matter. There would always be some other inbred, bomb-making asshole to take the last one's place. Our only hope was to make it home before one of those guys found his mark.

CHAPTER 28

SLIM THE DICTATOR

IT FELT LIKE A LIFETIME since our platoon sergeant was whisked away from us by a medical helicopter. Even though the vast majority of us hated Gunny's guts, we loved him as a leader. He made our lives a living hell. He ran us ragged with endless missions, tower guard shifts, and made us carry untold pounds of shit we didn't think we needed. At the same time, we were his. He didn't let anyone else screw with us, Afghans included.

It should go without saying we all loved and respected Slim. He was trying his hardest to fill the void that Gunny left behind. Command-wise he was more than capable. Slim was a combat leader through and through. The real problem was, without Gunny there to calm down Slim's more psychopathic tendencies, things had started to fly off the rails.

One night I was tossing and turning restlessly on my shitty cot when Slim barged into the shower bay. "Second Squad, wake the fuck up! Wake up," Slim slammed a baseball bat on the tile floor, creating an ear-splitting cracking sound. I thought we were under attack.

We rolled out of our cots and stumbled into the open area of the bay. None of us had any idea what was going on.

"Which one of you pieces of shit left garbage in the fucking guard towers?" Slim screamed.

We all exchanged confused glances.

"Um, what?" I managed to get out.

"Shut the fuck up," Slim yelled in my face.

I balled up my fists and bit my lip. I wanted to punch the crazy asshole in the fucking mouth.

"Get the fuck outside!" Slim screamed so loud his voice cracked. "Go!"

We all slowly walked outside, still unsure of what was going on. We lined up in the motor pool next to where our trucks were parked. Slim and Tooth paced back and forth in front of us.

"You think you assholes can just destroy this place?" Slim growled. He was asking us questions, but wouldn't let us get a word in edgewise. "So we're going to make sure we get right," Slim continued. "Start sprinting!"

We started running half-assed across the massive boulders that covered the motor pool. All army bases were covered in gravel to keep the ever-present dust storms of Afghanistan under control. For some reason, Spartan was covered in massive ankle-breaking boulders instead of gravel. While running, it took every bit of control and focus not to roll your ankle. Not that Tooth or Slim cared; they just stood there screaming at us.

Poor Oldies went down first. His old joints just couldn't hold up to the abuse. Not that it mattered.

"Why the fuck are you stopping, Oldies?" Slim screamed.

Without a word, Oldies hobbled along, knowing any complaint wouldn't do any good.

"Fuck!" Nan screamed as he went down next. He'd been hiding an ankle injury for months. He had been wrapping it in layers of tape before going on foot patrols and taking insanely unhealthy levels of painkillers so he could keep up with us on missions. The wind sprints on the boulders were just a bit too much for him.

Cali and I helped him up and he limped along behind us.

The boulders were wreaking havoc on my back. At some point in the last few months, I had started getting shooting pains going down my ass and into my left leg. At best it felt like someone was stabbing me in the lower back. At worst it would make me unable to get out of my own bed. The pain made it hard to do anything, especially sleep.

I self-medicated with pills Gong gave me that did nothing to dull the pain. I was worried I was going to end up like Grandpa. I didn't want to get sent home to some army medical butchers to make it even worse with some botched surgery. I was afraid to tell anyone about the chronic pain for fear of sounding weak.

Each step across the boulders sent lightning bolts up my leg and into my back. I openly screamed curses and insults at Slim and Tooth. "You fucking crazy asshole!" I snarled as I tripped over another boulder.

"You want to go, mother fucker?" Slim yelled at me. "I'll take my rank off, and we can go!" He rushed at me and got in my face. He knew as well I as did I wasn't going to swing at him. If he thought I would, he wouldn't have come near me. I was about two times his size and had a mostly undeserved reputation for being a fighter back in the U.S. And no matter how pissed I was at Slim, and even though I really wanted to sometimes, I would never lay a hand on him.

"Fucking low crawl," Slim commanded. A low crawl is also known as an army crawl. You lie down and drag yourself along with your arms with your face on the ground. He wanted us to do that on massive goddamn boulders.

"You got to be shitting me," Nan said with a look of concern on his face. "He's finally fucking lost it."

"He never fucking had it, man." I shook my head. We were waiting for him to change his mind, but it never happened. We slowly laid down on the jagged rocks only for him to yell at us again.

"Stand the fuck back up! Stand up!"

We all jumped back up to our feet.

"Get the fuck out of my sight," Slim barked at us, and we all scampered back to the relative safety of the shower bay.

That sort of thing became routine for Slim and Tooth. Even when Slim didn't do it, his insanity emboldened the other team leaders. Kitty was the worst of the group. Mostly because she wouldn't lift a single solitary finger to help anyone work, but would flip out on her team if her gear wasn't all nice and set up for her whenever she needed it. Tooth dubbed these little punishment sessions "The Gun Line."

Being unoriginal, he stole the name from the Eddie Murphy movie *Life*. In the movie, a prison guard, nearly as redneck as Tooth himself, declares that if anyone crosses "The Gun Line" they will be shot. It really spoke volumes about what he thought about the soldiers in his charge.

Another night we were standing out in the rocks, my back was on fire, and I hadn't slept in what felt like days. We stood with the same weapons we had with us on that night's patrol and because I was Slim's gunner, I had an M240B machine gun in my hands. Kitty was screaming at us alongside Perro and Tooth.

"Down!" Perro yelled. At that command, we were supposed to drop down to the push-up position, weapon and all. We all smacked into the rocks, our weapons clattering against the ground, and grunted with pain.

"Up!" We were supposed to leap back to our feet. By then, pulling myself to my feet required an intense amount of effort.

"Go!" Then we were supposed to run in place with our weapons held out in front of us. Slim repeated this process so many times I lost count.

Finally, after three solid hours of this, Perro stopped and Kitty stepped forward. "Weapons out!" she screamed, and we held them out. She started walking down the line looking at them for cleanliness. Obviously, that was a test we couldn't pass. We had just spent hours slamming our weapons onto dusty rocks. She stepped in front of me and took one look at the dust-coated machine gun in my hands. "What the fuck is this shit, Kassabian?" she yelled in my face.

I stared into her eyes not saying a word. My blood was boiling, and it was taking everything in my power not to strangle the life out of her.

"You're just going to stand there like a retard?" she snarled at me.

I shook with anger, and I wanted to smash her across the face with my machine gun. Instead, I just turned around and walked away.

"Get back here, you piece of shit!" Kitty yelled. I heard Perro and Tooth saying something about leaving me alone, but she obviously didn't listen.

I walked away before I punched her. I knew if I stayed, I wasn't going to be able to control myself. M240 in hand, I walked across the rocks trying to control my racing heart. I fumbled with a pack of cigarettes and stuffed one in my lips and lit it after a few attempts. I could still hear Kitty throwing abuse my way from somewhere behind me.

I heard feet stomping across rocks, and I turned around to see Kitty storming toward me. "Get back here, you fucking pussy!" She cried.

I snapped.

I ran at her. I cocked the M240 in my arms as if it was a football and sent it flying in her direction. It slammed into the rocks right in front of her feet. "That's it, mother fucker!" I roared at her. Fists balled, I advanced on her. I saw the look in her eyes change from anger to sheer terror.

Suddenly, I was stopped dead in my tracks. It was as if I'd hit a cement wall. I looked down and saw Casey's short, stocky figure standing in front of me.

Casey was a team leader in the commander's personal security detachment. He was a semi-professional mixed martial arts fighter, and everyone knew not to fuck with him. Casey and I used to spar and fight in Texas before we deployed, and we were good friends. "Be cool, Joe. Bitch isn't worth it," he said in his deep, gravelly voice.

Kitty didn't see a friend looking out for me, she saw a fellow NCO sticking up for her and once again advanced on me, screaming insults and abuse.

Casey turned to her. "Look, bitch, I'm doing this for *him*. If you don't back the fuck off, I'll let him go."

She stopped dead in her tracks, turned, and quickly escaped the area.

Casey guided me over to a bench and sat down with me. "You all right, brother?"

"I...just snapped." I shook my head.

"It happens, man. Sometimes you just have to let them know you aren't to be fucked with." He slapped me on the shoulder. He offered me a pack of cigarettes. I took one and lit it.

"I think I broke my M240."

"I saw that. Good distance. Your form could use some work, though." I couldn't help breaking out into nervous laughter.

Slim came out from his tent with Perro, both of them were laughing. They had watched the whole thing. "You all right, Joe?" Slim asked. He sat down next to me. I was still shaking, and he saw that. "You gonna shoot me?" he asked, grinning.

As much as I wanted to punch him in the face, I couldn't hate him. He had created a monster he couldn't control. "Thinking about it." I smiled.

"Hey man, I don't care that you put that bitch in her place, but don't throw your weapon like it's a javelin again, all right?" He laughed a little and put his arms around me.

"Next time I'll just shoot the fucker."

"Please," Perro added.

Somehow, nothing came of the incident. I got demoted for using Facebook, but not from threatening to kill an NCO and throwing a machine gun through the air. I wish my angry outburst had tempered the brewing insanity of my squad's team leaders, but it didn't.

Creep, someone we all hated, brought out the beast in Slim. Creep had never managed to figure out how to stay awake while on guard. He would set an alarm on his watch and then sleep right through it. He made whomever was on guard shift constantly ask where their relief was. Once he was awakened and pushed into a guard position, he would just fall asleep again.

Slim decided no matter what the commander said, Creep would have someone in the guard tower with him. That order effectively cut our already meager amounts of sleep in half and made us hate the little bastard even more.

To make things worse, Creep was an absolutely disgusting person. We rarely got more than one shower a week. But because most of us hated being covered in our own filth, we would wash ourselves with baby wipes or wet rags. Creep didn't do either—he didn't shower when he had the chance and he didn't wipe off. I'm pretty confident the guy never owned a toothbrush. Sharing the tiny confines of a guard tower with the human embodiment of a Dumpster was something nobody wanted to do.

I was the lucky one to be chosen first to spend the night with him up in the godforsaken, frozen guard tower. I bundled myself up in every piece of winter clothing I had and trudged out into the cold Afghan night. The wind was piercing and cut right through our shoddy guard tower.

"My fiancée says once I make sergeant, we can afford to buy a house," Creep said in his slow drawl. It was slow even for a redneck. He had been talking nonstop since the beginning of our guard shift.

I was pushed all the way against the side of the tower trying to escape his stink. I didn't bother to cover the bright cherry of my cigarette in the night anymore. I was hoping a Taliban RPG gunner would end my misery.

"Is that so..." I said. I could hardly believe he'd actually found a woman willing to have sex with him and wondered if he was lying. He *had* to be lying. At that point, I was just trying to remember what it was like to be warm.

"Yeah. When we get back, we should do a double date." He smiled. I was happy it was so dark I couldn't see his rotting rows of brown teeth.

"I think I'd rather jerk off with a handful of broken glass," I said, flicking the ash off the end of my cigarette. He finally got the hint that I didn't want to talk to him and went silent. At least that's what I thought. I turned to look at him and saw he was leaning against the tower, still standing, fast asleep.

I flicked my still-lit cigarette at him. It bounced off the side of his face, but he didn't wake up. Finally, I turned and smacked him as hard as I could on top of the helmet. He woke up with a start and stared at me through his huge coke-bottle glasses as if he had no idea what he'd done wrong.

"The fuck are you doing? Wake up, shit-bird!" I screamed at him.

"I..." he stuttered. "I wasn't asleep," he said with a straight face.

"Are you fucking high?" I shouted. My breath clouded up in front of my face and mixed with the cigarette smoke. "You know what, just go tell Slim what you just did and I'll finish this goddamn shift by myself."

"But—" Creep started.

"Shut your cock holster and go before I fucking shoot you," I yelled in his face. I pushed him toward the tower's stairs with mitten-covered hands. He slowly turned and trudged down the stairs. If I had known what was going to happen next, I would have just kept my mouth shut and let the idiot sleep.

I finished my guard shift and was replaced by Lip from First Squad. I walked through the freezing night, my eyes watering from the blasting wind. I was stopped dead in my tracks by the sight of Second Squad soldiers filling sandbags by the shower bay.

They were all clad in various states of winter dress and filling up small, green sandbags up with handfuls of rocks. (Spartan had no actual sand.)

"The fuck is going on?" I asked Oldies, who was filling a bag nearby.

"Creep fell asleep on watch again," he said, his fatigue showing on his face.

"And?"

"Slim is making us build a fighting position in the bay; that way he isn't too far from his bed."

"No fucking way." I shook my head. I walked past the toiling soldiers and stepped into the shower bay where I saw Slim, Perro, and Kitty standing. Next to them was the beginning stage of a sandbag bunker being formed in the middle of the bay.

I dropped my weapons on the cold tile floor, stripped off my body armor, and went outside to help everyone dig.

While we filled the bags, we could hear the team leaders listening to music and laughing.

"Fucking assholes," I cursed.

"You used to be one of them," Guapo giggled.

"Yeah, but I wasn't that bad, was I?"

"Not really, but we still hated you," Nan said, scooping up a handful of rocks.

"If it makes you guys feel any better, I hated me too," I said.

"It does a little, actually," Nan said with a smile.

I noticed Creep was nowhere to be found. "Where the hell is Creep?" I asked to no one in particular.

"Slim decided that punishing him didn't work, so he's going to punish us while Creep watches," Nan said.

"That's the dumbest shit I ever heard. How is that going to fix anything?"

"Maybe he's hoping one of us will finally just shoot him." Guapo shrugged, a pile of rocks in his hands.

A terrible rap song started playing over the speakers the team leaders had set up. It was just repeating one lyric over and over again.

"Who the hell is this?" I winced.

"It's Tyga, man," Guapo said. "This song is tight."

"He's just saying 'Rack City Bitch' like, a thousand times. How is this music?" Nan asked.

"What does that even mean?" I shook my head.

"Tits?" Nan quipped.

"Maybe. But a city of tits?"

"It's got to be a strip club," Cali offered. "He's talking about money, too."

"Ah, is that what 'tens, tens, twenties, and fifties, bitch' means?" I asked.

"Who throws tens at strippers? That's just bad economics," Nan said. "I don't even throw singles."

"You guys are retarded." Guapo laughed.

"*We're* retarded? You're the one who likes this shit," I said.

The song ended, and we worked in silence. I hefted a heavy bag of rocks onto my shoulder and followed Nan through the bay doors. The team leaders turned and looked at us.

"Could you be filling those bags any slower?" Kitty sneered.

Before I could make a smart-ass remark, Nan broke out into song. "Rack City, Bitch!" He shouted.

"Rack, Rack City, bitch!" I parroted after him.

The team leaders looked at us as if we'd lost it.

"Tens, tens, twenties on your titties, bitch!" Nan bellowed as he plopped down a sandbag. In the background, Guapo's piercing witch-like cackle echoed off of the walls of the bay.

Creep sat at the edge of his cot not saying a word while we made what seemed like endless numbers of trips outside to fill sandbags. Finally, after a few hours, our shitty sandbag bunker was complete. Even though it was colder than a Michigan winter outside, we were soaked through with sweat and exhausted.

"Why are you relaxing?" Slim snarled at us as we sat down on the cold tile floor. "What kind of shitty fighting position is this? There's no concertina wire, no weapon, no nothing!"

"You want us to set up concertina wire where we sleep?" I asked, shaking my head.

"You have five fucking minutes or you'll be taking it all back outside and trying again," Slim warned. He and the rest of the team leaders stomped outside.

"They want a fighting position?" Nan smiled. "Let's fucking give them one." He walked outside and a few minutes later came back with the explosives crate that was in one of the trucks and a roll of concertina wire. Guapo and Oldies started unrolling the shiny chrome wire in little zigzags through the bay. The razor-like tips of the wire kept getting caught on their clothes, making them speak only in curses.

Nan cracked open the explosive crate and produced a Claymore mine and several bricks of C-4 plastic explosive. He unspooled several feet of wire, propped the Claymore up by the door, and assembled it.

"Where the fuck did you get that?" I gasped. I hadn't seen a Claymore since basic training.

"It was in Slim's truck." Nan laughed to himself as he played around with wires.

"Do you even know how to set that up?" I asked, watching him intently.

"No clue," Nan giggled. He finished screwing in the wires and stood up. The only part of the mine that wasn't set up was the actual detonator. At a glance, it looked primed and ready to go. Next, he pulled the strips off the back of the bricks of C-4 and stuck them all over the walls. Guapo got in on the insanity by grabbing one of our M240B machine guns, placing it in the bunker and loading it. He cackled some more when he ripped the charging handle back.

"This went from zero to sixty real mother fucking quick." Oldies shook his head. He reminded me of Roger Murtaugh and how he was always "too old for this shit." Right down to the bushy mustache and receding hairline.

"That's the only way to do it, man." I smiled at our explosive-laden madness.

"The loaded two-forty is a nice touch," Machete noted. "But I have the cherry on top." He ducked into his shower stall, a place that smelled so bad none of us dared to venture, and came out holding two rocket launchers.

"Should I even ask where you got those?" Oldies scratched his head.

"I stole them from those Dealer guys months ago," Machete said. He leaned the two rocket launchers against the side of the position and sat down on a pile of ammo boxes.

"Is it weird I'm not even surprised by that?" I asked. Everyone just shook their heads.

Slim and the rest of the team leaders confidently walked into the bay and immediately stopped where they stood. Slim glanced down and saw the slightly curved figure of a Claymore mine pointed right up at him. He was so close he could read the "THIS SIDE TOWARD ENEMY" that was stamped on the mine's plastic outer casing. His eyes slowly lifted away from the floor and followed the wires that were screwed into the top that led all the way back to Nan. He was holding the disconnected detonator in his hand.

"What...the...fuck..?" Slim stammered. He locked eyes with the barrel of the loaded machine gun pointed at him, manned by the cackling Guapo.

"Um, Slim?" Perro started pointing up at the blocks of C-4 that were all over the walls.

"You fuckers are nuts!" Slim yelled. First seriously, then he started to laugh so hard his pale face turned beet red and he doubled over. "I fucking love it!" The other team leaders started nervously laughing. "Where did you guys get those rocket launchers?"

"You don't wanna know, boss." Machete gave him a little finger-gun motion. Machete had a tendency to call everyone "boss." A habit that drove me fucking insane.

"Noted," Slim said. He walked over to the dry erase board we used to plan missions and organize tower guard. He picked up a marker and next to where it said "Tower One" and "Tower Two" he wrote "OP Creep."

"You'll be manning our new OP here throughout the night like it was a guard tower." He smiled.

All of our faces dropped. We thought the punishment was building that stupid bunker in the middle of the freezing cold night. We never actually thought we would have to man it. To make matters worse, he wrote my name next to the first shift even though I had just gotten off one.

"Kassabian, you have first watch. Everyone get some sleep while you can," Slim ordered and walked back out of the bay with the other team leaders in tow.

Everyone slowly shuffled back into their stalls to sleep. I walked back to where I'd dropped my gear and put it back on. I dragged my feet over to the bunker and sat down on a pile of uncomfortable rock-filled sandbags. I glanced down at my watch; it read 0330. "Fuck this,"

I said to no one. I leaned my head against the side of the bunker and went to sleep.

A few weeks later, our squad was sent packing to FOB Walton to get our trucks worked on. Also to spend ungodly amounts of money on nicotine and energy drinks at the base's store. The few hours we spent at Walton were dedicated to doing as much damage as humanly possible.

In their chow hall, we filled our pockets with stolen snacks. We broke into the showers that we weren't allowed to use and used up all of their hot water. Most of the guys took the opportunity to trim their body hair and leave it all over the shower area. It got to the point where elements of our command structure started watching us like hawks while we were at the base.

"Second Squad!" Slim yelled at us. We were all in various stages of working on our trucks. Oldies was switching out his fifth or so windshield of our tour. The rest of us were trying to patch up the many leaks and cracks our trucks had accumulated over the last few weeks. "Go up to the company building and stand by," Slim ordered and walked off.

I almost felt sorry for the soldiers of our company who were stuck at Walton. Our first sergeant, a few senior NCOs, communications soldiers, and our long-lost former First Squad leader, Olly, all lived here. There were about three mechanics who tried their best not to be seen or heard. None of them really had jobs.

We trudged across Walton's gravel roads and made our way to our company building. It was a massive wooden shack that was clearly put together by people who had no idea what they were doing. It was still better than an Afghan shower bay, though. We walked up the building's creaky stairs and went inside.

Standing in the room in front of us was Gunny. He had his ever-present crooked smile on his face and was wearing a brand-new uniform.

"Holy shit," Nan said. "Shouldn't you be in a hospital or something?"

"You really thought I was going to stay in a hospital?" Gunny smiled.

We all filed through and shook his hand. I couldn't keep from hugging the bastard. Last time I'd seen him, he was dying on a road in a godforsaken part of Kandahar.

"You guys are making it seem like I was hurt badly or something." Gunny chuckled.

"So you're back? You're going to be our platoon sergeant?" I asked with probably a little too much hope in my voice.

Slim stepped into the room followed by the team leaders. "Yep," Slim smiled. "Thank fucking God for that."

I looked around, and everyone looked happy for the first time in a long while. We weren't happy that we would have to load that extra twenty pounds of shit Gunny always made us carry back into our bags. We weren't happy we would start having to cut our hair and shave again. We were just happy everything was back to normal.

"So, I heard something about an OP Creep?" Gunny asked the room full of soldiers and we all started laughing.

CHAPTER 29

TAKING A BREATHER

MY TOTAL INABILITY TO SLEEP was starting to take its toll. Sometimes I would go several days only getting a few minutes of sleep at a time. I would blank out momentarily in the middle of something like eating, walking on a patrol, or taking a dump. I'd wake up with a start, not entirely sure what was going on around me.

No matter what I tried, I couldn't sleep. Nan gave me some of the pills he was prescribed, but they had no effect. I would lie on my cot half-drunk and high from sleeping pills. Sleep would still elude me.

I thought no one caught on that I was actively putting their lives in danger. I was never caught with my eyes closed when it mattered. I assumed most people just thought I had the mid-deployment malaise that everyone else had.

I should have known better. One day, while in the middle of what seemed like an endless string of cigarettes, Slim and Gunny approached me. "How are things going?" Slim asked with genuine kindness. I could tell he was legitimately worried about me. That made me feel even worse.

"I'm good," I answered.

"We can see that you're hurting," Slim pointed out. I guess I wasn't as good as faking it as I thought.

"You look like a corpse," Gunny added helpfully. He was right, my eyes and face were more sunken than normal. When you're moving through the world half asleep, you kind of forget to eat. I was surviving off mostly caffeine and nicotine.

"Thanks." I gave a weak smile.

"Seriously, you look terrible even for you," Gunny continued. "We're sending you and a few other people to FOB Walton to relax for a few days."

I gave him a weird look. "Relax?" I asked. "I...don't understand."

"There's a little camp inside Walton for people..." Slim began.

"I don't need a day off. I'm not a pussy," I interrupted.

"Well," Slim smiled and put his hand on my shoulder, "you don't have a choice. You, Nan, Kitty, Machete, and Perro are leaving today. Pack enough shit for three days."

I groaned and stomped away to pack my bags. Maybe because they were making a few other people go, they weren't really onto me falling apart yet. Or maybe we were all going crazy at the same time. I knew why they were sending Nan. The dude had lost his mind when he was blown up by a grenade. Something in his head got scrambled.

As for Kitty and Perro, I could only guess Kitty was going because whenever there was an easy duty or a way to get out of work, she would be there. I didn't really understand why Machete was going. Maybe they hoped he would finally take a shower.

I ducked into my little shower stall and started shoving things into my backpack without really looking. I slapped my combat gear on and awkwardly waddled outside trying to balance my bag, rifle, and my helmet in my hands. The others who were picked for our wonderful retreat to the base were down the street, ready and waiting for our ride.

I plopped down in the rocks next to Nan.

"This is fucking stupid." Nan said.

"Why would they send us to Walton to relax? It's down the fucking street!" I added.

"Remember, before you get too pissed, people actually live full-time at the place we are being sent to for relaxation." Nan gave a little smile and adjusted his glasses.

"Mother fucker." I cursed.

"Look at it this way, they have the internet there. We can load up on new porn," Nan said, fumbling around in his pocket for a pack of cigarettes.

"I don't know man. I prefer the old standbys. They've been good to me."

"There's plenty of fish in the sea, bro," Nan said, lighting his cigarette.

First Squad had finally climbed into their trucks and pulled them out for us to get in for the ten-minute drive to FOB Walton.

As we drove through the gates of FOB Walton, I watched the gate guards scramble around and pull the security gate out of the way as if we had Taliban hot on our heels or something. Most of them were wearing more gear than any of us in the trucks. It was hard not to notice that their gear still looked brand new. Mine was a shit-brown color highlighted by splashes of blood and dip spit. I looked like a modern art masterpiece.

The trucks pulled up next to a compound hidden away behind another wall of Hesco baskets. Hanging over the gate was a little sign that read "The Oasis."

"That's the name they're going with?" Nan laughed as we climbed out of the trucks.

"Doesn't that imply some kind of body of water?" I pointed out, shrugging.

We walked through the doors and into a small tent. The tent's air conditioning was the best thing I had felt in a long time. We had air conditioners back at Spartan, but they were so overworked and choked with dust they struggled just to make our areas livable.

A fat guy sat behind a little desk and welcomed us to The Oasis. "Hey, guys!" he chirped. He was way too happy. I glared at him. "Go ahead and sign in." He pushed a little clipboard toward us. "And we'll go around back and turn in your weapons for your stay."

Our eyes all got wide.

"Turn our weapons in?" Nan stuttered a little. "What if we get attacked?"

"Come on man, you're at Walton. You're safe here." The fat guy smiled. "I want you to think of this place as a safety zone," he began.

I stopped him. "I'll give you my weapons if you don't finish that sentence." I groaned, signed my name, and walked through to the other side of the tent.

The Oasis was a big area with tents set up in nice neat rows. It had a little seating area in the middle, with nice picnic tables flawlessly lined up. It all looked just a little too groomed for being in the middle of Kandahar.

"Your weapons, please?" the fat guy asked me with his hands out. I handed over my rifle, grenade launcher, and pistol. The fat guy fumbled with all my weapons but eventually put them all into a locker. One by one, we each handed over the one constant we had had in Afghanistan.

Your laptop could break, your sleep could be interrupted, your wife or girlfriend could leave you, but you knew your weapon would always be there for you. I felt naked with my empty holster slapping against my hip as I walked. I turned around and started walking to the tent Nan and I had signed into.

"We are going to chow," Kitty called out.

"Have fun." I waved back at them.

"No, we are all going to chow as a squad," Kitty insisted. Even though she rarely acted like it, she still technically outranked me. I didn't care. Gunny sent me to Walton to relax and possibly even to sleep. Kitty wasn't going to stop me from doing that.

"Nah, I'm good." I kept walking.

Nan nudged me a little. "She could make our stay here a living hell. Just listen to her," he said.

"I'm sick of that bitch. She thinks she's in charge of our vacation? Fuck her," I shot back a little too loud. She heard me say it. What I had meant to be just a bit of minor insubordination was about to get much more severe.

"*What* did you say?" Kitty screamed at me.

I went all in. "Fuck you!" She'd already heard me; might as well go for it. "Quit acting like your rank fucking means anything, you useless fuck!" I spat.

Nan took a little sidestep away from me.

"We'll see what happens when Slim finds out about this," Kitty said and stomped out of the compound toward the chow hall.

For some reason it was never explained to me why Slim would always humor her. Or at least he did to her face. He would hang out with us afterward and we would laugh about how badly we pissed her off but never got in trouble.

Nan laughed and offered me a cigarette. He must have seen that I was shaking with blind anger. I steadied the cigarette and put it in my mouth. Nan lit it for me. I heard laughing somewhere behind us. I turned and saw the fat guy locking his weapons locker.

"What's so fucking funny?" I snarled, smoke coming from my mouth.

"Calm down, tiger." The fat guy smiled. "That shit always happens once units get here." He laughed a little harder. "Dickhead NCOs think they can micromanage the relaxation of soldiers who are already at their breaking point." He walked back to his front office tent.

Nan started laughing. "You mean there's more Kittys out there?"

"God, I hope not," I said through clenched teeth.

Nan and I walked into our tent to find a surprise: the whole tent had been partitioned into individual rooms with pieces of wood. Inside each room, which all had locks on the doors, was a real bed. I sat down on my bed to find it felt like what dreams are made of. My ass sank into the cloud of a mattress. I laid back into the miracle mattress and let its incredible comfort engulf me.

My door opened and Nan came in and sat on my bed. "You want to check out their gym?" he asked.

"Of course," I said, getting up.

We walked across the rocks and into another tent. It was the first time I had been in a purposefully-built gym in nearly a year. Machines were in gleaming rows with dumbbells all set in their own notches on a shiny new rack.

"It isn't as good as what we have at Spartan," I complained.

"You mean the rusty barbells, mismatched dumbbells, and broken treadmill? Or is working outside in the dirt under the blazing sun what you're missing?" Nan said.

"It builds character."

"It builds tetanus," he said.

We decided to work out. We dragged their clean and pristine weights outside onto the rocks. A small Indian guy who was in charge of keeping the gym clean came out and yelled at us, but we ignored him.

Perro walked by as I dropped a barbell loaded with weights and it clanged off the rocks. "What, were you homesick?" he laughed.

"Something like that," I panted.

After our workout, I went to the shower trailer. It was gleaming white and spotless. There were no masses of pubic hair clogging the drain or the sounds of anyone jerking off in the shower next to you. Absent were the six inches of standing water at the bottom that refused to drain. I turned the shower on and burning hot water came out of the chrome showerhead with enough pressure to make me step back.

I stepped into the shower, and even though the water was brutally hot, I stood there and let it scald me. It felt amazing. It was my first real shower in a few weeks. It was a nice contrast to the short, horribly cold ones with no water pressure we were forced to take at Spartan. I stayed in the shower until the water started to go cold on me. I had stained the pearly-white shower brown with the built-up filth from my body.

Nan and I met up to go to the chow hall. We were in a weird daze and not really sure of what to do. We had no patrol or guard shifts to get ready for. We had nothing to rush around for. Normally, we had to slam down food whenever we could get it, often at strange times. If we waited until after we got back from patrol, there wouldn't be any food left. Being stuck at Walton, we had all the time in the world to eat and go back for seconds even though we weren't supposed to.

We filled our pockets with energy drinks and snacks, even though we didn't really need to steal them anymore. We were so used to stealing shit from Walton's chow hall it just felt weird leaving without bulging pockets. The Hooligans used Walton as little more than a giant mark. Even though we had logistical and supply units from our company stationed at Walton, we could never get anything from them.

When Gunny took over, he unleashed us on Walton as if we were criminals. Like when we stole the air conditioner from Camp Nathan Smith. He always told us, "They have so much they won't notice it's missing." I don't know how much of that was true, but I know I didn't care if they did notice. Gunny would tell us what Camp Spartan needed and let us loose on Walton to steal it.

The best score we ever had was after Bugsy was out walking around having a smoke and noticed a massive shipping container full of mattresses. At the time, we were all sleeping on army-issue cots that were hard to distinguish from the concrete floor. Bugsy ran to Gunny and told him about what he saw. Gunny had us round up all our trucks and rush over to the container. We shoved mattresses anywhere they would fit. We strapped them to the sides of our trucks with rope and stacked them on top next to our gunners. Somehow we were never caught.

Now Nan and I walked around the base and stopped at the bazaar. The bazaar was a tiny shanty town built near the base's wall and staffed by locals. In some failed attempt to bolster the local economy, they let a few Afghans sell whatever they could get their hands on to the soldiers that lived on the base.

That mostly meant buying badly bootlegged DVDs, purses, and clothes. If you talked to the right person, you could buy weed, booze, and old Soviet military gear. Nothing had a set price, and you could try to talk them down or threaten them with physical violence to get a better deal.

I only used the bazaar to stock up on the newest movies that were out in the U.S. It was a hit or miss type thing. Sometimes the bootlegs you bought were near perfect, other times the person videotaping the screen had only managed to get half the movie. Sometimes the damn DVDs were blank.

After we'd loaded up on bootleg DVDs, we retreated to our tents in the Oasis. I sank into my mattress, but I still couldn't sleep. I stayed awake and stared at the ceiling of my tent as it rippled in the wind. Everything in my being was exhausted. I was so tired it physically hurt.

Everything ached, and I hadn't slept in so long that everything kind of felt disconnected, as if I was staring out just above a bonfire. My eyes burned and were blood red. I started to think I might have to talk to someone. I got out of my bed and walked down the narrow plywood hallway to where Nan was staying. I knocked on his door.

"You awake?" I asked.

"Why?" He groaned.

"Um, I think I'm going crazy?" I mused.

"All right, I'm awake."

I pushed his door open and saw him propped up half-naked in his bed. "Why do you think you're going crazy?"

I went through everything that had been happening to me. The total lack of sleep, the nightmares when I did fall asleep, and the impact it had been having on me.

"Jesus, man, maybe you should talk to someone."

"Can you imagine what people would say about me if I had to see a shrink?" I shook my head. "Gunny would take my team leader position in a heartbeat."

"I thought you hated being a team leader." Nan laughed. He popped a cigarette in his lips and lit it not seeming to care we were inside a tent.

"I do," I assured him. "I hate everything about it and my soldiers are retarded. But if I get fired, I could get sent to First Squad or another platoon or something."

"None of that will matter if you lose your fucking mind," he pointed out.

"Fuck." I knew he was making sense, but I didn't want to hear it. We had always been told that if you needed help, no one would ever stop you and it would stay between you and your command. Everyone knew that was a bunch of shit. As much as I loved Slim, I knew he would eventually tell someone I was going crazy. It would trickle down to the soldiers, and none of them would ever respect me again. I would be called a pussy and a coward for it. I would lose my position and probably be kicked over to a different platoon. There was no way I could do it.

"I can't." I shook my head.

"I know." Nan shrugged.

"You're not going to tell anyone are you?" I asked.

"Hell no, dude. It's not like you went running around telling people I threatened you with a grenade."

"Or you that you stabbed me."

"Or that I stabbed you." Nan laughed, smoke escaping his mouth. "I'm going to go email Satan," he said, getting up. Satan was the name he had given his wife. I had known Nan for over two years, and that was the only name I ever heard him call her. He insisted to everyone that he really did love her. "You try to get some sleep." He patted me on the shoulder and walked out of the room. The sounds of his flip-flops echoed down the plywood hallway.

Back in my room I sank into my mattress. I stared up at the tan tent ceiling until I drifted off.

I awoke a short time later on the floor in a puddle of sweat. My heart was slamming in my chest, and I had an overwhelming sense of dread and fear. My room was trashed. My bags were thrown everywhere, and my clothes were scattered. I saw my cell phone shattered in pieces on the ground.

I panicked and ran outside. It felt like my world was closing in around me all of a sudden. I couldn't sleep, I had nightmares, but I never thought I was actually crazy. At first, I tried to tell myself that someone had snuck into my room and wrecked it for reasons not known to me. But I knew that didn't make any sense. Waking up on the floor in a trashed room really drove home what I was trying to dodge: I was losing my goddamn mind.

I lit a cigarette and paced. I was still exhausted, but there was no way I was going back in there. It was the scene of where my mind had finally snapped. I sucked down one cigarette and then another. Eventually, I did go back to my room. Somehow it seemed like even more of a mess than when I'd first woken up in the middle of it. I rummaged around in the piles of clothes and gear I had thrown everywhere and found a pill bottle. I popped it open and ate a few sleeping pills.

I walked outside and laid down on a bench in the smoking area. The edges of my world got foggy and the stars in the crystal clear night sky started blurring together. Whether I blacked out from the narcotics in my bloodstream or actually fell asleep, I don't know. I slipped off into the first stress-free sleep I'd had in a very, very long time.

CHAPTER 30

SAYING GOODBYE TO CAMP SPARTAN

THE TIME HAD FINALLY COME to pack up our Camp Spartan home away from home. A new National Guard unit that had just gotten to Afghanistan was going to replace all the platoons of our company at all the far-flung bases we were scattered to. We would be moving into Walton with the logistic and supply units. Not everyone was happy about that.

"How the fuck are some weekend warriors going to keep a lid on Kandahar?" Cali wondered aloud. National Guard soldiers were known throughout the active duty army as being subpar at best. Politely called "citizen soldiers," the National Guard only trained for a few days out of the month. Their gear was made up of hand-me-downs from the older shit the active duty didn't want, and almost every single soldier I had ever seen looked as if they had either been pulled from some shitty ghetto or the buffet line.

"To be fair, we haven't exactly done a great job at that either," Nan said with a laugh. He was telling the truth. Almost daily attacks around the city were normal. The Afghan police were losing nearly one guy a day to shootings, bombings, and grenade attacks. Most of them had stopped showing up to work months ago.

"They're going to get massacred," I said, kicking little rocks around while we sat out on the smoking bench. "We've spent the last couple months pissing everyone and their mother off in this slum. Summer is just around the corner...doesn't sound promising for them."

"They're going to take one look at those pudgy Nasty Girls and know they can take them," Cali said. Nasty Girls was the loving nickname active duty gave the National Guard. We weren't very creative.

"Do we have to train them when they get here?" I asked.

Nan took a drag from his cigarette and blew smoke through his nose. "I heard Perro and Slim talking about it. Only a few of us are going to stay back here and train them. The rest of us are going to Walton," Nan answered.

"Great," I puffed smoke out of my mouth. "So only a few of us will get killed because of their stupidity rather than all of us."

"See? And you said you were a pessimist," Nan joked.

We started packing our bags and various loose ends a short time later. It was unbelievable how much bullshit a soldier managed to accumulate when they only had living space equal to a hallway closet. I stuffed pile after pile of bootleg DVDs into my duffle bags.

A bunch of my clothes had gone missing over the course of the past few months, which freed up a bunch of space. It happened almost every time a group of soldiers lived together. Everyone wore exactly the same thing and eventually your shit would get mixed together. No matter how hard you tried, eventually you would find yourself wearing someone else's shirt or pants.

Of course, some of the people in my squad were just no-good, thieving dickheads. There was a saying, "There is only one thief in the army; everyone else is just trying to get their shit back." You could catch someone red-handed wearing something of yours and when confronted, they would just shrug and say they thought it was theirs. You could never really tell whether someone was lying or not.

I had stacked my duffle bags neatly outside my shower stall and thrown away probably two dozen bottles filled with dip spit. I swept out piles of cigarette butts and empty Rip-It cans. I looked down the bay; everyone seemed to be doing the same thing.

We heard a rumble at the gates, stopped working, and meandered our way outside. Half-dressed and unshaven, we lumbered to the front gate to see the newcomers. Their trucks were all uniform, neat, and clean. Their windows had stickers on them as if they'd just come off the factory floor.

The trucks came to a stop, and the doors kicked open. Fresh-faced soldiers climbed down from their trucks and landed on the rocks. Their gear was crisp and brand new. There were probably a few tags still attached somewhere. They saw the huddle of humanity that had gathered by the shower bays and looked shocked.

We were gaunt and sunburned. We stared at them with hollow eyes and sunken faces. Most of us had dust caked on our faces and weren't even wearing shoes. We looked like extras from a George Romero movie.

"Welcome to the thunder dome, bitches." Cali smiled. He spat out a wad of dip spit for effect.

"Oh, Cali, be nice to our new guests," I said, laughing.

"Should I show them to the shower stalls they will be living in or the bathroom facilities that don't function?" Nan asked.

"Maybe the guard towers we've spent the last five months furiously masturbating in," Guapo offered.

"Those are my favorite." Cali guffawed.

An overweight sergeant with unblemished gear walked up to the group of us. It may have just been because he was wearing an ill-fitting helmet, but he gave the impression of looking down his nose at us. "Can you point me to the TOC?" he asked. Without a word in response, I pointed to the Afghan bathhouse where our dark, dank, TOC resided. "Is that how you talk to an NCO?" the fat sergeant snorted at me.

"To be fair, I didn't even say anything to you." I shrugged and walked back to the shower stalls.

On Slim's orders, it didn't take long before all our bags were piled outside near our trucks. Even he looked excited to get out of that place. It was one step closer to going home. I saw Slim stuff handfuls of grenades and ammo into his bags from our ammunition point—the same point that had the badly repaired grenade that Nan had threatened us with a few months back. I asked Slim why he was pilfering the ammo point.

"Fuck these guys," Slim cursed. "We still have a few more months in this shithole, and I don't want to find myself lacking a grenade at a bad time."

"Fair enough," I nodded. "You might want to leave that one, though." I pointed to a grenade that was wrapped in tape and placed away from everything else.

"Why?"

"Just trust me." I slapped him on the back and walked out.

We stuffed our bags into our trucks. It was a tight fit because the MATV wasn't designed for a cargo load. Our rucksacks and bags were haphazardly lashed down with bungee cords and rope anywhere we could fit them. Normally, when units switch out, the outgoing unit is supposed to give the incoming unit a tour of the area. Like what the Dealer soldiers did for us.

This time was a little different. We weren't leaving Afghanistan yet, and we were taking over a different area around Walton, so we didn't really have time to dick around and teach these guys how to survive in Kandahar. The majority of us were getting sent to Walton as soon as possible while Slim, Perro, and Cali were going to stay behind and half-ass their way through the tour of the area.

The same National Guard unit was taking over all the outlying bases we had been running over the course of the last several months. That included taking over training the Afghan police, dealing with the locals, and most important, living in those horrible stalls we had called home.

A lot of the guys acted as if they were pissed that we were being moved out. They were being forced out of a place that no one had any business living in, but it was a place we had turned into a kind of dysfunctional home and now someone was taking it away.

Not me. We were moving to the closest thing there was to a paradise in the middle of Kandahar. I was excited. Our missions would be entirely mounted, and we wouldn't have to live with the Afghan police anymore. I tried to hide my excitement while everyone bitched and complained about losing our beloved Spartan to a unit of weekend warriors.

The looks of disgust and revulsion on the faces of the guardsmen as they surveyed where they were going to be living were priceless. "Where are the bathrooms?" a guardsmen asked no one in particular.

"Over there, champ," Memphis said in his thick southern drawl. He pointed to the line of dingy port-o-johns. Most of them were overflowing with shit, piss, and discarded *Maxim* magazines.

"In case you were wondering what that smell was," Guapo cackled. The guardsman didn't say anything in response. His face sank.

Our little unscheduled tour brought us into the shower bay next. Ammunition sat discarded all over the tile floor. In front of the massive fighting position we had to build as punishment, C-4 explosive was still stuck to the walls and a Claymore mine was pointed toward the doors. The whole bay smelled like fermented dip spit and cigarette smoke with a slight tinge of sweaty balls. That was home.

"You know, I thought you guys were idiots for saying you were going to miss this place. But now that these assholes are moving in...I don't even know how I feel," I struggled with the words.

"You know it's okay to hate something and still miss it," Nan said. "This place is miserable, but we made it our own little world. Shit, Walrus's kid was conceived here." He gave a small smile. "Whether we like it or not, this pile of shit shower bay is a part of us now."

"Goddamn, that's depressing." I shook my head.

"Isn't it, though?" Nan laughed.

Some of the Guardsmen started bringing in their bags and plopping them down in front of certain shower stalls. I saw a guy set his rucksack down in front of the stall I had called home just an hour before. He peeked his head inside and looked around in disgust.

"It could be worse," I mumbled to him.

He gave me a nasty look. "How, exactly?"

"You know those tents outside? That's where our Third Platoon lives." I gestured outside. "You live in the middle of one of the worst parts of Kandahar City now, the possibility that someone fires some rockets at you in the next few months is pretty high. Would you rather have some tent fabric or an Afghan bathhouse between you and that explosion?"

The guy didn't say anything. He still had the same look on his face. He slowly turned back to his bags and started pushing them into my former stall.

With our bags packed and our home being desecrated by National Guardsmen, it was time to say goodbye. We climbed into our trucks and pulled out of Spartan. You would have thought we would have been happy or excited to be one step closer to going home. We weren't. We all sat in silence staring out the windows of the truck. We rolled out of our tiny world and into Kandahar City.

CHAPTER 31

HUGO CHAVEZ THE PSYCHIATRIST

ONE OF THE DOWNSIDES TO living in something that could reasonably be called a society again was that we had to start following certain rules. Every few months, the army regularly made its soldiers go through health screenings. I began to think it was just because they had brought us back in from outside their base and were afraid of what diseases we might have brought with us.

Like Kandahar Air Field, Walton had some soldiers who would never actually leave its walls during their tour in Afghanistan. Walton would become their whole world and their whole war.

Unlike where we had just come from, Walton had actual doctors, nurses, and medical specialists. They had medications other than ibuprofen and water. Our medics tried their best out in the wilds of Kandahar City, but unless you were bleeding to death, they generally lacked helpful medical knowledge.

On our unit's orders, we woke up early one morning and lined up outside the aid station. The aid station was a huge wooden building that was bigger than any structure we had at Spartan. The floors were uneven, and the building was nothing more than a glorified wooden shack. We sat in the waiting room and read months-old *Maxim* magazines that were full of half-naked women.

I noticed they had a weapons rack in the waiting area. Before we were allowed to talk to one of the medics, we had to turn in our weapons. That's when it hit me: these weren't normal checkups. We were being psychologically screened.

"Fuck, I think we have to talk to a shrink," I half whispered, half yelled. A young looking woman sitting behind the desk in the waiting room shot me a dirty look.

"Why do you think that?" Nan asked.

I pointed to the weapons rack. "Why else would they be disarming us?"

"Shit, you're right." Nan looked surprised.

"Do we lie or tell the truth?" Machete asked.

"When do you ever tell the truth to an army doctor?" I retorted. You had to lie about injuries or mental issues or your unit's leadership would think you were just some pussy trying to milk the government for a paycheck or were trying to get out of work.

A young soldier called my name from a clipboard. I glanced around and slowly stood up. I handed my rifle over to Nan and followed the young soldier into a separate room. I sat on an uncomfortable wooden bench and waited.

"The medic will be with you shortly," chimed the young soldier; she walked out of the room, leaving me there with my thoughts.

The room was mostly bare. The walls were empty; everything was a plain plywood pattern and smelled like disinfectant. The door swung open again and in walked the medic. "Hi, Specialist, how are you feeling today?" he asked, smiling.

"Wonderful," I deadpanned.

"I see according to your records you sought help for sleep disturbances in the past?" he asked.

I was immediately speechless. I had no idea they actually had access to our medical records.

"Um, yeah," I stammered.

"How's that going?" he asked, taking a closer look at me.

I looked like a walking corpse. If insomnia had an awareness poster, I would have been on it. "I think you already know the answer to that." I half-smiled at him.

"Yeah. You look pretty rough. When was the last time you had a full night's sleep?"

"Probably the last time I was in America," I tried to joke, but I knew even that wasn't true. When I was in Tampa Bay, I couldn't sleep unless I was shitfaced.

"Don't worry, this is completely normal," he tried to reassure me. "Your unit has been beaten up, and it's to be expected that you're feeling the effects."

"I was just hoping for some more powerful sleeping meds," I said flatly.

"I'm going to put you in for a psych screening. Drugs won't fix this alone," he said, writing something down on a piece of paper.

"What? But I..."

"Look, man, you only have a few months left here in the country, and when you get home, you're getting out, right?"

"Well, yeah," I answered. There was nothing I wanted more than to get out of the army.

"Maybe it's time you start worrying about *you* then. Because the army sure fucking won't. Just take the screening for me?" He patted me on the shoulder. He handed me a little paper slip with an appointment date on it and walked out of the room.

Fuck, I thought. How in the hell was I going to explain this without being labeled a pussy? I stuffed the paper in my pocket and walked back into the waiting room.

I collected my rifle from the rack and walked back to our tents. When they moved us to Walton, they stuffed us into giant tents that had long rows of beds and plywood floors that creaked with every step. No walls or sheets were erected to provide any privacy. The massive open area made me miss the cozy confines of my shower stall. It probably didn't help that my cot was right next to Memphis, and he still smelled like a Dumpster.

I sat down on my creaky bed and fished around in my pocket for my appointment slip. I had to go back the next day. That date didn't mean anything to me at first, but as I thought about it, I realized I would miss a mission. The mission was nothing special. Just to drive around to Afghan police bases to make sure they were actually reporting for work. *But I would have to miss a mission.* That wasn't something anyone was allowed to do unless they were close to dead or they were on leave.

I walked over to Slim's tent and opened the shoddy wooden door. The NCOs' tent had plywood sheets built up into walls so that each person had his or her own room. The walls were uneven and shot off at odd angles. Even though it looked like something you would see in a slum, I was jealous of their level of privacy. I knocked on the door labeled with "Staff Sergeant Slim" and entered because I had no manners.

Slim was sitting on his bed playing on his laptop. "What's up, man?" he asked, removing a massive set of headphones from his head.

"I had to talk to the doctor today..." I started.

"About your back?" he asked. He knew my back pain was nearly crippling me. Some days I needed help getting out of bed. I was eating so many ibuprofen pills I was probably causing myself irreversible kidney damage. Nothing kept the pain at bay.

"No..." I handed him the slip, and he took it from me.

Slim studied it and glanced up at me. "Oh, shit," he began. "You aren't going to kill yourself or some shit are you?"

"God dammit, dude, no," I spat, snatching the paper slip. "I just can't sleep, and they are freaking out over it."

"So just get some drugs and move on," he said turning back to his laptop.

"Yeah, whatever. I'm not in trouble for missing the mission am I?" I asked.

"No. These missions here are bullshit. No worries. I'm pretty sure we could just not go on them and no one would give a shit except maybe Gunny."

"Hasn't that been true of all our missions since day one?"

"We just have to survive for a few more months. I don't care if they have us cleaning toilets, as long as they send us home on time," Slim said. I was in agreement. I just wanted to go home.

The next day, I walked back to the wooden building and sat in the waiting room again. The overly cheerful female soldier behind the desk took my rifle, and I went and sat in a different room. It wasn't the one where I'd talked to the medic the day before. It was a big empty room with just two chairs facing each other. It looked more like an interrogation room than somewhere you would go to get healthcare.

I sat down in one of the seats and waited. After a few moments the door to the room flung open and in walked a short, fat captain. His uniform was a few sizes too small, and he was wearing huge safety glasses. He was a dead ringer for Venezuela's dictator Hugo Chavez, and it was kind of funny. He sat down on the chair opposite me and smiled.

"Nice to meet you, Joseph. I am Captain Hugo." He beamed.

"Hi," I groaned. The guy was overwhelming. He had that fake happiness that customer service people have that makes you hate them.

"I hear you're having a hard time sleeping?"

"Yeah...I've tried everything, and it's not working. Maybe if I can get something stronger ..." I began.

"I don't believe in giving drugs to people," he said, still smiling.

"Why am I here then?" I asked.

"Something is causing you not to be able to sleep. I want to find out what that is so we can work it out."

"God dammit," I swore under my breath.

"What was that?" he asked through his ceaseless smile.

"Oh, nothing. So how do we go about working this out?" I was there under Hugo's orders. It wasn't like I was allowed to leave.

"We go back to traumatic incidents you've been through, and we will talk about them. I will make you focus on certain aspects of them until you're comfortable."

My expression sank. That sounded like the last thing on earth I wanted to do. Before I could open my mouth to say anything, he handed me another appointment slip. It was dated for the next day.

"We will start tomorrow morning." He gave me a wide, fake smile, then he got up and walked out of the room.

I left the building still trying to understand what I had gotten myself into. I was running scenarios through my head trying to figure out a way to get out of these appointments. I went back to my tent and resigned myself to being psychoanalyzed the next day. I thought it over and came to the conclusion I was going to try to work with him, even though I really didn't want to.

I wasn't afraid I'd be thought of as a pussy by my comrades; just going to the appointments was enough to do that. Complying wouldn't make that any worse. And there was always the small chance it would actually help. I lay sleeplessly on my cot as my thoughts sprinted through my head.

The next morning I sat up on my cot, having achieved a few fitful minutes of sleep throughout the night. My eyes burned, and hot, blinding pain shot up my back. Those sensations had become my morning companions over the course of the last few weeks. I grabbed onto one of the tent's support beams and hauled myself to my feet.

I walked out of the tent and stomped across the rocks to the aid station. I pushed the wooden door open and prepared to sit down in the waiting room, but the smiling girl behind the desk motioned for me to go back. She took my rifle and set it aside. I would never get used to being unarmed. The wooden floor creaked and moaned as I walked down the hallway to the room set aside for Hugo and me.

Hugo was sitting and smiling in his little metal chair. "Please sit." He motioned with his hand. His creepy fake smile made what was left of my hair stand on end. His teeth were almost too white. I sat down in the metal folding chair he had set out for me. "Okay, we are going to start slow," he began. "This type of therapy is very...aggressive." He never stopped smiling.

"Aggressive?" I asked. His wording made me think he was going to hook my head up to a car battery and shock the piss out of me.

"It is not easy to go through. You will see." He smiled. I looked around the empty room. What was he going to use in aggressive therapy?

"We are going to start from the beginning. From your childhood."

I had a few choice stories picked out for when he brought that up. "Okay...so..." but before I could say anything he cut me off.

"Wait," he interrupted. "I am going to be moving my finger back and forth like this." He moved his finger back and forth in front of my face. "I want you to follow it back and forth while you tell your story. Don't focus on me at all."

I was literally speechless. That was the treatment. He was going to attempt to finger-wag me back to the picture of mental health.

He made that "treatment" sound like it was the be-all end-all of therapy. It was so aggressive! The asshole was just wiggling his finger at me while I was supposed to pour out my heart to him. Follow his goddamn finger waggle and I would be fucking cured. I would sleep like a baby, and all my nightmares would just vanish. Fuck him. Fuck that whole goddamn aid station that made me think I needed this finger wiggling bullshit.

I stood up in my chair so fast it fell over behind me.

"What's wrong...?" he glanced down at his paperwork. "...Joseph?" The asshole who wanted to help me had never even bothered to learn my name.

"Fuck this," I spat. I stormed out of the room and down the hallway. I walked into the waiting room and grabbed my rifle and kicked open the aid station door. I stomped across the rocks, kicking a few into the air as I went. I'd made my squad think I was a pussy for absolutely no fucking reason. I didn't even get any better sleeping pills out of it. He could have at least given me some pain medicine to misuse like a normal army doctor.

Not too long after that, Slim and Gunny tracked me down. It was quickly reported to my unit that I had stormed out and told an officer to go fuck himself. I told them what had happened, and they laughed.

"He wagged his finger?" Slim laughed. "Was that seriously his idea of a cure?"

"Apparently. He made it sound like it was cutting-edge shit, too," I said.

"No wonder so many people are killing themselves." Gunny shook his head. "Are you going to be okay?" I could tell he really cared about me. He cared about all of us, even if he didn't know how to show it.

"Yeah, I'll live." I shrugged. My sleeping issues weren't going to solve themselves, and I was falling apart at the seams. I didn't want them to know that, though. What I was going through wasn't any different than what any of the other soldiers were going through.

Ever since Nan had gotten blown up, he took a flying leap off the deep end. Slim would regularly snap and attack his own soldiers, whom he considered his friends. I don't think Pip ever recovered from being covered in Gunny's blood. I heard Sal had to retreat to a special room in the hospital at the airfield where he would spend time with a service dog. We were all in various stages of losing it. Afghanistan had broken our minds and most parts of our bodies.

I kept telling myself I only had to hold it together—whatever was left of me—for a few more weeks. I could keep forcing my body to function on a few scant minutes of sleep. I could wince through everyday life and try to ignore the burning in my spine. Everything would be better once I got home.

At least that's what I kept telling myself.

CHAPTER 32

OPERATION GRIZZLY GANG-BANG 2: ELECTRIC BOOGALOO

IT WAS OUR LAST BIG mission. We dubbed it Grizzly Gang Bang Two because we knew it was going to be as big a cluster fuck as the first one. Unlike the first operation, we weren't hunting down any Taliban warlords or capturing anyone important. We weren't even going to try to go out and get in a fight.

Instead of sitting on our asses and counting the days until we flew out of that godforsaken hellhole, we were going to take out the National Guardsmen for a big, useless operation. We were supposed to go into one of the biggest villages in our area, door to door, and collect biometric data from everyone there.

The village in question was a hotbed for IED construction. Even though everyone knew the second we stepped foot in that village every Taliban member would haul ass, we were going anyway. What it was really about was showing the National Guard unit how to conduct a large-scale operation. It was nothing but a huge dog and pony show, but with real terrorists involved.

"This is fucking stupid," Nan said, loading gear into his vest.

"Yep," I agreed.

"We are going to stroll into an IED factory four fucking weeks before we go home and get blown to shit for what fucking reason?" Cali snarled.

"Hearts and minds?" I suggested.

"We are putting those fucking guardsmen up front," Guapo smiled. "Let *them* find all the tripwires and become heroes and shit."

"Fuck yeah," I agreed.

The door to the tent swung open, and Slim was standing there wearing his gear. With him were three short and incredibly overweight women. Their uniforms were stretched to the max, and they didn't have a neck between them.

"Listen up, fuckers," Slim barked. "These are the Female Engagement Team." He motioned to the fat girls standing behind him. "Their job is to interact with the women in the village...and do some shit." Slim looked confused and turned to the fat girls. "What do you do again?"

"We tell them about the inclusive Afghan government and how women are part of the system now," one of the fat girls piped up.

"I'm sure in between forced marriages and ass whoopings, they will care very much about the government system," I said.

The three fat girls sneered at me.

"More like the Female Eating Team," Nan whispered as he nudged my arm. We both fought back laughs.

Slim smiled. "They'll be joining in a few of the advance teams going into the village during the operation."

"So while we are looking for IED makers, they are going to be trying to talk to the women? I'm sure the men are going to love that." Nan shook his head. Afghanistan was, and probably still is, an incredibly conservative country. Women weren't allowed outside of the house without a male escort and even then they wore full body cover.

At no time were we ever allowed to search them or talk to them. Just looking at an Afghan woman was enough to invite the jeers and insults of the local men. It didn't matter if the American soldier involved was a man or a woman; they saw us all the same.

I assumed that collection of fat chicks had never actually gone out and done the job they said they did or they would have known that already.

"Chimera will be joining us on this operation so we can sweep the whole village at once," Slim droned on. Chimera was the unit that lived down the road and took over for the Dealer soldiers that had shown us the ropes when we first got to Afghanistan. It was the unit Sal got sent back to.

Chimera had dealt with worse luck than we had during our deployment. They'd been blown up on more than one occasion. They were on the way home, as we were, and no doubt just as pissed about taking part in the operation.

"Do we really have to do this shit now?" I complained to no one in particular.

"I know it's stupid. But someone higher than Rocky wants this dumb shit to happen, so here we are," Slim said, shaking his head. "We aren't going to be running out there trying to start anything. We all go home, boys."

"Right," I nodded.

Slim turned around and left the tent, the fat girls at his heels.

"You really believe him?" Nan asked.

"About not starting shit or all going home?"

"Both."

"Nope," I answered. "Starting shit is what we do, and we have been way too lucky so far."

"In the movies, someone always dies right before they are supposed to go home," Cali whined.

"If you're lucky, you might just be that hero," I said, and laughed.

"Man, fuck that, I don't need any buildings named after me," Cali said. On every military base, every building, no matter how unimportant, was always named for a dead soldier. Walton was named after some long-dead soldier who did something heroic on his way out.

"Just think, someone could be taking a shit or jerking off in the Cali Latrines." Nan giggled.

"I'd be so fucking honored." Cali spat a fat wad of dip spit into a bottle.

We loaded into the trucks and slipped on our headsets. Slim's iPod clicked on, and the entirely overplayed "Dirt Road Anthem" started playing. Oldies' legs popped through the turret and his ass sank into its seat right next to my head.

"I swear, if we die on our last mission, I'm going to haunt the fuck out of you, man," I swore over the headset.

"Count me in on that," Memphis added.

"What if *I* die?" Slim laughed.

"You have no right to haunt me. You can only haunt people who outrank you. You'd have to haunt Gunny or Rocky," I answered.

"They would probably still kick my ass," Slim said.

Our trucks rolled out of the gate and onto the crowded highways of Kandahar. After thousands of missions, I had stopped looking out my window as we navigated our way through traffic. That time was different. My heart raced; my eyes darted out of my tiny sliver of a window. I was scared again.

I hadn't felt scared since the night everyone got shredded by those grenades. After months of not giving a shit about what happened to me, wandering through the days totally numb to the danger that surrounded me, I was suddenly terrified. I could tell I wasn't the only one. Slim's eyes were all over the place. Oldies' turret flew back and forth as he scanned everything with his heavy weapon.

We all knew we just had to make it through this cluster fuck that had been slapped together at the last second, thought up by some asshole who didn't care that we were supposed to be going home in a few weeks. All the survival instincts we had ignored over the last year had suddenly snapped back into our minds. We just wanted to live.

Our trucks left the crowded city and we ambled on into the countryside. Tall brown mountains flanked us as we kicked up dust on the crater-pocked dirt road. Every time we bounced across a crater, the fact that each one was once an IED blast or a rocket impact wasn't lost on me. In the past, I had never thought about it.

"There it is." Memphis pointed through the windshield at the mountain ahead of us. The village looked like any other Afghan village: mud shacks slapped onto the side of a mountain in the middle of nowhere. Scout helicopters buzzed down low over us, sending up blinding clouds of dirt and dust. They crested up over the mountain and did low passes back and forth.

"When was the last time we had air support?" Oldies asked.

"Never?" I joked.

"Nah, that one time we got fucked up over by Camp Grizzly," Slim corrected us.

"Still, makes me a little nervous," Oldies' voice crackled over the headset.

"Why?" I asked.

"Because some asshole up top thinks this is going to go so bad we are going to need helicopters," he said.

"Oh, shit." It suddenly struck me. "First Chimera and now helicopters."

"All Grizzly elements," Rocky's voice came over the radio. "Long Knife reports possible fighters in the vicinity of the village. Keep your eyes open." Long Knife was the call sign of the helicopters.

"God dammit!" I cursed. "I fucking told you, Slim!"

"Calm down, they're probably going to run off now that they heard the choppers," Slim said.

I'm not sure if he was trying to reassure me or himself.

The order to dismount off our trucks and march into the village came over the radio. I grabbed my rifle, double-checked my grenade launcher, and climbed out of the truck. Its heavily armored door slammed behind me. I walked around the truck where Slim was kneeling.

"Remember, I'm going to haunt the living fuck out of you." I squatted next to him and heard a distinctive *rip*. I glanced down at my pants and saw they had torn wide open from my crotch to my knee. I wasn't wearing any underwear.

"*That* might fucking haunt me," Slim laughed.

"Off to a great goddamn start aren't we?" I shook my head. Though the breeze felt amazing, the last thing I wanted to do was go running into a massive operation with my dick hanging out.

In squad-sized elements, we advanced across the rocky trails and into the village. Chimera soldiers fanned out along the outer edges of the village to make sure no one got in or out. Our trucks were positioned with heavy weapons to support us should anything happen. Scout helicopters zoomed back and forth over our heads. The amount of military power brought to the tiny, nondescript village was impressive.

Our forward squads started knocking on people's doors and forcing their way into houses to start the biometric process. The people were furious about what we were doing, and angry shouts started coming from the doorways.

"Hearts and minds," I laughed to myself. I leaned against the cracked mud-brick façade of a house. The small street we were on didn't leave a lot of room for any space between us. Thad and Dirty from First Squad were opening the door of the house across the street from me and we were nearly touching shoulders.

The only thing that kept racing through my mind was how easily one burst of machine gun fire would have torn us to shreds. One IED would have turned us into little more than dust and gore. My hands shook, and my eyes darted as I attempted to light a cigarette.

"Get your fucking spacing!" Slim screamed. He saw the same thing I did and was scared. Soldiers ducked into tiny alleyways and doors trying their hardest to get out of the possible lines of fire.

We went uninvited into the houses and shook the places down looking for weapons. I ducked into a small doorway and started throwing things around. The man of the house came forward and screamed at me in Pashtu, so I cross-checked him against the wall with my rifle. I noticed his eyes darting between my face and my exposed dick. A normal person probably would have worried about being in such a vulnerable position, but the rifle I had pushed into his chest evened the playing field.

"See anything?" Machete asked me, coming in behind me carrying his M249 machine gun.

"Nope. Let's move on."

After Machete and I left the house, more soldiers carrying biometric gear went in after us to take the angry old man's fingerprints. We moved through the town slowly but methodically, making sure we didn't miss a single house or resident. I tore through countless houses and compounds, never finding a thing.

"You know, for this being an IED-making hotbed, there seems to be a serious lack of bomb-making shit," I said, sweating profusely. Even with my new draft hole, the heat was stifling. No matter where you went in the village, the heat assaulted you as if it was on the Taliban's side. The inside of each house felt like a brick oven, though the Afghans never seemed to mind.

"Faulty intelligence? That would *never* happen," Bugsy said dryly.

"Looks like we're creating a healthy recruiting base for the Taliban now, though." I smiled, taking another long pull from my camelback. The water tasted like hot plastic.

"What, from all the raiding or you running around showing everyone your dick?" Bugsy laughed.

"Little bit from Column A, a little bit from Column B," I replied.

"Hold where you are!" came an anxious voice over the radio. I didn't recognize it. "Possible HVT."

An HVT was a high-value target, meaning all the biometric crap had paid off. We all took a knee, some of us behind a defensive area, but most of us just on the side of the small village road. I felt the warm breeze on my still-exposed junk. I looked up to see three small children giggling and pointing at my partial nakedness.

"Let me guess...some random dude who stole shit off an army base," Bugsy said. Any Afghan who worked on one of the many military bases had their biometric data archived. If they got booted off base for whatever reason, they would pop up in our biometric system as being a possible member of the Taliban.

"That's giving them too much credit." I shook my head. Just then, with no warning, the ground shook so violently it nearly knocked me on my ass. A deafening explosion ripped through the air, and a massive dirt plume shot up into the air.

"What the fuck was that?" Bugsy screamed.

"*Fuck.*" I pulled myself back to my feet and looked down the village street to the rest of the soldiers. "Is everyone okay?" I yelled.

"Yeah," Machete called back.

"I'm good," came Cali's voice.

"All Spartan elements, status report," Slim's voice boomed over the radio. Everyone mercifully answered back they were okay. I looked around, and all the Afghans had vanished from the streets.

"Keep your fucking eyes open," I yelled. My eyes darted to all the open doors, windows, and rooftops that surrounded us. It was coming. My heart slammed in my chest and I gripped my rifle so hard my knuckles turned white. Seconds turned to hours as I waited for the Taliban to commence shooting us to pieces trapped in that shitty little village.

But it never came. Up the road a few hundred meters where the Chimera troops were, an IED had gone off. It wasn't even close to them when it blew. Someone, somewhere must have been spooked and set it off way too early.

"All Grizzly elements prepare to exfiltrate," Rocky's voice said over the radio. I breathed a sigh of relief and motioned for the soldiers around me to get the hell out. We didn't manage to hit every house as we'd planned, but I think we managed to scare off the IED maker. Even if it was by accident.

Even though we wanted to rush out of that village as fast as possible, we didn't. We moved out as slowly and as deliberately as we'd moved in. I was even more nervous on the way out. The only thing I could think of was that the bomb was nothing but a sign for waiting fighters in the mountains somewhere. My rifle followed my eyes as I checked, double-checked, and re-checked every nook, cranny, and rock as we made our way down the crowded village roads.

Every electrical connection to a generator was a possible tripwire. Every loose pile of dirt was an IED. Every window was concealing the barrel of a rifle. Every single step on the way back to the trucks was going to be my last. I was certain of it. I was so nervous that I suddenly noticed I wasn't breathing. When I reached the trucks, I gasped for breath.

I struggled with the heavy door and climbed inside. The air conditioning was a blast of freezing cold and immediately turned all my sweat icy. I took my helmet off and dropped it next to Oldies' feet. Sweat poured down from my unkempt hair and stung my eyes.

"What the hell was that?" Oldies asked, peering down from his turret.

"Not really sure," I yelled over the truck's loud diesel engine. "Shit just kind of exploded for no reason."

"Afghanistan problems," Oldies laughed. Slim and Memphis's doors both swung open and they climbed inside. I leaned over and put my headset back on, and they did the same. "Guess you won't be haunting me," Slim joked.

"Not from a lack of you trying." I shook my head.

"Like *that* was the first time we almost died."

"We really have to stop making this a thing." I laughed. It felt like I had decompressed a million times over once we started laughing together. The truck slowly crept into line with the others, and the convoy started back toward the Kandahar City skyline.

CHAPTER 33

LEAVING WALTON

OUR DUFFLE BAGS WERE PACKED and piled at the end of a large cement surface. The stars hung in the night sky as we awaited our final ride out of FOB Walton. We, of course, had been told the helicopters would be coming for us hours before, but they never showed. Something you learn early on in the army is that whenever you're told that transportation is coming, it will inevitably be several hours late.

We all used our duffle bags as uncomfortable pillows in an attempt to get some sleep, but everyone was fully awake. We were all too anxious to get on the coming helicopters to sleep. Every single time the wind blew a little too hard we sat up from our duffle bags and stared into the sky waiting to see the big gangly form of a Chinook helicopter come into view.

"I think these assholes run off black people time," Oldies cursed, staring up into the sky.

"That's racist," Memphis drawled.

"Mother fucker, *I'm* black."

"You're not black, you Cosby sweater-wearing mother fucker," Memphis joked.

"He's got a point, bro," I said. "You're the whitest black guy I've ever met."

"And *he's* from Detroit," Memphis added, pointing at me. I didn't even bother to correct him.

"Fuck you guys," Oldies said, rolling over on his stomach and showing us his back.

I started to drift off into a fitful sleep when I thought I heard the sound of helicopter blades chopping through the air. I opened my eyes and stared into the sky and didn't see anything. The stars still shone overhead in the empty void.

Where the fuck is this thing? I thought. As if something up above was answering my question, the large form of a Chinook helicopter emerged from the darkness. It had no lights and was painted pitch black. It was hiding in plain sight.

The helicopter's rotors sent dust and rocks flying throughout the area, and we ducked for cover. Several people's bags were sent tumbling across the helipad, and they tried in vain to chase them down while getting beaten by hurricane-force winds. Another two Chinooks landed on the crowded helipad. Slim got off his bag, balanced himself with an awkward crouch, and braced himself on his rifle. He turned to face us: his squad sitting in a loose circle on the rocks holding onto our bags for dear life.

His mouth moved, but we couldn't hear a single word over the deafening thud of helicopter blades. After a few attempts, he quit trying to talk and frantically pointed to one of the Chinooks. He grabbed his bags in both hands, his rifle smacking off his chest from the sling it was attached to. He ran to the helicopter in a low crouch and we followed.

Thankfully I was a large guy, so the rotor wash from the helicopters didn't threaten to sweep me away. Others weren't so lucky. Out of the corner of my eye I saw a short blonde girl from one of the other platoons get blasted off of her feet and dragged across the helipad as she tried to run to the helicopter. Her bags tumbled across the concrete after her.

We crammed into the innards of the helicopters and piled all our bags in the middle. We sat on cargo nets and, with the back ramp of the helicopter still hanging open, we slowly lifted into the air. A soldier who was strapped to the helicopter with a long piece of cord stood on the ramp. He had a machine gun in his hands as he stared over the expanse of empty Afghan countryside.

As we flew over Kandahar City, I saw the brightly lit form of Walton fade away, swallowed by the darkness of the rest of the city. Not a single light could be seen in what could easily be mistaken for a dead city. Like something out of a bad zombie film.

The helicopter banked sharply and sent all our bags crashing down onto Kitty who was seated across from me. I laughed, but my mean-spirited laughter was completely drowned out by the sounds of the helicopter.

After about forty-five minutes, we dipped back to the ground and landed at Kandahar Air Field. Mercifully, the engines of the helicopter powered down and I was able to hear something other than painful ringing and pounding. We pushed and shoved our way out of the crowded helicopter and onto the tarmac. A long line of buses waited for us.

If I thought the inside of the helicopter was small, then the bus was microscopic. Wearing full combat gear and carrying all our belongings, we could barely fit through the door of the bus, let alone sit down. I smashed into a seat and felt someone push against me and try to sit in what was left of the seat.

I was so tightly packed into the bus I couldn't move. Stuck to the ceiling of the bus was a sticker that depicted a jet bombing tiny stick figures with the caption, "We will free the shit out of you."

The buses drove on for what seemed like longer than our flying time in the helicopters. Probably because I could hardly breathe inside of that moving sardine can.

We stopped in front of a sea of tents somewhere on the outskirts of Kandahar Air Field. The bus doors slid open and we piled out as fast as we could. Some people could do little more than toss themselves out of the bus and land like a sack of shit on the dirt.

Tents were set up in a small city with massive generators between each one. Slim led us to the tent we were allocated. On the way, I saw several showers and toilet trailers set in a row with a little wooden walkway built around them.

"No more shitting in a port-o-potty." Cali smiled.

"It's about the little things in life," I said.

We walked into our new temporary home, and I was taken aback by how many beds they had managed to smash into the small tent. With a few inches of clearance on either side, bunk beds were lined up with little room for anything else. The top bunk was maybe six inches away from the tent's ceiling.

There was so little room, we were forced to put our bags in the same bed we planned to sleep in. I put my rifle under the mattress and my arms around my bags and drifted off into a night of restless sleep. The next morning, I woke up to Slim shaking my bed and yelling at me to get up.

"What's going on?" I asked still half asleep.

"We have PT," he said.

I looked him up and down and saw he was wearing the horrible vinyl army short-shorts that we had to wear to do physical training.

"Seriously?" I thought he was joking. I sat up and smacked my head on the upper bunk's support beams. Wincing, I looked around and saw several other people changing into their PT uniforms. "You got to be kidding me," I groaned. I rolled out of my bed and started searching through my bags for a PT uniform. I couldn't believe we finally had no missions to do and Slim had woken us up for this bullshit.

We all lumbered outside wearing stained, gray PT shirts. They said "Army" in big, bold letters on the front and were paired with tiny shorts. I felt objectified by everyone who walked past us.

"Fall in," Slim ordered.

We all lazily stood at attention. The hot Afghan sun was cresting overhead and already burning my skin. After a few minutes of stretching, we took off into a lazy jog down the dusty roads of the tent village.

We jogged on, huffing and puffing the shit-caked, dust-filled air. Our lungs worked overtime trying to find tiny oxygen molecules in the middle of all the air pollution. I coughed and gagged on dirt and debris, but I didn't care. We were leaving Afghanistan. It didn't seem real yet. It felt like any minute Slim would turn around and scream in my face and we would just go on living in that hellhole forever. It was real, though. Every single step we ran down that road brought us one step closer.

CHAPTER 34

CLOSING THE BAR AT MANAS

THERE WE WERE, ALL LINED up in our full combat gear, standing in front of the massive plane we were about to get on. We were finally going to leave Afghanistan. It was actually happening. But we weren't going home yet; we had one more stop in the middle. A tiny Air Force base called Manas in the former Soviet country of Kyrgyzstan, a country whose name is nearly impossible to pronounce with an American tongue.

We marched in two single-file lines into the belly of the Air Force transport jet. The walls of the jet were lined with steel bench seats and in the center was the seating section of a passenger airline bolted to the floor. A few ratchet straps secured the section to the walls for good measure.

We filed into the seats one behind another with no regard to how big any individual soldier was. I was squeezed into one of the center seats. It was an area that was too small for someone even half my size. My knees were in my chest, and the ballistic plate from my vest pushed down on my groin where my rifle was also smashed. My legs started to go numb before we even took off.

The plane taxied for a few seconds, and the big jet took to the air. Unlike an actual passenger jet, which is nice and quiet on the inside, the big Air Force jet was just a few octaves quieter than a Chinook helicopter. Everything shook and rattled as we lifted into the air. I don't think there was any sort of sound insulation between the passengers and the roaring jet engines. It didn't feel like the jet was taking flight as much as it was stumbling accidently into the act of flight.

When leaving a combat zone, a jet doesn't do a standard take-off. It rockets straight up into the air going as fast as mechanically possible and zigzags through the clouds. It was meant to dodge ground fire and possible surface-to-air missiles that routinely target flights out of

Afghanistan. I don't know if it worked, but I do know that it did a fantastic job of making everyone vomit into their mouths.

After fighting through the air to our cruising altitude, we settled into what was mostly a normal flight. It was a long couple of hours to Manas, during which my legs transformed from being merely numb to burning with pain. I didn't care. At some point during that flight, the jet was going to leave Afghan airspace. I was getting the hell out of there, my legs be damned.

"Ladies and gentlemen," crackled the voice of the flight captain over an intercom. "We are officially outside of Afghan airspace."

The cargo hold erupted with cheers. We all pumped our fists into the air. We high-fived and hugged each other. Our time in Afghanistan was finally over.

A few hours later, the jet landed with a bounce on the runway in Kyrgyzstan. The jolt suddenly brought life back to my dead limbs. We slowed to a stop, and the rear ramp dropped down. I tried to get to my feet, but I was wedged too deeply in my airline seat prison. The guy next to me dropped his shoulder and gave me a boost to my feet. I stumbled and had to lean against the wall for support while my legs tried to remember how to function correctly.

I struggled off the jet and onto the tarmac. The air was so clean in comparison to where we had just come from that I had to stand there a minute and breathe it in deeply.

We were surrounded by huge snow-capped mountains, and the sky was a flawless blue. Far behind me was the brown palette of Afghanistan and its hazy air. Manas could have been heaven on earth.

We were pushed into a building that was cooled by the best working air conditioning system I had felt since we had left proper civilization.

An Air Force airman was standing in front of a big pull-down screen with a PowerPoint slideshow playing on it. The airman clicked a button on a laptop and cycled through some slides. They were the rules of Manas. No weapons anywhere, and because we were slated to be flying back to the States, we weren't allowed to leave the base. And the base bar had a two-beer limit.

"Did he say beer?" Nan shot forward in his seat.

On my last deployment to Afghanistan, I had passed through Manas. I remembered that the rule at the bar was a two-beer limit— *if* your commander actually let you drink. But the rumor around Manas was that no army units had ever been allowed to drink when they came through. The combined destruction that would have visited Manas had they let a whole company of soldiers just back from Afghanistan get drunk would have shocked the Air Force's delicate sensibilities.

"Drink up, boys," Rocky called from the back of the room.

We all erupted into cheers and high-fives so loudly that the Air Force guy giving the rules briefing gave up trying to talk and walked away.

"Oh, man, he's going to regret that." Slim shook his head.

"So when does these pussies' bar open?" I asked.

"Well, it's like four in the morning, so I'm assuming not right now," Nan said, glancing at his watch. We filed out of the building and found our way to the tents we would be staying in. The Air Force's massive, modern barracks complex towered over our ratty tents.

It was a huge tent lined with bunk beds. Unlike the ones in Afghanistan, there was plenty of room for everyone. The bedframes weren't just ramshackle handmade pieces of shit, and the mattresses looked and felt brand new. In the middle of the room were weapons racks equipped with locks for us to store all our weaponry.

I changed and went into the shower building that was next to our tent. Individual shower stalls with frosted glass doors lined the walls. Every surface was gleaming white tile. I climbed into the shower stall and turned it on. Without hesitation, piping hot water blasted against my face. It had been so long since I'd felt actual water pressure. I looked around and thought about how much more comfortable these shower stalls would have been to live in.

Showered, I collapsed into my bunk bed. The mattress was the most comfortable thing I had felt since Tampa. I tried to close my eyes, but it didn't do any good. None of us were sleeping. We were all way too excited, even though we still had no idea when we were actually leaving for the States.

Once you arrive in Manas, they just shove your unit on the next flight going out, whenever that might be. It could be a day or a week. The wait made minutes go by like hours and days go by like weeks. I took my watch off so I wouldn't obsessively glance at it. I gauged the passage of time by what meal we were about to eat.

The base had several entertainment buildings. They were packed full of airmen, video games, and computers. Bugsy and I were sitting in one of them waiting for our turn to use the computers when we overheard an airman complaining that the chow hall had run out of ice cream. Bugsy and I gave each other furious looks.

I wanted to say something. Without warning, I was almost thrown in a rage. I wanted to explode on the kid. I wanted him to know that while he spent his time drinking beer and playing video games, good kids were getting torn to shreds on some shitty Afghan street thousands of miles away from home. He enjoyed hot showers and a warm bed while guys not even old enough to buy beer were at Spartan and Grizzly and the Reserve just wanting to call their parents and let them know they were okay. They just wanted to live another day.

I didn't say anything, though. I stopped myself. That place, Manas, was that kid's war. That was *his* deployment. I couldn't be mad at him for some shit he would never understand. Instead, Bugsy and I got up and left the building. We paced around Manas, chain smoking cigarettes and avoiding human contact.

The sun slowly inched down behind the towering mountains, and we went out into the night hunting for the bar. We followed a massive horde of Marines who were hooting and hollering their way down the street. If anyone knew how to hunt down Air Force booze and women, it would be a group of Marines.

A weird tropical hut-looking building with neon lights had a huge line of airmen, soldiers, and Marines outside of it. Crowds of soldiers milled around on a big wooden deck that surrounded the tropical hut. I noticed big brown bottles in everyone's hands.

"Jesus, those things are like forties, man," Nan smiled looking at the massive beer bottles.

"It took five years and a few too many deployments, but I think I found something about the military that doesn't completely suck." I stared in awe. We waited our turn in line down into the bar area. It looked like a regular chow hall with a bar in the middle. A huge projection screen stood against the wall with cable TV playing on it.

A squat-looking Asian woman wearing colorful clothes stood behind the bar at a register. She looked pissed—the way anyone tended to look after dealing with a bunch of soldiers. "What you want?" she barked at me. There was no menu, drink list, or anything. I honestly had no idea what to order.

"What kind of beer do you have?" I asked.

"One kind beer," she snarled at me. She slammed a huge bottle of beer on the counter. The bottle was dark brown and had a red label with Cyrillic letters scrawled on it. A giant number eight was in the middle of the label. "Six dollar." She held her hand out.

I fished around in my pocket and found some money. I walked off with my beer and found Slim sitting at a long table in the middle of the room. I sat down across from him and noticed the big projection screen wasn't just playing cable TV; it was playing a WNBA game.

"Enjoying the game?" I asked.

Slim winced as he took a drink from his bottle of beer. "It's just like the NBA." He shrugged.

"If you take away any of the reasons you would watch an NBA game," I said, motioning toward the screen.

"I don't know, that chick kind of looks like LeBron," Slim said and laughed.

I finally took a sip from my massive bottle of beer. It tasted exactly as you would expect a Soviet bloc country's bad Budweiser copy to taste. I made a face and Slim laughed.

"What? It just tastes like Bud."

"If they brewed it with burning tires." I shook my head.

It didn't take long for most of the squad to empty their beer and go back for another one. We were all feeling more than a little drunk. Our tolerance wasn't just low, it was practically nonexistent. The warmth of the booze flooded my body. Nan wasn't handling his booze well and was calling every girl who walked by our table a whore or a slut.

We made our way outside to the deck area where people had started blaring music from their laptops and had turned the place into some weird impromptu dance club.

People's cigarette smoke added to the atmosphere of loud music and flashing lights. Soldiers, airmen, and Marines started emptying onto the deck area and joining the party. Including an army major who looked like she was about fifty years old and walking with a cane.

The major was dancing her ass off. She was swinging her cane around in circles and breaking it down. Two massive black Marines sandwiched her, air fucking her so hard they probably should have been wearing protection. Air Force girls in short PT shorts were grind-dancing all over Marines and soldiers. Soldiers from my unit were just kicking over tables and shattering beer bottles on the ground.

A Marine near the laptop that was blaring music had stripped off most of his uniform and was vigorously humping the face of some Air Force girl, and she wasn't coming up for breath. Other Marines stood around cheering him on. Eastwood, one of the most poorly tempered senior leaders I had ever met, jumped into the party and was humping some army girls on the dance floor with a beer in his hand.

"I love sluts!" Nan cheered and sent his empty beer bottle flying into the crowd of dancing people. I didn't hear it shatter. I put some distance between myself and the massive amount of repressed sexual energy that made up the deck dance club. I'd just sat down at a table near the entrance with Slim, Nan, and Cali when Rocky emerged from inside the bar.

Rocky's lip was bulged to its limit trying to contain a massive amount of dip. He spat a fat wad of spit, and it splattered on the deck.

"You know, it's funny," he growled, "we are acting like this is some insane party, but to these people, it's just another day. It's a different war around here."

"What fucking war?" Slim cursed. "These faggots make the same paycheck as us, get to drink, and don't even have to carry weapons."

I shook my head. "I joined the wrong branch."

"I thought you had a dick, Kassabian," Rocky laughed, and a little dip spit came out.

"My reputation precedes me," I said.

"Only bitches join the Air Force." Rocky spat again. "Someone has got to go to faraway lands, meet a different culture, and kill it. That someone is us." After dispensing his wisdom, he staggered away without another word. I found out later he went outside and dominated the cornhole game against any and all comers for the next couple hours.

I lost count of how many third-rate Russian beers I had and went back to the bar for another. The tiny, angry Asian woman told us she didn't have any more beer. We had drunk them clean out. I gave up and started walking back to our tent.

Nan and I staggered across the shifting rocks and attempted to find our tent. I was too drunk to successfully light my cigarette so it dangled uselessly from my lips as I tried my best not to fall over. In our drunken stupor, our tent seemed much farther away than it had a few hours before.

I collapsed into my bed, drunk and tired. As fun as that night was, none of us wanted to be there. We got drunk, broke things, and nearly started fights. We screamed, yelled, and fantasized about being home. As happy as we all seemed, our heads weren't out on that deck. They were in Fort Hood, Texas.

CHAPTER 35

THE LONG WAY HOME

I WAS KICKED AWAKE SOMETIME before the sun came up and told to grab my bags. We weren't leaving quite yet. We had to go through customs first. Balancing what felt like about one hundred pounds of gear on various parts of my body, I made my way across Manas with the rest of the soldiers in my company.

We lined up in front of a big tan warehouse. I dumped all my bags on the ground and sat on top of them. A fat Air Force guy strutted around at the entrance of the warehouse with a microphone in his hand. I noticed his spotless uniform had creases in it. He had time to diligently iron his uniform before showing up to work that morning. I hadn't even brushed my teeth.

The Air Force guy paced around in front of us while he explained what we couldn't bring on the chartered Ryanair flight we would be getting on. No fluids over ten ounces, no fingernail clippers, knives, or anything else you would think you wouldn't be able to bring on a civilian flight. I had heard this briefing before, and it was mostly just for show. As long as you weren't trying to smuggle back any war trophies, explosives, or weapons, they would just let you walk.

After he was done reading from his script, the Air Force guy opened the door to the warehouse and we slowly walked inside. Little wooden stations were set up to dump your gear on and some tired-looking airmen rifled through it to make sure you weren't trying to commit any kind of international crime.

I walked up to the stall when it was my turn and dumped all my bags out. A fat guy wearing rubber gloves started rifling through it. He opened every little pocket on every uniform and unfolded everything. From the time I was seventeen, I had spent way too much time going through airports, so I knew a little trick to sneak things through customs.

Customs agents, military or civilian, were usually fat, lazy bastards who hated to actually do their jobs. If you place contraband you don't actually want in an easy-to-find place, they will dutifully find it and think they've done their job—leaving your good shit securely unmolested by their Cheetos-dusted fingers.

I left a knife in the pocket of one of my uniforms for that fat bastard to find. Like clockwork, he pulled it out. "You can't take this home," he said, his eyes staring daggers at me.

"Shit! Sorry." I faked surprise. "I totally forgot about it."

The fat guy put it in a little crate labeled "contraband." He would probably take it for himself after we were gone. Then that fat bastard did something I'd never seen before: He kept going through my shit. Hidden in the liner of one of my jackets was a bag of tiny pink pills. I had hidden a cache of over-the-counter cough pills to help me sleep through the incredibly long plane trip back to America. "If you have anything in here you shouldn't, you need to tell me, because if I find it, you'll be charged," the fat guy said for about the third time.

"Yeah, I have a rocket launcher in my shower bag," I sneered.

The fat guy opened my shower bag to check. He took out my bottle of body wash, my fingernail clippers, and razors.

"You can't have these either," he said, placing them into the contraband crate. That was just punishment for being a smartass. After proving that he had more power than I did, he tossed my shit into a pile and told me to move along.

I stuffed all my gear back into the bags and shuffled my way to a lobby area. From there we were stuffed into rickety Russian buses with broken seats and trucked out to an airport.

Manas International Airport was a pile of crap. Its main terminal looked like it was vintage Soviet 1950s design. Wreckage of MIG fighter jets was strewn everywhere. The rusted, burned-out husk of a huge Russian transport jet lay in ruins by the side of a runway. By comparison, the various Air Force jets on the runway stood out as beacons of the modern world.

A big white jet with "Ryanair" painted on its side crept down the runway. Ryanair was probably the Department of Defense's favorite airline—a cut-rate Irish airline that cuts corners wherever they can to save money. I was surprised they still had a bathroom. They were always staffed with the angriest bunch of Eastern European stewardesses who would ignore you and pretend they didn't understand what you were saying.

The flight from Central Asia back to the States was a grueling one. Spending nearly twenty hours crammed into an airline seat was bad enough, but when you can't wait to get home from a war, it's nearly unbearable. You could only sleep so much of the flight away. Naturally, anyway.

I went into my bag and fished out the little baggie of pills I had smuggled through customs. I upended the bag into my mouth and washed it down with a bottle of water. It didn't take long for me to start fading from the sleeping pills pumping through my bloodstream. I closed my eyes and drifted off to sleep before the flight even took off.

A jolt woke me as the plane bounced off the tarmac. I was awake but too blitzed on sleeping pills to really understand what was going on. I noticed my face was wet and tried to wipe away a massive amount of drool. "What's going on?" I slurred to Thad, who was sitting next to me.

"We're in Germany, bro." He clapped me on the shoulder. "Halfway there!" he cheered, squeezing past me and getting in line to walk off the plane. I got up and stumbled my way into the terminal. I plopped down in a seat next to someone I didn't recognize and stared mindlessly at a TV that sat in front of me.

I was trying to fight off the effects of the pills by forcing myself to stay awake. I was worried that if I fell asleep, I would be left behind. I'm not sure if it was paranoia due to the intake of way too many sleeping pills or whether I just didn't trust my fellow soldiers at all. I wasn't going to take the chance.

My hands and feet tingled, and my brain struggled to comprehend what was going on around me. It took me the better part of an hour to figure out the news channel I had been watching was actually in German. A loudspeaker kicked on and announced that our flight was restocked and refueled, and we were good to take off once again. We all got back onto the plane. I crashed into my seat and was out as soon as I leaned back.

I woke up to a jolt again. It wasn't the plane landing that time, though. It was Thad slapping me and cheering. "We're in the States, dude!" he yelled.

I looked out the window and saw the lush green landscape of Bangor, Maine. The plane slowly came to a halt and once again we were kicked off. We walked through the terminal and were greeted by lines of old people and war veterans. Each of them wanted to shake our hands or hug us.

The number of people and close human interaction freaked me out. It felt like the walls were closing in. I broke into something resembling a jog to get through them all.

Breathing heavily, I walked up to a drink stall and bought several Red Bulls. I slammed them down back to back in an attempt to counteract all the sleeping pills I'd eaten.

Before long, we were pushed onto a different plane and started the last leg of our trip to Texas.

I had to sit next to one of our mechanics, whom I hated. He smelled terrible and wouldn't stop talking about how many women he was going to bang when he got back to Texas. I wished the sleeping pills had killed me. I tried to ignore him for the last four hours of the trip.

I had my face pressed against the window watching the clouds go by. By now the infusion of caffeine had me shaking like mad. I stared hard through the clouds trying to catch any glimpse of the brown landscape of Texas under us.

I slumped back into my seat. It hadn't seemed that long ago I was on a plane just like that one, but going the other way. For a second it felt as if the last year of my life had never actually happened. It was all just a blur.

The burning pain in my spine and the never-ending ringing in my ears were a reminder it was real. The handful of pills I had to take to sleep, only to awaken screaming and punching the air were a reminder it was real. Any sudden loud noise that would send me ducking as if a rocket had just screamed overhead was a reminder it was real. My bloodstained gear was a reminder it was real.

The plane skipped across the runway and everyone erupted into wild cheering. I joined them. I screamed at the top of my lungs and pumped my fists into the air. For the first time in a long time, I was feeling actual happiness. The plane slowed to a halt, and the door creaked opened. It was moving impossibly slowly.

We got up and pushed each other down the aisles like refugees fighting over food. We were all exhausted, and our legs were cramped from endless hours of travel, but at that very moment, we were energized by twelve months of unbridled carnal wanting. No one in the world wanted anything more than the people on that plane wanted to get off.

We rushed out onto the tarmac to be greeted by the overpaid old guys that made up every chain of command in the military. They all shook our hands. None of them had any idea what we had done over the last year. I was willing to bet that my brigade commander wouldn't have shaken my hand and told me "good job" had he known I had been drinking smuggled booze on a rooftop and hurling the empty bottles onto innocent passers-by only a few months before.

We filed into an airport hangar and turned our weapons in at a desk. The one constant I had over the last year of my life was taken from my hands for the last time. I saw Grandpa was behind a desk further down, filling out paperwork. I vaulted the counter and wrapped that old bastard in the tightest hug I had ever given another man in my life.

"Hey, brother!" he said when he realized it was me. "Welcome home." He grinned at me.

"Thanks, man. How's the back?" I asked.

"Fucking terrible." He shook his head. "You should go get on that bus, man, you can't miss your own homecoming." He pointed to a line of buses that were going to take us to some parade field.

"Yeah, I guess." I hugged him again and walked off.

Walrus stopped me on the way; I noticed a little limp in his step.

"What's up, fatass?" I gave him a hug.

"'Sup fucker. Drinks later?" he asked.

"Fuck, yeah. I'll call you when I get home." We shook hands, and I climbed onto my assigned bus.

The buses snaked through the back roads of central Texas. Police cars and motorcycles sped along next to us flashing their lights and sirens as they went. The buses were so close together during the trip I was pretty sure we were going to wreck. Survive Kandahar and die in a fiery bus accident outside of Fort Hood. That would be our luck.

During the trip, no one talked. We stared out the windows taking everything in. Now that the one thing we wanted more than anything else was right in front of us, it didn't seem real. In Afghanistan, all of that was just an abstract thought. Nothing but future hopes and dreams. Now that everyone's hopes and dreams were coming true we were frozen in place.

The buses pulled up to a parade field near our company headquarters. There was a massive group of people waiting for us. They were holding signs and banners, toting around kids or pushing them in strollers. The crowd started screaming when we pulled into view. Their cameras went off like the muzzle flashes of a hundred machine guns. I wondered how far you could see that flash at night while on patrol.

The bus doors slid open and we marched out into a neat formation. Our first sergeant and commander stood in front of us.

Rocky, looking hungover and haggard from days of travel, straightened his uniform up and turned to face us. "Go see your families! Dismissed!" he ordered in a bark.

Everyone flooded to their loved ones. The family members rushed forward to hug their husband, wife, child, or significant whatever. I dropped my bags at my feet and lit a cigarette.

The reality hadn't set in yet.

While my body was standing there in Texas, my mind would never leave Afghanistan. The blood-soaked mountains of that country would be with me until the day I died. My rifle was silent from then until forever.

That war, though. That war would never truly be over for us.

ACKNOWLEDGMENTS

First and foremost I would like to thank the soldiers of my unit, who will not be named. Even though I hated the vast majority of the people I served with, we will always be connected. We will be family members that you don't really like but still talk to from time to time. We threatened each other with grenades, stabbed each other, and sometimes beat each other's asses. But I will always love you anyway.

Thank you to the soldiers of the Second Squad "Hooligans" who helped jog my memory while I went through the long process of writing this incredibly flawed account of our little war. You know who you are.

A huge appreciation to the one other soldier I will actually name, Sergeant First Class Albert Brodeen. He was our first platoon sergeant and the only man who ever led me during my time in the U.S. Army and motivated me to be a better soldier. One day out in field training before our deployment, he told me to write a diary. Or, as he put it, "We are living history. You need to document it," which started me down what turned into a four-year-long road of writing this book.

Thank you to my sister and long-suffering editor, Amy Good. She took my retarded, ape-like writing style and turned it into a functioning book. Trust me when I say it was ugly as shit before she got her hands on it.

Last and not least to Hamid Sawari, our interpreter. If left to our own devices in Afghanistan, our attitude would have eventually gotten us killed. Hamid was always there to smooth things over with the locals, the Afghan police, and the Afghan army to ensure our survival for another day. When the going got tough, and any other interpreter would have abandoned us, Hamid picked up a weapon and fought side by side with us. I'm glad to say that after several years of trying and writing countless letters to congressmen, he safely immigrated to America a few years ago. He is as big a part of the Hooligans as Slim or me.

ABOUT THE AUTHOR

JOSEPH KASSABIAN was born and raised in the Metro Detroit area of Michigan and enlisted in the U.S. Army in December of 2005 at the age of 17. He served multiple combat tours in support of the Global War On Terror, including the one covered in this book. In 2013, he exited the Army with an Honorable Discharge and began a career in writing.

CONNECT WITH JOSEPH KASSABIAN

Sign up for Joseph's newsletter
and find out more information at:
www.joekassabian.com

Facebook Page:
www.facebook.com/joe.kassabian.5

Twitter:
@jkass99

Instagram:
joekassabian

BOOK DISCOUNTS AND SPECIAL DEALS

Sign up for free to get discounts and special deals
on our best-selling books at
www.TCKpublishing.com/bookdeals

Made in the USA
Las Vegas, NV
23 December 2022

64010259R00144